Resource Allocation and Productivity in Education

Recent Titles in
Contributions to the Study of Education

Assessing What Professors Do: An Introduction to Academic Performance
Appraisal in Higher Education
David A. Dilts, Lawrence J. Haber, and Donna Bialik

Encounters with Difference: Student Perceptions of the Role of Out-of-Class
Experiences in Education Abroad
Michael R. Laubscher

Public School Reform in Puerto Rico: Sustaining Colonial
Models of Development
José Solís

Diversifying Historically Black Colleges: A New Higher Education Paradigm
Serbrenia J. Sims

Socialization and Education: Essays in Conceptual Criticism
Wolfgang Brezinka

The Importance of Learning Styles: Understanding the Implications for
Learning, Course Design, and Education
Ronald R. Sims and Serbrenia J. Sims

Achieving Racial Balance: Case Studies of Contemporary
School Desegregation
Sondra Astor Stave

The Politics and Processes of Scholarship
Joseph M. Moxley and Lagretta T. Lenker, editors

The History of American Art Education: Learning About
Art in American Schools
Peter Smith

Moral Development Theories—Secular and Religious: A Comparative Study
R. Murray Thomas

An Integrated Theory of Moral Development
R. Murray Thomas

The Condition of English: Literary Studies in a Changing Culture
Avrom Fleishman

Resource Allocation and Productivity in Education

Theory and Practice

Edited by William T. Hartman and
William Lowe Boyd

Contributions to the Study of Education,
Number 71

GREENWOOD PRESS
Westport, Connecticut • London

Library of Congress Cataloging-in-Publication Data

Resource allocation and productivity in education : theory and
    practice / edited by William T. Hartman and William Lowe Boyd.
        p.   cm.—(Contributions to the study of education, ISSN
0196-707X : no. 71)
    Includes bibliographical references and index.
    ISBN 0-313-27631-5 (alk. paper).
    1. Educational productivity—United States. 2. Educational
productivity—Canada. 3. Education—United States—Finance.
4. Education—Canada—Finance. 5. Resource allocation.
I. Hartman, William T. II. Boyd, William L. III. Series.
LB2806.24.R47   1998
379.1'1'0973—dc21   97-33963

British Library Cataloguing in Publication Data is available.

Library of Congress Catalog Card Number: 97-33963
ISBN: 0-313-27631-5
ISSN: 0196-707X

First published in 1998

Greenwood Press, 88 Post Road West, Westport, CT 06881
An imprint of Greenwood Publishing Group, Inc.

Printed in the United States of America

The paper used in this book complies with the
Permanent Paper Standard issued by the National
Information Standards Organization (Z39.48-1984).

10 9 8 7 6 5 4 3 2 1

Copyright Acknowledgments

Every reasonable effort has been made to trace the owners of copyright materials
in this book, but in some instances this has proven impossible. The author and
publisher will be glad to receive information leading to more complete acknowledgments in subsequent printings of the book and in the meantime extend their
apologies for any omissions.

Contents

Introduction and Overview

William Lowe Boyd and William T. Hartman

After years of talking about improving educational productivity, people now are actually trying to do it, largely because of mounting public pressure for more effective schooling.[1] Better educational productivity has become a national imperative because of the challenge we face in international economic competitiveness and the demands upon our changing economy and work force. At the same time, few observers believe that we can continue to escalate spending on public education in search of better results (Odden & Clune, 1995). Instead, pressures are mounting for both better results *and* more-efficient use of resources. Increasingly, as the Consortium on Productivity in the Schools (1995) argues, we need to be better at "using what we have to get the schools we need."

Serious efforts to improve productivity in education require nothing less than a "paradigm shift" in approaches to policy-making and the management of schools (Boyd, 1992). For far too long, policy and management have focused mainly on *inputs* for schools, while neglecting attention to systematic, data-based assessments of the *outcomes* of alternative policies. Such input-driven approaches, as Eric Hanushek (1981) has long complained, can easily amount to little more than "throwing money at schools," because there is no evaluation of the efficiency of alternative policies. Even now, in the face of escalating demands for more-efficient and more-effective results, school reformers still confront many school districts and school authorities who remain wedded to the traditional, input-driven, nonevaluative approach to resource allocation (Odden & Clune, 1995).

This book presents research and analysis that increase our understanding of the processes affecting educational productivity. Only in recent years have researchers begun to probe beneath the surface of state and federal policies and school district budgets to determine how resources actually are allocated and utilized at the various levels within school districts, from the school board down to the school, the classroom, and individual students. Only recently have schools and administrators had available new sophisticated tools of computer technology and software to facilitate more-efficient resource management. Here, many important questions need to be answered: What are the implicit theories or rules of thumb that school boards, school administrators, and teachers use in making decisions about resource allocation in classrooms, schools, and school districts? How are these practices related to the promotion of student achievement? How are the availability of new technologies, data analyses, and databases affecting decision making? What patterns of resource allocation and utilization emerge at the various organizational levels? What differences do these patterns make for organizational outcomes and the improvement of educational productivity? These questions are at the heart of the collection of papers presented in this book.

BACKGROUND

Resource allocation in education is a complex hierarchical decision-making process. Each level in the organization makes decisions to distribute the resources under its control to units or individuals at the next lower level. The state and federal governments appropriate funds for education and allocate them to school districts. School boards make decisions on the level of taxes to levy locally for education and set policies for the distribution of the combined amount of money available to the district. Working within these policies, district-level administrators allocate resources (generally in the form of personnel, supply, and equipment funds) to individual schools. Resources come to the school with various administrative, legal, and political constraints attached to their use. At the building level, principals (and others) distribute resources among various instructional, support, and administrative departments or functions in the school. The resources that are received by the departments are allotted to individual classrooms; and, finally, within classrooms teachers decide how their efforts, attention, and available resources are allocated to students.

Although these decisions determine the adequacy and equity of resources available to educational programs, these decisions at lower organizational levels have received little systematic study. Several factors have inhibited the ability of research to inform and improve resource allocation practices in schools. First, the usual financial accounting practices in school systems conceal more than they reveal about resource allocation. As noted earlier, only very recently have school systems begun to take advantage of modern computer technology and software to create sophisticated financial information systems. Second is a lack of sufficient research on which to build theories, explanations, or even advice of more than an anecdotal nature. Third, the wide range of procedures for resource allocation procedures that can exist in educational organizations inhibits generalizations. Finally, resource allocation processes are complicated and involve numerous individuals and groups, and the interpretation of results tends to vary with individuals' organizational or disciplinary perspectives.

The purpose of this book is to examine microlevel resource allocation practices from a variety of levels within the educational system: school board, district administration, building level, and classroom. A number of the chapters focus on a particular organizational level and present research findings about the policies and practices common to that level. The findings suggest both the causes of the practices and their implications for improving school effectiveness.

OVERVIEW OF THE BOOK

The book opens with three chapters that set the stage for what follows by discussing the policy, political, and information problems affecting the pursuit of educational productivity. Next, actual resource allocation in education is examined in a series of chapters dealing with each of the primary organizational levels within the local educational system. Finally, the book concludes with a chapter presenting a conceptual synthesis, reflecting on the contents of the book, and offering a "policy framework" for school resource allocation.

In Chapter 1, "Productive Schools from a Policy Perspective," William Boyd argues that school reform is approaching a dangerous crossroads in many postindustrial nations. With aging populations and many competing demands for tax money, support for school reform could evaporate if the productivity of public schools is not improved. A disenchanted public could increasingly favor the path toward privatization and disinvestment in public education. Thus, school reform efforts could be imperiled if we do not (a) deliver and publicize positive results, and (b) help avoid or minimize the damage wrought by the adoption of simplistic "panacea" solutions. Success in school reform, however, is complicated by disagreements about the goals to be achieved, about the policy designs to achieve these goals, and about "what works" and how to explain the answers to an impatient public. Drawing on examples from systemic reform efforts in Britain and the United States, Boyd discusses how these disagreements and associated issues play out in the formulation of policy for school reform and the need to develop strategic responses to these problems.

Chapter 2, "The Politics of Educational Productivity," by William Boyd and William Hartman, explores how knowledge about the management of productive schools relates to the typical practices of school administrators. After reviewing research on what administrators do and don't do to promote educational productivity, the authors advance several alternative explanations for the traditional tendency to neglect instructional improvement and student outcomes. Although this tendency is now diminishing, due to mounting demands for better outcomes, this chapter discusses the variety of micropolitical factors that can impede efforts to improve educational productivity.

Chapter 3, "The New Politics of Information in Education," discusses the far-reaching consequences of the utilization of new financial analysis technologies. The authors—E. Vance Randall, Bruce S. Cooper, Sheree T. Speakman, and Deborah Rosenfield—are pioneers in the development and application of powerful, new financial analysis software in education. In this chapter, they discuss five dimensions of the politics of information associated with the shift from district-level to school-site financial analysis. Using vivid examples from school districts, they illustrate how the changes in the level of analysis alter the accountability and personalize the process:

> No longer are problems in school finance some esoteric issues far away at the district or state level, done by faceless participants. Instead, the new politics of information starts with local information, affecting the lives of identifiable students. As other data are related to costs—such as teacher behaviors and student achievement . . . —the stakes rise and the constituents become engaged. It is then that the five dimensions of information politics come together.

Chapter 4, "The Role of the School Board in Resource Allocation," by Elaine Chichura and William Hartman, examines the unique functions played by boards of education. They must combine the economic and political dimensions of the formal organization of public schools to provide and maintain both an appropriate educational program and an efficient delivery of the chosen services. This chapter reports on a case study undertaken to examine, in detail, the roles of four Pennsylvania school boards in the resource allocation process. First, a description of the formal and informal roles of school boards in the budgetary process was developed to explain how resource allocation decisions were made. Second, the objectives, motivations, and constraints that affected the decision-making behavior of the school boards were examined using three theoretical approaches: the rational model (use of formal goals and objectives in budgetary decisions); the bureaucratic model (rules and regulations of an organization); and the political model (power, special-interest groups, and public choice theory). The actions and choices of school boards and their members were systematically scrutinized to evaluate which theoretical model or combination of models best explained the role of the board when making resource allocation decisions.

In Chapter 5, "Reconciling Equity and Excellence: Resource Allocation in School Districts," Peter Coleman, Stephen Easton, and Linda LaRocque note that discussions of fiscal resource distribution frequently focus upon balancing equity or excellence policy goals, which are perceived to be in competition. Their discussion of equity and excellence in school districts proposes a broader definition of resources than has typically been used. Drawing upon data from an intensive qualitative study of ten school districts in British Columbia, Canada, they show that high-performing districts approach resource allocation decisions in ways that differ from those of less-successful districts.

This and other empirical work on schools and school districts suggest that resource allocation activities that focus upon the use of nonfiscal resources, such as teacher incentives and family contributions, and link these with fiscal resources in appropriate ways can indeed have a positive effect on outcomes. This emphasis upon nonfiscal resources, labeled "productive" by the authors, allows a reexamination of notions of equity and excellence that suggests that the opposition between them is a false one. Both goals are attainable, given a broader conception of resources and more-careful resource use; consequently, the authors propose a resource allocation model for school districts that would contribute to both equity and excellence in policy.

Very little research is available on how schools actually allocate the resources that are received from higher levels. Chapter 6, "Understanding Resource Allocation in High Schools," by William Hartman, presents the results of an intensive study of the resource allocation practices of four high schools in Oregon. First, the considerable range of practices found among the schools is described, along with the districts' policies and methods for transferring resources to the schools. Second, alternative theoretical explanations for the actual allocation processes observed are proposed. These range from a rational model emphasizing achievement of goals, to a bureaucratic model, to political models featuring power or public choice theory. The quantitative and qualitative evidence for the appropriateness of each model are reviewed, and the dominant resource allocation behaviors and causes in the high schools are identified.

In Chapter 7, "Allocation and Distribution of Resources in High Schools," M. Barbara Sartori examines in detail the budgeting processes in four Pennsylvania high schools to understand how available resources were distributed among instructional, support, and administrative units. This study involved both a description of the resource allocation processes in high schools and an analysis of the objectives and motivations of high school principals and others involved in the budget process as they made these decisions. Use of a case study approach allowed discovery of the informal rules and processes as well as the formal process. Attendance at budget meetings, interviews with school personnel, and analysis of budget documents provided evidence to evaluate the appropriateness of each model of resource allocation. As a companion study to the school board analysis presented in Chapter 4 and the high school analysis in Chapter 6, the same three decision-making models—rational, bureaucratic, and political—were used to interpret the behaviors and attitudes of high school level personnel. This provided a consistent line of inquiry across several organizational levels, and in two separate states.

In Chapter 8, "Transcending the Effects of School Size on the High School Curriculum," David Monk uses data from the *High School and Beyond* data set to analyze the allocation of resources across various areas of the high school curriculum. Past research has shown that substantial variation exists in the deployment of curricular resources among high schools of a comparable size. In other words, although size may play an important role in the development of curricula, there are situations in which small high schools are able to overcome the constraints imposed by small size and, in fact, offer impressively diverse and in-depth curricula. Similarly, there are large high schools that are either unwilling or unable to take advantage of the flexibility larger size offers in the development of curriculum. In these large schools with minimal curricula, the tendency is to offer large numbers of sections of a relatively small number of undifferentiated courses. Because school and school district reorganization have been widely pursued for many years as a means of broadening the curricular opportunities of students, particularly at the secondary school level, Monk notes that his results "demonstrate the upper bounds on how successful such policies are likely to be. The findings suggest that focusing solely on the school size related sources of curricular inequalities will not be adequate if the goal is to eliminate inequalities in curricular opportunities among high schools."

Chapter 9, "Resource Use and Student Achievement in Elementary Schools," by Richard A. Rossmiller, is concerned with resource allocation at the elementary classroom and student level. It is unique among microlevel studies of resource allocation in that it focuses on a large sample of individual students over a three-year time period. Two different types of resources were considered: student time and expenditures per student. The analysis of student time examined the relationships between allocation and use of time in elementary school classrooms and cognitive outcomes exhibited by students. Results from the reading and mathematics areas revealed wide variation among individual students in the amounts of time on-task and off-task, a disappointingly large amount of process time, and inconsistent relationships between achievement test scores and the amount of time on-task in these subjects.

An analysis of the relationship between expenditures attributed to specific students and student achievement indicated inconsistent, but generally positive, relationships between expenditure per student and time on-task, and negative correlations between expenditure per student and achievement. For regular students, schools and teachers were allocating resources among students unrelated to performance on achievement tests. Rossmiller concludes:

> The results of this study underline the complexity of the educational process and the difficulty of attempting to understand student achievement and growth based only on the events that occur within the school. Although our unit of analysis was the individual student, thus avoiding some of the problems encountered in research based on school- or district-wide data, we were not able to account for a large percentage of the variance in either student achievement or student gains. Our results suggest that the search for a single education production function is futile. Rather, we believe that there are many valid education production functions, that is, that the most-efficient and most-effective combination of resources will be a function of the specific student as well as many situational variables. Perhaps that is why the teacher is such an important element in the educational process. It is classroom teachers who must make hour-to-hour and minute-to-minute decisions about how to use most effectively the resources available to optimize learning for the students in their classrooms. Thus, teachers are in a very real sense the primary managers of the resources society allocates for the education of children.

In his thoughtful concluding chapter, "A Policy Framework for School Resource Allocation," Douglas E. Mitchell reflects on the contents of this volume and raises stimulating questions about the meaning of productivity in education and the implications of competing conceptions of education as an economic good. It is altogether fitting, we think, that the book ends with a discussion of the broader issues Mitchell raises. He argues:

> To analyze school productivity, it is necessary to assume that education is a product, generated by applying pedagogical techniques to students seen as "raw materials." . . . At least three other conceptions of the economic nature of education highlight the limitations of productivity analysis. . . . The economic value of schooling, and the means for enhancing that value, take on very different meanings if education is viewed as a social service, an investment in human capital formation, or a means of generating cultural identity. These broader and more-complex conceptions of the economic value of schooling may ultimately prove more fruitful in explaining school resource allocation problems and outcomes than the current emphasis on production function analysis.

NOTES

1. See, for example, Consortium on Productivity (1995); Cooper, Sarrel, and Heinbuch (1994); Ferguson (1991); Ferguson and Ladd (1996); Hedges, Laine, and Greenwald (1994); Hanushek et al. (1994); Picus and Wattenbarger (1996); Rothstein and Miles (1995); Verstegen (1994).

REFERENCES

Boyd, W. L. (1992, November). The power of paradigms: Reconceptualizing educational policy and management. *Educational Administration Quarterly, 28* (4), 504–528.

Consortium on Productivity in the Schools (1995, October). *Using what we have to get the schools we need: A productivity focus for American education.* New York: Institute on Education and the Economy, Teachers College, Columbia University.

Cooper, B. S., Sarrel, R., & Heinbuch, S. (1994, Summer). Making money matter in education: A micro-financial model for determining school-level allocations, efficiency, and productivity. *Journal of Education Finance, 20* (1), 66–87.

Ferguson, R. F. (1991). Paying for public education: New evidence on how and why money matters. *Harvard Journal on Legislation, 28,* 465–498.

Ferguson, R. F., & Ladd, H. F. (1996). How and why money matters: An analysis of Alabama schools. In H. F. Ladd (Ed)., *Holding schools accountable: Performance-based reform in education.* Washington, D.C.: The Brookings Institution.

Hanushek, E. A. (1981). Throwing money at schools. *Journal of Policy Analysis and Management, 1,* 19–41.

Hanushek, E. A., with Benson, C. S., Freeman, R. B., Jamison, D. T., Levin, H. M., Maynard, R. A., Murnane, R. J., Rivkin, S. G., Sabot, R. H., Solomon, L. C., Summers, A. A., Welch, F., and Wolfe, B. L. (1994). *Making schools work: Improving performance and controlling costs.* Washington, D.C.: The Brookings Institution.

Hedges, L. V., Laine, R. D., & Greenwald, R. (1994). Does money matter? A meta-analysis of studies of the effects of differential school inputs on student outcomes. *Educational Researcher, 23* (3), 5–14.

Odden, A., & Clune, W. (1995, December). Improving educational productivity and school finance. *Educational Researcher, 24* (9), 6–10, 22.

Picus, L. O., & Wattenbarger, J. L. (1996). (Eds.) *Where does the money go? Resource allocation in elementary and secondary schools.* Thousand Oaks, Calif.: Corwin Press.

Rothstein, R., & Miles, K. H. (1995). *Where's the money gone? Changes in the level and composition of education spending.* Washington, D.C.: Economic Policy Institute.

Verstegen, D. (Ed.). (1994, Summer). Special issue: Further evidence on why and how money matters in education. *Journal of Education Finance, 20,* 1.

Productive Schools from a Policy Perspective

Desiderata, Designs, and Dilemmas

William Lowe Boyd

In many postindustrial nations, school reform seems to be approaching a dangerous crossroads.[1] Difficult policy choices will have to be made in societies that are increasingly impatient for better results in school performance and student achievement. Moreover, these choices will have to be made in the face of adverse economic, demographic, and sociopolitical trends. The combination of budget deficits, economic competitiveness pressures, diminishing faith in the welfare state, and soaring numbers of senior citizens threatens support for children's services. The inescapable consequence is increasing demands for efficiency, value for money, measurement of results, and accountability in education (Guthrie, 1993). In the United States, for example, we face criticism for a "productivity crisis" in primary and secondary education. In other words, although we keep spending more, we see little improvement in student achievement (see Hanushek et al., 1994; Odden, 1994a).

With many competing demands for government money and an aging population—who, unlike children, can vote—how long can the interests of children and school reform capture adequate support if we don't show better results? The dangerous crossroads we could be approaching in some nations is one where a disenchanted public will increasingly favor the path toward privatization and disinvestment in public education (Boyd, 1987).

The stakes are very high in this, both for our societies and for equal educational opportunity for all children. In the high-tech postindustrial age, education is a key to success in the increasingly important knowledge and information industries. Winston Churchill had it right when he said, "The empires of the future are the empires of the mind." The same thought is reflected in the slogan "Microsoft's only . . . asset is the human imagination."

Thus, in our increasingly interdependent and economically competitive world, international forces are producing an imperative for more-productive schools. (Note that I didn't say more-*effective* schools; I said more-*productive* schools because they need to be cost-effective or *efficient* as well as effective.) Thus, the demand is not only for effective schools but for quality and efficiency at the same time. With well-educated and quality-conscious consumers and parents in Western nations, the demand for quality, for information on school performance, and for choice of schools seems inescapable. The "genie" is out of the bottle on these matters, and no amount of wishful thinking by educators can put it back in.

So, we live in a time of high stakes, ferment, and challenge in school reform. The "clock is running" on our efforts, and we could wear out our welcome, politically, if we do not (a) deliver and publicize positive results, and (b) help avoid or minimize the damage wrought by the adoption of simplistic "panacea" solutions.

In responding to these issues, I believe that our problems revolve around competing views regarding

1. the "desiderata of school reform" (that is, the desired essentials or goals we want to achieve),
2. dissensus about the policy designs to achieve our goals,
3. dilemmas about what works and about how to explain the answers to an impatient public.

In a nutshell, then, my argument is that we are trying to "decant the elixir of school reform" in the face of differing desiderata, diverging designs, and perplexing dilemmas of determination, dissensus, and dissemination.

Given all the controversies that surround school reform, one has to agree with Judith Chapman (1991) that virtually all aspects of the topic are what Gallie (1964) called "essentially contested concepts." We can and do have big disagreements about nearly every feature of education policy and practice. This occurs not just among the public, the parents, the politicians, and the political parties, but also among teachers, school administrators, school reformers, and educational researchers.

Our ability to resolve these disagreements is impeded by two major dilemmas:

1. The difficulty of determining what works and why, and
2. Even if we know the answers to the first dilemma, the difficulty of explaining and "selling" what works (and policy to achieve this) to policymakers, the public, and (even) to educators

This chapter discusses how these dilemmas play out in the formulation of policy for school reform or, put another way, for more-productive schools. In this discussion, I draw mainly on the experiences of the two countries I know best, the United States and Britain. In closing, I argue that because of the political problems we face, we need, more consciously than ever, to develop strategic responses to these dilemmas.

THE DIFFICULTY OF DETERMINING
WHAT WORKS AND WHY

Our difficulties in improving the productivity of schools revolve around our problems in determining what works and why. Although our knowledge is improving, we still have a limited grasp of the "production function" in education, that is, how the inputs and processes of schooling combine to produce student learning outcomes (see, for example, Hanushek, 1986; Monk, 1992). Despite extensive research efforts, the complexity of the mix of variables involved in teaching and learning in diverse social contexts tends to confound efforts to achieve a "science of education," often leaving us with a sense of indeterminacy (McDermott, 1976).

To make things still more complex, education policy is generally intended to improve performance at the incompletely understood "micro" level (that is, classrooms) by altering—or working through— variables at the "macro" and "meso" levels. We have disagreements about strategies for doing this and about how to balance "bottom-up" and "top-down" approaches to school reform. School reform's evolution over the past fifteen years has reflected these disagreements. Macro policy strategies have ranged from "intensification" (increasing the rigor and standards of what already was being done) to "restructuring" the system, either incrementally (one school at a time—for example, the Coalition of Essential Schools) or holistically ("systemic school reform" [see Smith & O'Day, 1991]); and from centralization to decentralization and school-based management, and then on to a hybrid that might be called "centralized devolution."

More-specific policy remedies have included a wide range of prescriptions, from various "effective schools" practices to Total Quality Management, to performance incentives and penalties, to school choice plans, to privatization and "contracting out" the management of schools. Finally, there are promising and even more-specific reform packages, such as Robert Slavin's "Success for All" schools, Henry Levin's "Accelerated Schools," and James Comer's "School Development Program."

How should choices be made from among all these competing policy ideas for reforming schools? When the experts cannot themselves agree, policymakers and the public are especially prone to rely on their own biases and possible misconceptions. This is unfortunate because research has revealed a great deal about what makes schools effective and about the process of school improvement.[2] Yet, we are still disadvantaged by our own disagreements about which policies are best and, indeed, about the extent to which any policy created *outside* of schools can actually change behavior *inside* of schools. As Fullan and Miles (1992) argue, "all large-scale change is implemented locally" (p. 752) and involves a learning process. But, they point out that this does not mean that "only the local level counts," for they emphasize that "change is systemic" (pp. 751–52). As their insightful discussion makes clear, our cutting-edge knowledge about how to design and manage school reform is increasingly sophisticated but not widely understood in the education community, let alone by impatient policymakers and the public.

Our policy disagreements about what works are epitomized by the fundamental and long-running dispute about whether spending more on schools helps improve student achievement. The leading skeptic about spending on schools is Eric Hanushek, an economist whose research has warned against the folly of "throwing money at schools" (Hanushek, 1981, 1986, 1994; Hanushek et al., 1994). Hanushek's key point is that although more spending for schools obviously can be beneficial, the essential and generally missing step in practice is to compare alternative policies and evaluate how effectively (productively) the money actually is being used. Without this step, one can only guess about how wisely (or ineffectively) money is being spent. Moreover, the current political and economic reality is such that we are unlikely to get significant increases in funding for education (Odden & Clune, 1995), so, as the report of the Consortium on Productivity in the Schools (1995) emphasizes, we must get better at "using what we have to get the schools we need."

Apart from his key point, which seems indisputable, Hanushek's research conclusions have been challenged in recent years by a number of studies.[3] In particular, Hedges, Laine, and Greenwald (1994) reanalyzed the data Hanushek used (from thirty-eight articles and books published from the 1960s into the 1980s) and found strong ties between student achievement and both per-pupil funding levels and teacher experience. The dispute between Hedges et al. and Hanushek revolves, in part, around the use of different methodologies (Hedges used "meta-analysis"; Hanushek used a method called "vote counting") and partly around how the results are interpreted (Viadero, 1994). When a reporter from *Education Week* asked other experts who was right in this conflict, the answer she got was that "maybe both sides are" (Viadero, 1994, p. 6).[4]

This "non-conclusion" is emblematic of the indeterminacy impeding efforts to guide policy with research. The frequent lack of consensus among experts in the education research community is summed up by Christopher Cross's observation that "for every study in education research, there are an equal or greater number of opposing studies" (as quoted in Kaestle, 1993, p. 29). At its worst, education research at times comes dangerously close to looking like a caricature of science.

Happily, education research is not always in dispute or disarray and does make a difference (see, for example, Boyd & Plank, 1994). Hanushek's research and studies responding to it, documenting the circumstances under which money does make a difference, have played a part in the overdue "paradigm shift" in education policy and management from a focus on inputs (for example, spending levels and resources) to a concern for outcomes (Boyd & Crowson, 1981). However, in a fascinating turn of events, the concern in the United States for better outcomes in student achievement has led us full circle: "Systemic school reform," as codified in the "Goals 2000: Educate America Act" (passed in March 1994), seeks higher student learning outcomes for all children. Its intention was to encourage our fifty states to voluntarily (a) adopt rigorous standards and curriculum frameworks, (b) link them to a strong testing or performance assessment system, and (c) establish "opportunity to learn" (OTL) standards specifying the minimum resources and opportunities that schools should provide to give all students a fair chance to learn the more challenging curricular content upon which they will be tested.[5]

The idea of opportunity to learn (OTL) standards (also called "school delivery standards") immediately proved to be controversial on political as well as pedagogical grounds (Kirst, 1994). In fact, it proved to be "dead on arrival" because it not only raised the old problem of trying to determine, in some reasonable way, what minimum inputs and practices ought to be in place in all schools but added the explosive issue of which level(s) of government should have the responsibility for determining, financing, and enforcing such standards (see Porter, 1993, 1994). The old-fashioned, input-oriented approach to school policy and management tried to do part of this, but it only assumed a linkage to student outcomes rather than trying to assess this systematically.

In the United States, the dispute about the relationship between resources or inputs and student outcomes was intensified in 1994 by the confluence of two events, one academic and one political. In October 1994 the Brookings Institution published *Making Schools Work: Improving Performance and Controlling Costs* (Hanushek et al., 1994), the report of a distinguished panel of economists concerned about the economics of educational reform. This report argues that the productivity and performance crises of American schools will continue until three fundamental deficiencies in their management are corrected:

1. Inattention to the efficient use of resources
2. Lack of performance incentives
3. Neglect of evaluation and experimentation

The report notes that not just school administrators but also school reformers have been deficient on all three of these counts. It cautions that additional spending is unlikely to improve the schools if it is spent in the usual manner, that is, without evaluating the results of alternative policies. Indeed, the authors of the report note, "Because current operations are so inefficient, additional resources can be found by making better use of current funds. . . . [T]here is no question that sizable overall inefficiencies currently exist. The possibility of tapping into poorly used resources makes budget-neutral reform less constraining" (pp. 8–9).

The political event that made this report all the more threatening was the stunning Republican victory in the November 1994 election. With the Republicans in control of Congress for the first time in forty years, and the right wing of their party in ascendance, war was declared against big government and what were perceived to be the many inefficient and unnecessary government programs and agencies that had been created by the Democrats. The flavor of this activity was captured in the blunt title of a policy discussion held in Washington in December 1994 by the "Project for the Republican Future." It was called "What to Kill First: Agencies to Dismantle, Programs to Eliminate, and Regulations to Stop."

Key aspects of the national systemic school reform effort underway in the U.S.A. were in danger of becoming casualties of their efforts. Although the "Goals 2000: Educate America Act" and the long policy-development process leading up to its passage (which began about 1986 with the work of the National Governors Association) enjoyed broad support from Republican as well as Democratic governors and legislators, this bipartisanship evaporated in the heat of the Republican electoral victory. Conservative think tanks called for the elimination of the Federal Department of Education and a dramatic diminution of the federal role in education. Two former Secretaries of Education, both highly visible Republicans with presidential aspirations, published an article with similar recommendations. In a piece coauthored with Dan Coats, a Republican senator from Indiana, Lamar Alexander and William Bennett wrote,

By signing off on HR-6 [The Improving America's Schools Act of 1994] and Goals 2000, President Clinton transformed a nationwide reform movement into a federal program . . . [usurping the proper and legal control of education by local and state governments]. . . . Clinton has even created something akin to a national school board, the National Education Standards and Improvement Council. Almost as worrying is the resurrection of inputs, resources, and services as gauges of education quality. Three decades of research show no reliable link between what goes into schools and what children learn there. Yet Goals 2000 and HR-6 affirm the routine assertion of the education establishment: If you're not happy with school results, more money and regulations will improve them. (Alexander, Bennett & Coats, 1994, p. 42)

They concluded their article by calling for the repeal of HR-6 and said that "it's time for the Federal Government virtually to withdraw from elementary and secondary education and relinquish the authority it has seized in this domain. . . . Insofar as any education functions stay in Washington, their guiding principles should be choice, deregulation, innovation, accountability, and serious assessment keyed to real standards in core subjects" (p. 44).

Although President Clinton eventually triumphed over the "Gingrich" Republicans, the provisions for the implementation of the Goals 2000 Act were weakened, and the momentum behind it slowed considerably. The systemic reform effort is not dead at the federal level, but the real progress toward national standards is being pursued in a more decentralized way at the state level.

Assessment—whether of student performance, schools, or programs—is central to school reform in national systemic efforts such as those underway in the United States and Britain. For Hanushek et al. (1994), assessment should emphasize cost-effectiveness, not mere effectiveness, as desirable as that is in itself. Thus, in one example, Hanushek et al. (1994, pp. 66–67) discuss intensive early education programs for disadvantaged students that rely, in part, on one-to-one tutoring. They note that Slavin's "Success for All" program produces significant improvements in student performance, but that its cost, which exceeds that of typical federally funded programs for disadvantaged students, is a problem. By contrast, a variant of one-to-one tutoring developed by George Farkas and his colleagues at the University of Texas at Dallas costs substantially less, and "initial estimates of performance gains appear similar to those of Success for All" (p. 67).[6]

The neglect of assessment, evaluation, and cost-effectiveness analysis in education in the past has several causes. Such studies cost money, involve tricky conceptual and technical problems (Linn, 1994; Monk & King, 1993), and can cause political problems (Darling-Hammond, 1994). Those being assessed in any sphere rarely welcome the "opportunity" to be held accountable. In the quasi-monopolistic environment of public education, the lack of performance incentives and the associated low costs to individuals (teachers and school administrators) of inefficient behavior have often discouraged efforts at not only assessment but even school improvement (Boyd & Hartman, 1988; Driscoll & Boyd, 1995). To the extent that one agrees with this analysis, the inefficiency and productivity crisis in education is an inevitable consequence of government schools being a complacent, subsidized monopoly.

Not surprisingly, then, controversies abound over new testing and assessment programs, and over the introduction of "report cards" on schools. Yet, an irresistible wave is running in this direction in countries like Britain and the United States. For example, Alexander, Bennett, and Coats (1994) asserted that there should be "wide-ranging choices for families among excellent schools that differ on many dimensions [and a] fundamental right to flee a bad or unsafe school for a good one (plus tests that make it possible to know which are which)" (p. 44). This is exactly what the Conservatives (also known as the "Tories") were trying to do in England and Wales when they introduced the publication of "league tables" comparing schools on student test performance. As they have learned from the ensuing controversy over the use of raw test scores unadjusted for the social intake of schools or for measures of "value-added" by schools, it is no simple matter to arrive at tests that "make it possible to know" a good school from a bad one. This is likely to be a hard lesson for Alexander, Bennett, and Coats, as well.

One of our problems in determining what works is being able to resist the lure and dangers of simplistic solutions for complex problems, the genre Fullan and Miles (1992) call "impatient and superficial solutions" (p. 747). League tables for rating schools were such an idea, at least in their initial simplistic formulation. Using only raw test scores assures that schools with advantaged intakes of students will look better than schools serving mainly disadvantaged students. As the *Guardian* (November 21, 1994) editorialized, "Just using raw results is relatively meaningless because clever intakes produce clever results." Happily,

the debate in Britain about this policy has produced a more sophisticated understanding of the issue, and both the Conservatives and the
Labour Party are on record as favoring the introduction of league tables
with measures of the value-added by schools. Although such measures
still had not been introduced as of May 1997, this turn of events is a
good example of what I called for earlier: efforts to minimize or, if
possible, avoid the damage wrought by the adoption of simplistic
solutions.

The British debate over league tables and, more broadly, over the
entire sweeping and controversial reform agenda undertaken by the
Tories has enriched our knowledge about both the complexity of education policy and how policies work in practice—sometimes in ways
that neither their advocates nor their critics anticipated (see, for example, Vann, 1993; Whitty, 1994a, 1994b). In the case of league tables, the
debate and efforts to achieve better measures of school performance
have revealed numerous new issues but also produced promising improvements (Budge, 1994; Fitz-Gibbon, 1994). For example, Michael
Barber (1994) suggested the use of three indicators: raw test scores, a
value-added measure, and a "school improvement index." With "New
Labour" in power, following their spectacular general election victory
in May 1997, and Michael Barber playing a key role in advising the new
government on education policy, the long-called-for value-added measures may at last be introduced.

Improvements are certainly needed because the current league-table
approach not only demoralizes less-advantaged schools but distorts
and biases both parental choice of schools and school admission
practices. Under the school choice policy in effect, there is evidence
that many schools are choosing students as much as or more than
students are choosing the schools, and that schools are favoring the
admission of students who can boost their test scores (Beckett, 1994;
see also Adler, 1993; OECD, 1994). Moreover, the present system is
likely to lead to greater social class segregation in schools. Willms
(1992) writes,

> If parents choose schools on the basis of unadjusted [league table] results
> . . . they will be more likely to choose [the highly ranked] high social-class
> schools. And if those exercising their right to choose are disproportionately
> represented by middle-class parents, the reform will tend to increase
> social-class segregation between schools, making the system less com-
> prehensive. A study of the first cohort of Scottish secondary pupils whose
> parents were eligible to make placing requests confirmed this fear: high
> social-class parents were more likely to choose schools outside their catch-
> ment area, and they more often chose high social-class schools and older
> schools. . . . If the Government's agenda is to diminish the reputation of

comprehensive schooling, thereby setting the stage for a return to selective schooling, a national monitoring system with unadjusted comparisons between schools and LEAs will advance that agenda. (p. 20)

In summing up his assessment of the social and political context of monitoring systems, Willms (1992) asks, "Can monitoring systems appear as Torgerson's (1986) third face of policy analysis, where knowledge and politics are not deadly antagonists?[7] The experiences with monitoring in both the U.S. and the U.K. indicate that knowledge and politics may never be the best of friends, but they might appear as spirited rivals" (p. 26).

The tension between knowledge and politics often obscures our ability to learn what works and why. The more that performance and assessment are emphasized, the more the temptation for those being evaluated to engage in gamesmanship and, sometimes, outright cheating. As noted earlier, where they can, schools will be tempted to admit only students who test well or, failing that, may seek ways to keep low-scoring students from being tested. Researchers in New York State found that this can be done a number of ways: "by flunking a child, placing him or her in a remedial grade, assigning him or her to special education or to a bilingual class" (Zlatos, 1994, p. 28). An elementary school in Oklahoma City that was placed on probation because of the poor test performance of its third graders "solved" the problem by simply ceasing to test most of its third graders (Zlatos, 1994). As the stakes on testing and assessment continue to rise, and in some places bonuses and jobs rest on the results (for example, in Kentucky), the temptation to cheat will increase. As a consequence, more monitoring and safeguards against this danger will be needed.[8]

A less flagrant but more insidious problem than cheating is the manipulation of statistics. In a celebrated case that is now part of American folklore, a doctor in West Virginia discovered that all fifty states were reporting that their students were testing above the national average (Cannell, 1987). This remarkable accomplishment, now referred to as the "Lake Wobegon effect," after a mythical town in Minnesota where all children are above average, was achieved by the use of old, unadjusted test norms. This kind of creative use of statistics is also reflected in what Weiss and Gruber (1987) call "the managed irrelevance of federal education statistics." Of course, Americans don't have a monopoly on this propensity, which Mark Twain called being "economical with the truth." Writing in Barron's, Donlan (1994) reported:

Brazil's economy minister, Rubens Ricupero, explained his policies on government statistics in a way that every U.S. Secretary of Commerce will recognize. He said, "I have no scruples. The good things we publicize, the bad things we hide." For telling such a truth, he was immediately dismissed. (p. 39)

EXPLAINING AND GAINING SUPPORT
FOR WHAT WORKS

Even when all the problems just outlined are overcome, and school reformers are in general agreement about what works, they still face the task of explaining and gaining support for their recommendations. This is often harder to do than anticipated. Three impediments frequently stand in the way:

1. The difficulty of explaining complex ideas
2. Overcoming anxiety and resistance to ideas that are "foreign" and not fully proven
3. Overcoming misconceptions and biases

With the adoption of increasingly ambitious reform designs, such as the national "systemic" school reform plans in Britain and the U.S.A., and demands for the publication of assessment results on schools and school districts, those advocating or affected by such policies find themselves facing far more complexity than is involved in less-far-reaching reforms. Here, we are confronted with what has been called "the costs of understanding." Writing about the complexities of education voucher plans, van Geel (1978) observed:

> The more complex the idea, the more likely it will be misunderstood and both intentionally and unintentionally misrepresented. . . . [The more] unanswered, complex questions about the actual design and operation of [a policy idea] . . . [the more this adds] to the confusion and anxiety. In short, the costs to the reformer of trying to get people to understand [a complex policy idea] are high and the costs of understanding for those being introduced to the . . . idea are also high. (p. 346)

In the United States, the "systemic school reform" agenda covers a vast canvas that is imposing to the eye and the ear.[9] The "Goals 2000 Act" is 155 pages long, and its companion piece, HR-6 ("The Improving America's Schools Act of 1994"), is far longer. Apart from the objections of the Gingrich Republicans referred to earlier, the systemic reform effort has run into substantial problems in trying to explain and communicate the meaning and details of the whole reform plan to those outside of elite policy and professional circles. Fuhrman (1994) has described these problems in some detail, noting the difficulties in "articulating the nature and intent of [the] reforms:"

Many policymakers, educators and analysts are having problems explaining the role of coherent, standards-based policy in providing direction and support for changes in teaching and learning. In policy rhetoric, it frequently appears that reforms consist only of standards and assessments. Other central components, like support for classroom change through focused and enhanced teacher education and professional development, are less visible. The broader social agenda, like providing for children's health and security, also gets short-changed in reform discussions. Public skepticism is understandable in reaction to messages suggesting that setting standards and measuring achievement, in and of themselves, can somehow lead to better teaching and learning.

In states such as Connecticut, public confusion is expressed as concern that common standards may mean lower standards. Many urban and rural educators and parents worry that the standards discussion means new rules without new solutions to persistent problems of poverty. In Ohio, Pennsylvania, Kentucky, Virginia, and other states, confusion has also fueled virulent opposition to outcomes-based education, a version of standards reform that frequently includes affective outcomes as well as academic standards. (p. 3)

Similar and, indeed, much more acute problems have been experienced in Britain. When the Tories imposed a more radical and, unlike "Goals 2000," nonvoluntary version of systemic reform on the education system in 1988, they derided the objections and relevant expertise of professional educators. In a paper that should be required reading for American reformers, Paul Black (1994) presents a penetrating analysis of what went wrong in the efforts by British experts to help guide the government's development of a national assessment system to complement the new national curriculum for England and Wales.

Black (1994) notes that "the difficulties with TGAT [the Task Group on Assessment and Testing, which he chaired] lie in the interface between technical possibility and the public, political, and professional understanding of assessment and testing" (p. 200). He asks, in conclusion, a series of crucial questions for the development of assessment systems, of which the following are particularly relevant for this discussion:

How can professional educators and assessment experts communicate effectively to the public in general, and to politicians in particular, about the strengths and weaknesses of various forms of assessment? The limited reliability and even more limited validity of externally set, timed and formal written examinations are not understood. Their apparent fairness and objectivity is appealing, and those who wish to see them replaced by other methods are regarded either as romantics or as defenders of an illegitimate professional wish to avoid public scrutiny. Thus, the motives of TGAT were called into question because the technical basis for much of the group's thinking was not understood. . . .

A subsidiary question . . . is of particular importance: Can the public understand that new models of learning show that traditional assessment systems are inadequate and damaging? . . . [Research shows that] the backwash effects of narrow testing are more damaging than had previously been thought, and yet they are hardly understood outside the teaching profession. (p. 200)

In the United States, the Republican Right reflects the same kind of impatience with the complexity of sophisticated testing that Kenneth Clarke and other leading Tory politicians in Britain evinced in their "discourse of derision" (Ball, 1990) against the teaching profession. Alexander, Bennett, and Coats (1994) invoked this tone in saying:

The public has serious misgivings about *the trendy schemes beloved of today's education establishment*—the very approaches on which money and legitimacy are lavished by HR-6 and the rest of the Clinton package. As [a recent survey by] Public Agenda reports, "the large majority of Americans are uncomfortable" with such things as "ending the 'tracking' of students, and replacing standardized, multiple-choice tests with new, more 'authentic' assessments." (p. 44, emphasis added)

It has to be acknowledged, however, that Alexander et al. raised a quite serious and valid concern in noting the public opinion gap reported by Public Agenda between the general public's views and those of elite school reformers.[10] This gulf between the reformers and the lay public has led to the kind of controversies Fuhrman referred to in mentioning the "virulent opposition to outcomes-based education" in states such as Pennsylvania. Indeed, the heated conflict in Pennsylvania over outcomes-based education (OBE), led by the fears of the Christian Right that it would be used to "brainwash" children into accepting repugnant values and attitudes, has had national repercussions (Pitsch, 1994; Boyd, Lugg & Zahorchak, 1996). The dispute over OBE is a prime example of the vulnerability of complex and less-than-fully-proven ideas to misunderstanding and misrepresentation.[11] State officials in Pennsylvania found it difficult to adequately explain their proposed plan for OBE even to educators, not to mention the general public. In consequence, through effective use of the "politics of controversy" (Block & van Geel, 1975), opponents of OBE succeeded in raising so many fears about the concept that educators and policymakers nationwide now tend to avoid the term "outcomes" in favor of "results." Moreover, leaders among the Christian Right carried the misunderstanding and misrepresentation a significant step further, by claiming that OBE is part of the Goals 2000 plan, which, as a result, should also be rejected (Pitsch, 1994).

This brings us directly to grips with the problem of overcoming misconceptions and biases. Part of the difficulty here is summed up by the newspaper humorist Josh Billings's colorful observation, "It ain't what you don't know that's so harmful, it's what you know that just ain't so." Sadly, developments in school reform in New Jersey vividly illustrate how what people "know that just ain't so" impedes reform. As Firestone, Natriello, and Goertz (1994) reported:

> Unfortunately, general understanding of the state's last major educational funding initiative, the Quality Education Act, leans more to mythology than history. Many people believe the QEA provided sufficient funding to substantially equalize spending between the rich and poor districts. Moreover, even before the bill passed, most people assumed that poor districts would mismanage new state aid dollars. Complaints about urban districts are still common—that they don't know how to spend the increased revenues or that they squander funds on increasing teachers' salaries, as if equalizing salaries between rich and poor districts were not an effective way to recruit and retain good teachers for urban children. Finally, fears were raised that Robin Hood bills like the QEA would undermine the state's educational success stories: its wealthy suburban districts.

> The problem with the myths surrounding the QEA is that they are not supported by the evidence. For the past three years, we have been studying the implementation and impact of QEA, not just by looking at the numbers from the Department of Education, but by going into schools in twelve districts: six poor, urban districts that were designated by the Court and targeted by the Legislature to receive additional funds, four wealthy districts that were originally slated to lose money under QEA, and two middle income districts. Our findings debunk the myths; specifically, we found that:

> • While QEA started to reduce the gap between rich and poor districts, a substantial difference remains.
> • For the most part, poor districts made good use of the money they received, but they turn out to have costs that other districts don't have.
> • QEA did not undermine the quality of the state's wealthier districts. (pp. 16–17)

Despite these findings, QEA in New Jersey was, and still is, regarded as a controversial and unsuccessful program. The Firestone et al. findings were dismissed and disparaged. When one high state official was told about the findings, he immediately responded that "the study must be flawed," even though he had not even seen the study.[12] The common view continues to be that the troubled urban school districts are "bottomless pits" of incompetence and failure, whereas the wealthy suburban districts are "crumbling lighthouses—models of exemplary practices and outcomes threatened by the shift of state aid to poor, urban districts" (Firestone, Natriello & Goertz, 1994, p. 17; see also CEPA-NJ, 1994a, 1994b).

CONCLUSION

The perception of urban school districts as "bottomless pits" is unfortunately not confined to New Jersey. It is widespread and symptomatic of the growing danger of both (a) disinvestment in failing public education systems and (b) increasingly "savage inequalities" dividing the rich and poor in our society (Kozol, 1991). Calls are mounting in the United States to "break up," "privatize," or otherwise radically reform troubled urban schools districts. Increasingly, it appears that major surgery is required. But *what surgery* and *with what consequences* for the patients? Thus, we end as we began, approaching a dangerous crossroads of public and political opinion about the reform and future of public education. Will the public and its elected representatives take the path toward positive reform, or will they proceed on the path toward privatization, disinvestment, and abandonment, policy directions that are already gaining support in many states, particularly for urban education?[13]

To recapitulate the argument I have made, the "clock is running" on our efforts to reform schools. We could wear out our welcome, politically, if we do not (a) deliver and publicize positive results, and (b) help avoid or minimize the damage wrought by the adoption of simplistic "panacea" solutions. But how can we do this, and what can we do about the problems we face in school reform, the "differing desiderata," "diverging designs," and "dilemmas of determination, dissensus, and dissemination" outlined earlier?

First, we need to acknowledge that much of the disagreement about, and resistance to, school reform is understandable and legitimate. Given the "essentially contested" nature of our domain, it would be quite surprising if we did not encounter these problems. As Fullan and Miles (1992, p. 748) argue, rather than misunderstanding and disparaging resistance, we need to recognize the legitimate basis of most resistance and seek to establish a dialogue and learning process that might resolve some of the objections or enable accommodations. In the case of the OBE conflict in Pennsylvania, for example, state officials might have been able to dampen the fire if they had abandoned the controversial affective/attitudinal outcomes much sooner.

Second, as well as listen to our critics, we need to acknowledge when we don't have the whole solution worked out. As Fullan and Miles (1992) note, "it is folly to act as if we know how to solve complex problems in short order" (p. 746) when the best we can do is to start a learning process toward solutions. Thus, despite the vast canvas on which systemic reform has been laid out in the United States, Odden (1994a) notes that "proponents of systemic reform barely address the management and organization structures that it requires . . . and usually skirt altogether the finance structure" (p. 105). As a consequence, researchers are now working rapidly to try to fill in these important gaps in the plan (see, for example, Monk & King, 1993; Odden, 1994a, 1994b; Wohlstetter, Smyer & Mohrman, 1994).

Third, we ought to try, where possible, to reduce the appearance of dissensus in the research community by making more-effective use of consensus panel reports by distinguished experts on the "best knowledge or practice." These reports should be informed by political as well as technical expertise to increase the likelihood of acceptance of their recommendations. Professional associations such as the American Educational Research Association could play a major role in promoting such reports.

Fourth, in our reports and presentations to the public and policymakers, we need to give more thought to how to explain and publicize our research and reform ideas in easy-to-understand, jargon-free language. When we present our ideas in arcane ways, we not only impede communication but make ourselves vulnerable to ridicule and attack. We are in the business of education and need to give thought to how to reach and educate our various publics, recognizing that we must begin at their own "starting points." The following example from an education conference is all too typical: It included a session to introduce educators to the implications of what "constructivism" means for teaching and learning. Three panelists presented three very different and rather sophisticated explanations of constructivism. From an academic and intellectual point of view it was fascinating and stimulating. But, from an educative or communicative point of view it was almost baffling for many of the teachers and administrators there. A graduate student who was in attendance said afterwards that he had to try to "translate" what the panelists were saying for the benefit of the teachers around him.

Fifth, I think we need to take seriously the recommendations by the Consortium on Productivity in the Schools (1995) and by Hanushek and his associates (1994) for much more attention to the productive and efficient use of resources, to the need for performance incentives, and to experimentation and assessing the cost-effectiveness of programs. If we do not take the lead in developing sophisticated accountability and productivity measures, others with less sophistication will impose simplistic measures upon us. Of course, I realize that many in the education community find economic approaches and talk of accountability, efficiency, and incentives disturbing, and perhaps even morally reprehensible when applied to the sphere of education, a domain they believe should be exclusively concerned with the needs of children and social justice. The difficulty is that there are also other people and other needs out there competing for the available funds, which even in the most affluent and generous society are never limitless. Thus, we must be better able to document our prudential use of scarce resources, to show what works, with what costs, and with what benefits for children and society. And we must recognize that what works is significantly affected by the incentives and motivations in play within our organizations. Incentives already exist, of course, but in too many schools and school systems the predominant incentives, whether intended or not, do not reward productive behavior (Boyd & Hartman, 1988; Odden & Conley, 1992). Rather than divisive, individualistic performance incentives, research and experimentation now favor "cooperative performance incentives" for schools as collaborative learning organizations (Richards, Fishbein & Melville, 1993). To the degree that we can craft policies to encourage efficient use of resources, constructive performance incentives, and careful evaluation of programs, to that same degree we will be moving toward more-productive schools.

NOTES

1. This is a revised version of a keynote address presented at the International Congress on School Effectiveness and Improvement held in Leeuwarden, the Netherlands, January 5, 1995.

2. See, for example, Bryk, Lee, and Smith (1990); Chapman (1990); Fullan (1991); Fullan and Miles (1992); Lee, Bryk and Smith (1993); Louis and Miles (1990); Mortimore et al. (1988); Reynolds and Cuttance (1992); Reynolds et al. (1994); Riley and Nuttall (1994); Rutter et al. (1979); Scheerens (1992); Teddlie and Stringfield (1993); Willms (1992).

3. See, for example, Ferguson (1991), Ferguson and Ladd (1996), Verstegen (1994).

4. According to Viadero (1994), Hanushek "now says the two studies are 'in complete agreement.' 'There are some places that use money ineffectively and some that use it effectively,' he said. 'If you throw money at schools, you get at about the rough average'" (p. 6).

5. For the intellectual work behind this, see Smith and O'Day (1991); O'Day and Smith (1993); and Clune (1993a, 1993b).

6. For an insightful comparative cost analysis of Slavin's "Success for All" schools, Levin's Accelerated Schools, and Comer's School Development Program, see King (1994).

7. In Torgerson's (1986) first face of policy analysis, knowledge replaces politics ("the positivist's dream"); in the second face, politics dominates over knowledge.

8. In Kentucky, part of the state's ambitious reform plan provides for bonuses of as much as $3,200 per teacher to schools where performance exceeds target goals.

9. Persons with access to the Internet interested in following developments in U.S. school reform can subscribe to the free electronic "Daily Report Card" provided by The National Education Goals Panel. This service presents a daily digest of news stories from across the U.S.A. relevant to progress toward Goals 2000 and the National Education Goals. To subscribe to this free news service via e-mail, send the following message (with a blank subject line) to LISTSERV@GWUVM.GWU.EDU: sub rptcrd Your Name.

10. For more information on Public Agenda's survey findings, see Wadsworth (1994).

11. For a brief but perceptive analysis of Pennsylvania's OBE controversy, see Hanushek et al., 1994, pp. 130–131.

12. Information from personal communication with William Firestone, December 15, 1994.

13. Unfortunately, some urban school districts behave in ways that keep the "bottomless pit" image alive. For example, the East St. Louis school district, which Kozol (1991) uses as a horrendous example of "savage inequalities," is notorious for patronage and wasteful spending (*Education Week*, 1995; Schmidt, 1995).

REFERENCES

Adler, M. (1993). Parental choice and the enhancement of children's interests. In P. Munn (Ed.), *Parents and schools: Customers, managers or partners?* London: Routledge.

Alexander, L., Bennett, W. J., & Coats, D. (1994, December 19). Local options: Congress should return control of education to states, school boards—and parents. *National Review*, 42-44.

Ball, S. J. (1990). *Politics and policy making in education.* London: Routledge.

Barber, M. (1994, May 3). Table manners. *Guardian Education*, 4.

Beckett, F. (1994, September 11). Hobson's choice for parents. *The Observer*, Schools Report, 3.

Black, P. J. (1994, Summer). Performance assessment and accountability: The experience in England and Wales. *Educational Evaluation and Policy Analysis, 16* (2), 191–203.

Block, A., & van Geel, T. (1975). State of Arizona curriculum law. In T. van Geel, with the assistance of A. Block, *Authority to control the school curriculum. A study supported by a grant from the National Institute of Education* (ERIC Document No. ED 125070).

Boyd, W. L. (1987, Summer). Public education's last hurrah? Schizophrenia, amnesia, and ignorance in school politics. *Educational Evaluation and Policy Analysis, 9* (2), 85–100.

Boyd, W. L., & Crowson, R. (1981). The changing conception and practice of public school administration. In D. C. Berliner (Ed.), *Review of research in education, Volume 9* (pp. 311–373). Washington: American Educational Research Association.

Boyd, W. L., & Hartman, W. (1988). The politics of educational productivity. In D. Monk & J. Underwood (Eds.), *Microlevel school finance: Issues and implications for policy* (pp. 271–308). Cambridge, Mass.: Ballinger Publishing Co.

Boyd, W. L., & Plank, D. (1994). Educational policy studies: Overview. In T. Husen & T. N. Postlethwaite (Eds.), *International Encyclopedia of Education,* 2nd ed. (pp. 1835–1841). Oxford: Pergamon Press.

Boyd, W. L., Lugg, C. A., & Zahorchak, G. L. (1996, May). Social traditionalists, religious conservatives, and the politics of outcome-based education: Pennsylvania and beyond. *Education and Urban Society, 28* (3), 347–365.

Bryk, A. S., Lee, V. E., & Smith, J. S. (1990). High school organization and its effects on teachers and students: An interpretive summary of the research. In W. H. Clune & J. F. Witte (Eds.), *Choice and control in American education, Volume I: The theory of choice and control in American education* (pp. 135–227). New York: Falmer.

Budge, D. (1994, December 9). Determined to grasp the value-added sword. *Time Education Supplement,* 10.

Cannell, J. J. (1987). *Nationally normed referenced testing in American schools: How all fifty states are above the national average.* West Virginia: Friends for Education.

CEPA-NJ. (1994a, January). Necessary but not sufficient: The impact of the Quality Education Act on at-risk students. *CEPA-NJ Newsletter.* New Brunswick, N.J.: Center for Educational Policy Analysis in New Jersey, Graduate School of Education, Rutgers University.

CEPA-NJ. (1994b, September). The myth of bottomless pits and crumbling lighthouses: Two years of New Jersey's Quality Education Act. *CEPA-NJ Newsletter.* New Brunswick, N.J.: Center for Educational Policy Analysis in New Jersey, Graduate School of Education, Rutgers University.

Chapman, J. (1990). *School-based decision-making and management.* London: Falmer Press.

Chapman, J. (1991, January). School effectiveness and management: The enmeshment of the qualitative and quantitative concerns of schooling. A keynote address presented at the International Congress for School Effectiveness and Improvement, Cardiff, Wales.

Clune, W. (1993a, September). The shift from equity to adequacy in school finance. *The World and I, 8* (9), 389–405.

Clune, W. (1993b). Systemic educational policy: A conceptual framework. In S. H. Fuhrman (Ed.), *Designing coherent educational policy: Improving the system* (pp. 125–140). San Francisco: Jossey-Bass.

Consortium on Productivity in the Schools. (1995, October). *Using what we have to get the schools we need: A productivity focus for American education.* New York: Institute on Education and the Economy, Teachers College, Columbia University.

Darling-Hammond, L. (1994, August). National standards and assessments: Will they improve education? *American Journal of Education, 102* (4), 478–510.

Donlan, T. G. (1994, December 26). Famous last words. *Barron's,* 39.

Driscoll, M. E., & Boyd, W. L. (1995). The politics of educational productivity revisited. In B. Levin, W. J. Fowler, & H. J. Walberg (Eds.), *Organizational influences on educational productivity.* Greenwich, Conn.: JAI Press, 215–238.

Education Week. (1995, March 1). Audit faults management in East St. Louis district, 4.

Ferguson, R. F. (1991). Paying for public education: New evidence on how and why money matters. *Harvard Journal on Legislation, 28,* 465–498.

Ferguson, R. F., & Ladd, H. F. (1996). How and why money matters: An analysis of Alabama schools. In H. F. Ladd (Ed.), *Holding schools accountable: Performance-based reform in education.* Washington, D.C.: The Brookings Institution.

Firestone, W. A., Natriello, G. J., & Goertz, M. E. (1994, September-October). The QEA: Myth & Reality. *New Jersey Reporter, 24* (3), 16–25.

Fitz-Gibbon, C. (1994, December 9). Three routes to the wrong answer. *Times Educational Supplement,* 11.

Fuhrman, S. H. (1994). Challenges in systemic education reform. *CPRE Policy Briefs.* Consortium for Policy Research in Education. New Brunswick, N.J.: Eagleton Institute of Politics, Rutgers University.

Fullan, M. G. (1991). *The new meaning of educational change.* New York: Teachers College Press.

Fullan, M. G., & Miles, M. B. (1992, June). Getting reform right: What works and what doesn't. *Phi Delta Kappan,* 745–752.

Gallie, W. B. (1964). Essentially contested concepts. Chapter 8 of his *Philosophy and the historical understanding.* London: Chalto and Windus.

Guthrie, J. W. (1993). School reform and the "new world order." In S. L. Jacobson & R. Berne (Eds.), *Reforming education: The emerging systemic approach.* Thousand Oaks, Calif.: Corwin Press.

Hanushek, E. (1981). Throwing money at schools. *Journal of Policy Analysis and Management, 1,* 19–41.

Hanushek, E. (1986). The economics of schooling: Production and efficiency in public schools. *Journal of Economic Literature, 24* (3), 1141–1177.

Hanushek, E. (1994, May). Money might matter somewhere: A response to Hedges, Laine, and Greenwald. *Educational Researcher, 23,* 5–8.

Hanushek, E., with Benson, C. S., Freeman, R. B., Jamison, D. T., Levin, H. M., Maynard, R. A., Murnane, R. J., Rivkin, S. G., Sabot, R. H., Solmon, L. C., Summers, A. A., Welch, F., and Wolfe, B. L. (1994). *Making schools work: Improving performance and controlling costs.* Washington, D.C.: The Brookings Institution.

Hedges, L. V., Laine, R. D., & Greenwald, R. (1994, April). Does money matter? A meta-analysis of studies of the effects of differential school inputs on student outcomes. *Educational Researcher, 23* (3), 5–14.

Kaestle, C. F. (1993). The awful reputation of education research. *Educational Researcher, 22* (1), 23, 26–31.

King, J. A. (1994, Spring). Meeting the educational needs of at-risk students: A cost analysis of three models. *Educational Evaluation and Policy Analysis, 16* (1), 1–19.

Kirst, M. W. (1994, August). The politics of nationalizing curricular content. *American Journal of Education, 102* (4), 383–393.

Kozol, J. (1991). *Savage inequalities: Children in America's schools.* New York: Crown.

Lee, V. E., Bryk, A. S., & Smith, J. B. (1993). The organization of effective secondary schools. In L. Darling-Hammond (Ed.), *Review of research in education*, 19 (pp. 171–267). Washington, D.C.: AERA.

Linn, R. L. (1994, December). Performance assessment: Policy promises and technical measurement standards. *Educational Researcher*, 4–14.

Louis, K. S., & Miles, M. (1990). *Improving the urban high school: What works and why*. New York: Teachers College Press.

McDermott, J. (Ed.). (1976). *Indeterminacy in education*. Berkeley, Calif.: McCutchan.

Monk, D. (1992). Education productivity research: An update and assessment of its role in education finance reform. *Educational Evaluation and Policy Analysis*, 14 (4), 307–332.

Monk, D. H., & King, J. A. (1993). Cost analysis as a tool for education reform. In S. L. Jacobson & R. Berne (Eds.), *Reforming education: The emerging systemic approach*. Thousand Oaks, Calif.: Corwin Press.

Mortimore, P., Sammons, P., Stoll, L., Lewis, D., & Ecob, R. (1988). *School matters*. Berkeley, Calif.: University of California Press.

O'Day, J. A., & Smith, M. S. (1993). Systemic reform and educational opportunity. In S. Fuhrman (Ed.), *Designing coherent educational policy: Improving the system*. San Francisco: Jossey-Bass.

Odden, A. (1994a, Spring). Decentralized management and school finance. *Theory into Practice*, 33 (2), 104–111.

Odden, A. (1994b). Including school finance in systemic reform strategies: A commentary. *CPRE Finance Briefs*. Consortium for Policy Research in Education. New Brunswick, N.J.: Eagleton Institute of Politics, Rutgers University.

Odden, A., & Clune, W. (1995, December). Improving educational productivity and school finance. *Educational Researcher*, 24 (9), 6–10, 22.

Odden, A., & Conley, S. (1992). Restructuring teacher compensation systems. In A. Odden (Ed.), *Rethinking school finance*. San Francisco: Jossey-Bass.

O.E.C.D. (1994). *School: A matter of choice*. Paris: OECD/CERI.

Pitsch, M. (1994, October 19). Critics target Goals 2000 in schools 'war.' *Education Week*, 1, 21.

Porter, A. C. (1993, June–July). School delivery standards. *Educational Researcher*, 24–30.

Porter, A. C. (1994, August). National standards and school improvement in the 1990s: Issues and promise. *American Journal of Education*, 102, (4), 421–449.

Reynolds, D., Creemers, B. P. M., Nesselrodt, P. S., Schaffer, E. C., Stringfield, S., & Teddlie, C. (1994). *Advances in school effectiveness research and practice*. Oxford: Pergamon-Elsevier Science Ltd.

Reynolds, D., & Cuttance, P. (Eds.). (1992). *School effectiveness: Research, policy and practice*. London: Cassell.

Richards, C. E., Fishbein, D., & Melville, P. (1993). Cooperative performance incentives in education. In S. L. Jacobson & R. Berne (Eds.), *Reforming education: The emerging systemic approach*. Thousand Oaks, Calif.: Corwin Press.

Riley, K. A., & Nuttall, D. L. (Eds.). (1994). *Measuring quality: Education indicators—United Kingdom and international perspectives*. London: Falmer Press.

Rutter, M., Maughan, B., Mortimore, P., Ouston, J., & Smith, A. (1979). *Fifteen thousand hours: Secondary schools and their effects on children.* Cambridge, Mass.: Harvard University Press.

Scheerens, J. (1992). *Effective schooling: Research, theory and practice.* London: Cassell.

Schmidt, P. (1995, February 15). Looking the other way. *Education Week,* 23–27.

Smith, M. S., & O'Day, J. (1991). Systemic school reform. In S. Fuhrman & B. Malen (Eds.), *The politics of curriculum and testing.* London: Falmer Press.

Teddlie, C., & Stringfield, S. (1993). *Schools make a difference.* New York: Teachers College Press.

Torgerson, D. (1986). Between knowledge and politics: Three faces of policy analysis. *Policy Sciences, 19,* 33–59.

van Geel, T. (1978). Parental preferences and the politics of spending public educational funds. *Teachers College Record, 79* (3), 339–363.

Vann, B. J. (1993, December). *A personal reflection on school improvement in an era of increasing public accountability.* Unpublished masters dissertation, University of Leicester, U.K.

Verstegen, D. (Ed.). (1994, Summer). Special issue: Further evidence on why and how money matters in education. *Journal of Education Finance, 20,* 1.

Viadero, D. (1994, October 19). Does money matter? Both sides in debate have a point. *Education Week,* 6.

Wadsworth, D. (1994, November 30). Bridging the divide: What the public is telling educators that could help resuscitate school reform. *Education Week,* 38, 48.

Weiss, J. A., & Gruber, J. E. (1987). The managed irrelevance of federal education statistics. In W. Alonzo & P. Starr (Eds.), *The politics of numbers* (pp. 363–391). New York: Russell Sage Foundation.

Whitty, G. (1994a). Consumer rights versus citizen rights in contemporary education policy. Paper presented at conference on "Education, Democracy and Reform," University of Auckland, New Zealand, 13–14 August.

Whitty, G. (1994b). Devolution in education systems: Implications for teacher professionalism and pupil performance. Paper presented at conference on "Teachers in a Decentralised System," organized by the National Industry Education Forum at the Graduate School of Management, Melbourne, 26 August.

Willms, J. D. (1992). *Monitoring school performance: A guide for educators.* London: Falmer Press.

Wohlstetter, P., Smyer, R., & Mohrman, S. A. (1994, Fall). New boundaries for school-based management: The high involvement model. *Educational Evaluation and Policy Analysis, 16* (3), 268–286.

Zlatos, B. (1994, November 6). Scores that don't add up. *New York Times,* Section 4A, pp. 28–29.

2

The Politics of Educational Productivity*

William Lowe Boyd and William T. Hartman

Until recently, educational productivity was a bit like the weather: Everybody talked about it, but nobody did anything about it. Increasingly, however, people actually are trying to do something about improving educational productivity. In large part, this is happening because of mounting pressure for significant action. Though there have been few signs of increasing productivity, the costs of operating schools and colleges have been soaring. As Peter Brimelow (1987), Senior Editor of *Forbes* magazine, sees it:

> The issue is not complicated. First, you look at the input versus the output. In the U.S. since 1945, spending per K-12 pupil, when adjusted for inflation, has virtually quadrupled. This represents a productivity collapse of 75 percent, completely without parallel in any other industry. *And this is before any consideration of output quality*—the apparent deterioration of which has been the focus of national debate typified by the *Nation at Risk* report (emphasis in original).[1] (199)

---

*This chapter first appeared in David H. Monk and Julie Underwood (Eds.), *Microlevel school finance: Issues and implications for policy*. Cambridge, Mass.: Ballinger, 1988.

Indeed, on top of cost considerations, public concern about both the performance of our schools and our nation's economic "competitiveness" has become acute (Magnet 1988). Influential business leaders— such as David Kearns (1988), chief executive officer of the Xerox Corporation—now call our public schools "a failed monopoly," and many share Brimelow's (1986, 1987) dismal view of this domain.[2] Consequently, businesspersons, politicians, and the public alike have embraced the proposition that a key to improving our "competitiveness" is to improve the efficiency and effectiveness of our system of education.[3]

Thus, the educational "excellence" reform movement, as Secretary of Education William Bennett often reminded us, is committed, first and foremost, to improving the *results* of American schooling.[4] And, Bennett and the Reagan administration popularized the notion that we *know* how to do this, that we know *What Works* (U.S. Dept. of Education 1987a, 1987b). Moreover, they spread the idea that *what works doesn't require additional dollars*. What is needed, they argued—with support from an increasing number of scholars (Kirst 1983; Mann and Inman 1984; Rossmiller 1987; Walberg and Fowler 1987)—is more productive use of existing resources. Greater educational effectiveness, they proclaimed, can be achieved through greater efficiency in the management and operation of American schools.

At the same time, the educational "excellence" movement has raised, in a new way, perennial questions about equity and adequacy in the provision of educational services to all sectors of our diverse population. Many observers and participants have grave concerns about current school reform policies that tend to divorce excellence from equity considerations and also try to build improvements on top of underfunded, inadequate schools (Bastian et al. 1985; Fowler 1988). Thus, the politics of educational productivity revolves around the contest over whose conceptions of efficiency and equity in American schooling will prevail and, consequently, who will benefit and who will lose in resource allocation and decision making in the structure, operation, and outcomes of the educational process.

If, as Secretary Bennett has claimed, we know "what works," why aren't we doing more of it? Bennett believes that educators have been slow to apply what works because there is too little accountability of educators for producing desirable results.[5] Consequently, he championed a campaign to increase accountability. Despite occasional efforts in this regard in the past, real efforts to increase accountability have been just as rare as real efforts to increase productivity. Many in the public may agree with Secretary Bennett's view that the main impediments here are political ones, that teachers unions—and perhaps also school administrators (Rodman 1988)—are the villains blocking real improvement of American schooling.[6] Such rhetoric is common, but there is little systematic analysis of such assertions. To what extent, really, are our problems with educational productivity *political* ones, rather than *technical* ones associated with insufficient knowledge of what works? And, beyond these considerations, may *organizational* and *financial* factors also contribute significantly to the problem? These questions provide the point of departure for this exploratory chapter into this largely uncharted terrain.

To begin with, we need to deal at the outset with the scholarly view that we really know almost nothing about the educational production function, that is, "the relationship among the different inputs into and outcomes of the educational process" (Hanushek 1986, 1148). Although one can make a case for this view in the precise technical terms of economists, the models economists have used to explore this matter have been gross oversimplifications of the complexities of the schooling process. Thus, in an incisive critique, economists Byron Brown and Daniel Saks (1980) conclude that the models of the education production function "most used are also most useless" (112). The difficulties lie in the assumptions underlying the production function concept and their questionable validity in education. Problems abound with respect to the conception and measurement of outputs, inputs, and the relationships among them (see, for example, Brown and Saks 1980, 1981; Levin 1974; Hanushek 1972, 1979, 1986). This is not the place to delve into the specifics of these difficulties, but one example may convey a sense of the problems: Education production function studies typically use aggregate test scores or test score gains in which a single or average education production function is calculated for a group of students that is assumed to apply to all students equally. Yet, if children learn in different ways and at different rates—as they in fact do—then the application of a single educational production function for all students is inappropriate. This problem led Katzman (1971) to conclude, as Bickel (1986) put it, "that it was no more reasonable to conceptualize *the* educational production function than *the* agricultural production function abstracted from crop or geography" (185).

However, it should be noted that economists such as Eric Hanushek (1986) emphasize that public school educators generally are operating in disregard of what economists believe we *do* know. Consequently, for the purposes of this chapter we take the position that although we are far from having the technical command of the education production function implied by Secretary Bennett's rhetoric about what works, we do have useful and important knowledge, gleaned from research on instruction and effective schools (for example, Bossert 1988; Purkey and Smith 1983; Rossmiller 1987; Walberg 1984), that makes it impossible for educators to avoid responsibility for the practices they choose. In short, the burden of educational success no longer can be placed solely on the backs of children and their families.[7]

Thus, the central question of this chapter is, Why, until recently, has there been so little systematic effort by educators to improve educational productivity? Answers to this question help us understand why progress in improving school performance is so difficult, even now when pressure for better results is forcing attention to the issue. The roots of the educational productivity problem, we believe, are to be found in a complex tangle of technical, sociological, economic, and political factors. The result, we argue, is a political economy of public schooling that makes improvement in this arena difficult, but not impossible. In laying out our analysis, we first consider why educational productivity has become such an issue recently. Next, we review what is known about administrative efforts to increase educational productivity. In light of this discussion, we turn to our central issue, explanations for why so little usually is done to promote productivity. Finally, we consider forces and strategies likely to change this state of affairs.

THE EMERGENCE OF CONCERNS FOR EDUCATIONAL PRODUCTIVITY

The perennial concern of public educators has been the problem of securing adequate resources and facilities to provide access to schooling for all, regardless of their family background or geographic location. Thus, until the late 1960s, equality in education was understood not in terms of educational *outcomes* but in terms of *access* to favorable combinations of desirable inputs and recommended educational processes. The quest for "equal educational opportunity" in fact began from this point of view, based on a widespread belief that most poor and minority children were attending schools that were below average in staffing, resources, and facilities. But when *Equality of Educational Opportunity* (James S. Coleman et al. 1966) appeared, it created an immediate furor because it contradicted this belief. Indeed, its findings that educational services generally were provided rather equally (in terms of gross input categories) and that student achievement varied primarily according to social class background led to the popular, but erroneous, idea that schooling "doesn't make a difference." Not surprisingly, this touched off an extended scholarly debate and numerous reanalyses of the original data set (Jencks et al. 1972; Levine and Bane 1975). The Coleman report transformed the policy debate by redefining educational opportunity in terms of the *outcomes* of schooling. Further, it set in motion an urgent search for "effective schools" and instructional practices effective with disadvantaged children.

By the late 1970s, public concern was mounting over newspaper stories highlighting the declining average performance of American students on standardized tests and invidious comparisons with the test performance of students in other countries. Although the latter often were confounded by comparing "apples and oranges"—for example, the students of elite European secondary school systems versus the wider band of students gaining access in our comprehensive high school system (Kirst 1984, 73–93)—concern has continued to grow over unfavorable comparisons of the math and science performance of the middle band of students in the U.S.A. versus their counterparts in other countries. Moreover, contrary to widespread opinion, it isn't clear that our top students compare well with the top students of other nations. As Magnet (1988) notes, "The top 5% of the U.S. 12th-graders who took international calculus and algebra tests in 1982 came in dead last among the top 12th-graders of nine developed countries" (86).

By the spring of 1981 a growing sense of crisis was manifested by the release of another controversial Coleman report, *Public and Private Schools* (Coleman, Hoffer, and Kilgore 1981), and by the appearance of the first installment of an "unprecedented" three-part series in *Newsweek* magazine entitled "Why Public Schools Fail" (*Newsweek* 1981). It is not surprising, then, that following the Republican victory in the presidential election of 1980, equity in education increasingly was defined by the Reagan Administration in terms of competence or even "excellence" in student achievement outcomes. Indeed, with the release of the enormously influential *A Nation at Risk* report in 1983, achieving "excellence in education" was linked to national economic survival. Rather than fading into the obscurity most reports soon find, the rhetoric of *A Nation at Risk* caught on. With the increasing sense of a productivity crisis in American industry, in competition with foreign producers—and above all Japan—the "excellence" school reform movement has continued long beyond the brief "window of opportunity" forecast for it in 1983. In fact, as Jennings (1987) has argued, the "competitiveness" crisis linked to schooling has become "the Sputnik of the eighties."

On top of the "competitiveness" crisis, other forces have reinforced pressures for improved student performance and school productivity. Demographic trends pose the dual challenge of a rapidly expanding body of retired, senior citizens and a growing body of at-risk minority students, soon to constitute one-third of all American students. Because we moved from seventeen workers for every retired person in 1985 to three workers for every retired person in 1992, we no longer can afford high failure rates—if we ever could—among our increasing number of minority students, most of whom will need to become productive citizens if we are to maintain our standard of living (Hodgkinson 1985). Economic trends and constraints also have generated pressures for greater productivity in education. At the same time that evidence has mounted that more dollars spent do not necessarily produce better student outcomes (Hanushek 1981; P. Coleman 1986; Walberg and Fowler 1987), effective schools practices requiring few or no extra dollars have been documented that are associated with better outcomes (Mann and Inman 1984). Obviously, both of these points lead to greater concerns for cost-effectiveness and accountability.

Skillful and aggressive use of the federal "bully pulpit" to propagate the idea that we now know "what works" and its corollary, that greater accountability should be demanded, have been a key part of the contemporary politics of educational productivity. An important element of the federal effort has been the "Wall Chart" comparing the educational performance of the fifty states. Ginsburg, Noell, and Plisko (1988) assert that "the impact of the wall chart can be seen as completing the shift started by the Coleman Report to assess education primarily in terms of outcomes rather than inputs." The keen interest of the educational research community in the "effective schools" research (Purkey and Smith 1983), widespread attempts by school districts and even states to foster adoption of prescriptions coming out of this body of research, and occasional judicial attention to "minimally adequate" educational programs (van Geel 1987, 261–313), have lent credibility and legitimacy to the whole productivity movement.

Some significant milestones in this development are worth noting. First, the 1979 *Pauley v. Kelly* decision in West Virginia provided a detailed definition, largely in terms of educational outcomes to be efficiently achieved, of the meaning of the state's constitutionally guaranteed "thorough and efficient" system of public education (see van Geel 1987, 272). Then in the *Pauley v. Bailey* decision in 1982, Judge Arthur Recht provided a massive 244-page opinion elaborating the ways in which the state fell far short of providing this guaranteed "thorough and efficient" system (Sirkin 1985).

Second, although "most courts have avoided declaring that the state has a constitutional duty to educate effectively" and have been unwilling "to permit the schools to be sued for educational malpractice" (van Geel 1987, 261), the idea of a "right" to an effective education has been spreading. In a *Texas Law Review* article, Gershon Ratner (1985) has argued that state and federal constitutional law, and also the state common law of negligence, should be interpreted to impose a legal duty on public schools requiring them "to educate successfully in basic skills the vast majority of [their] students, regardless of the proportions of poor and minority students" (777, 781). Although legal scholars doubt Ratner's claim that the "effective schools" research could be used to convince the judiciary to accept this argument (van Geel 1987, 300), there are signs that educational leaders are beginning to adopt it. The most dramatic illustration has been the acceptance by the Council of Chief State School Officers of a plan embodying eleven *guarantees* of a high-quality secondary education for those students deemed least likely to finish high school (Olson 1987a, 1987b). These state guarantees include such bold provisions as

- An education program "of the quality available" to students who attend schools with high graduation rates.
- Enrollment in a school that demonstrates "substantial and sustained" student progress.
- Enrollment in a school with "systematically designed and delivered instruction of demonstrable effectiveness" and with "adequate and up-to-date learning technologies and materials of proven value."
- Information that would help identify at-risk students and report on school conditions and performance. The information must be "sufficient to let one know whether the guarantees are being met."
- Procedures that enable students, their parents, or their representatives to ensure that these guarantees are met (Olson 1987a, 17).

Thus, it seems that the "genie" of educational performance has gotten "out of the bottle." The upshot of these developments is that it is now clear that we are on the brink of what Murphy and Hallinger (1989) call a "third generation" concept of equity in education. The first and second generation concepts of equity in education focused, respectively, on access to schooling and on equality of aggregated resources. The third generation concept holds that state-of-the-art educational processes should be in place—and accessible to all, regardless of social class, tracking arrangements, and so on—even if we still lack the knowledge about the education production function to be able to guarantee equity in outcomes. Agreeing with Murphy and Hallinger, Rossmiller (1987) concludes that "most of the variables [found to be associated with school effectiveness] relate much more to the way in which resources are used—the processes of the school and classroom—than to the level of resources per se, thus lending support to the view that adequate resources are necessary, but not sufficient, to insure increased student achievement, and lending credence to the third generation equity issues" (567).

WHAT DO SCHOOL ADMINISTRATORS DO ABOUT PRODUCTIVITY?

In light of this background, we now can examine the evidence about what school administrators typically do about productivity. School administrators usually feel a strong sense of dual responsibility for both the maintenance and improvement of their organizations. They try to foster improvement while at the same time discharging their inescapable responsibilities for maintaining the day-to-day operation of their organizations. But, research shows that the latter dominate their activities. Indeed, systematic attention and concerted efforts toward the improvement of instruction and student achievement usually are conspicuous by their absence. In an extensive review of the literature, Boyd and Crowson (1981) conclude:

> Research on what school administrators actually do has shown that they spend nearly all of the time on organizational maintenance and pupil control activities despite rhetoric about the importance of instructional leadership.... [Thus] what may be most important is what school building principals *don't* do or do very little. .... [T]hey spend little time on the instructional program and entrepreneurship and much more time on disturbance handling. They do little by way of external public liaison activity and maintain a pronounced "inside" focus. Their resource allocation activity lacks economic muscle because they have little influence over the reward schedule for teachers.[8] (357–358)

Similarly, in their thoughtful review of the literature, Leithwood and Montgomery (1982, 309, 331) found that research suggests that *less than half* of elementary school principals actually attempt to improve their schools' instructional effectiveness. Instead, the emphasis for typical principals usually is on maintaining a smooth-running organization, with harmonious staff relationships, and on assuming that teachers are competent and "leaving teachers alone to teach." By contrast, effective principals are quite achievement- and task-oriented (Leithwood and Montgomery 1982, 320–323).

Studies in the Mintzberg (1973) mode, of how school administrators use their time, document the common neglect of instructional improvement and student achievement. For example, Martin's five high school principals spent almost 80 percent of their time on organizational maintenance tasks (53.9 percent) and pupil control tasks (23.8 percent). By contrast, only 17.4 percent of their time was spent on the school's academic program (Martin and Willower 1981). Moreover, Peterson (1978) found that neither of the two elementary principals he studied "spent more than 6 percent of his time planning and coordinating the school program, curriculum, or materials" (3). Though the categorization of activities by Peterson and Martin differs, neither produced encouraging findings. As Peterson (1978) noted, the time spent by principals on tasks associated with the technical or instructional core of the school "take[s] up less than 25 minutes in a six-hour day" (3).

It is vital to recognize, of course, that the Mintzberg-type studies overlook the importance of indirect leadership techniques, strategic actions, and one-time only activities, such as assignments in grouping teachers and students, which may be quite significant for the effectiveness of the educational program (Bossert 1988; Murphy, 1988). Moreover, serious concerns have been raised about the ability of the Mintzberg methodology to capture the reality of school leadership (Gron 1982). Nevertheless, these studies still raise some serious questions about the priorities of school administrators.

If school principals seldom spend much time on improving the curriculum and instruction, may they be exerting substantial leadership and influence via their role in evaluating teachers? Here, again, the research findings are disturbing. Principals generally view supervision and evaluation of teachers as ticklish and even risky matters; consequently, they tend to minimize their activity in this domain (Shapiro and Crowson 1985). Rosenholtz (1985) presents similar findings in her review of the evidence on "effective schools." She notes "an NEA survey in which fewer than 50 percent of the randomly sampled principals reported sufficient time for the accurate assessment of teachers" and cites "an even gloomier picture" presented by Natriello and Dornbush (1980–81). "In their sample, teachers reported receiving formal evaluations from their supervisors only once in every three years" (Rosenholtz 1985, 368).

If routine supervision and evaluation are often minimized, what about the remediation or removal of incompetent teachers? Here, it appears that action often is postponed or avoided altogether—at least until the situation is so flagrant that it both demands and facilitates administrative intervention. The fact that Bridges' (1986) book on this subject filled a void in the literature is evidence in itself of the extent of this problem.

Could it be that district-level administrators or other supervisory personnel are filling the frequent gap in supervision and instructional leadership on the part of principals? Research in this area is thinner than on the principalship, but what we do know is far from encouraging (Wimpelberg 1988). Though successful school improvement efforts generally have—and probably require—sustained support from the central office (Fullan 1982; Clark, Lotto, and Astuto 1984; Jones and Leithwood 1988; LaRocque and Coleman 1985; Leithwood 1988; Purkey and Smith 1985), studies of central office activities suggest that this occurs infrequently. As Wimpelberg (1988) summarizes this literature:

> Salley (1979–80) reported that curriculum and instruction are low on superintendents' lists of job priorities, regardless of the kinds of school districts they serve. In the same vein, Hannaway and Sproull (1978-79) found that chief and assistant superintendents spend an average of less than 1 percent of their time on instruction in schools and classrooms. Research by Pitner and Ogawa (1981) corroborates these findings. This literature appears to confirm a trend that Griffiths (1966: 102) had spotted in the 1960's: "This is the idea that administrators should have nothing to do with instruction."[9]

In sum, what probably occurs too often is what LaRocque and Coleman (1985) saw in their research and described as a kind of "mutual non-interference pact" between school principals and central office administrators. If this tendency is coupled with the common reluctance of principals to supervise and evaluate teachers, the "isolated teacher" syndrome associated with the dearth of supportive *professional* colleagueship in typical schools (Rosenholtz 1985), and the pervasive "treaties" underlying disengagement from teaching and learning (Powell, Farrar, and Cohen 1985; Sedlak et al. 1986), the upshot is "peaceful," but unproductive, "co-existence" all around.

In this context, as Murphy and Hallinger (1987) remark, there is increasing recognition that school "administrators are often inept managers of the technical core operations" (248) of their organizations. Clearly, teachers seem to feel that this is often the case (Urbanski 1986). In fairness to school administrators, though, it should be noted that until recently scholars and preparation programs in educational administration—reflecting the orientation of the field—also have neglected attention to organizational outcomes and student achievement (Erickson 1977, 1979). For example, Bridges (1982, 21–22) found that studies of organizational achievement were much rarer than of organizational maintenance.

Still, to return to an earlier theme, it could be argued that even though day-to-day administrative attention to improving instruction and student achievement is infrequent, school managers nevertheless discharge their responsibility here through periodic strategic actions, as in budget and allocation decision making. Research on this subject is again thin and again is not encouraging. Part of the problem is that educators have been slow to accept the idea that they have any substantial responsibility for student learning outcomes. Instead, they cling to the view that what schools do is give students an opportunity to learn, which they must be able and willing to seize. Even when outcome-oriented approaches such as PPBS (Program Planning and Budgeting Systems) are used, educators may be inclined, as van Geel (1973) found, to persist in taking an access- rather than outcome-oriented stance. Studies of school district budgeting are rare (Hartman 1988a). Those that exist suggest that the process is politicized and that the interests of employees often take precedence over attention to student and instructional needs (Levy, Meltsner, and Wildavsky 1974, 64). Usually, an incremental, bargaining model of budgeting is followed (Guthrie, Garms, and Pierce 1988, 223–235). In this context, discussions of how allocations relate to improved instruction and achievement are few and far between.

Studies of budgeting within school buildings are even rarer. However, we suspect that the findings of a recent comparative case study of budget decision making in four high schools, ranging from working-class to upper-middle-class student bodies, are representative of what usually occurs. In this study, Hartman (1988b) found:

> The possibility of linking distribution of resources to improving student achievement was *never* considered explicitly. No evidence was found that the use of any consistent achievement measures to provide information for decision making had been contemplated. . . . The primary objective of the allocation process in the four high schools examined was equality among teachers in workload and in their real instructional supply and equipment needs. In each school the allocation process worked differently, but functioned to distribute resources in such a way as to minimize conflict among school personnel and to establish a perception of fairness among teachers. Similar to Mann (1981: 4), this analysis found that "The current procedures for resource allocation at the building level have more to do with the equitability of adult working conditions than with the production of responsive learning environments for children."

In concluding this discussion of what school administrators do about productivity, we want to emphasize the strong contrast between descriptions of typical and effective schools. Speaking of elementary school principals, Leithwood and Montgomery (1982) provide a forceful summation:

> Whereas the effective principal acts as an instructional leader, leadership provided by the typical principal is largely administrative. The primary goal of these principals is a smooth-running organization with emphasis on keeping activities in the school manageable in the midst of pressures for change. . . . With respect to teachers, running a smooth ship places the principal's main emphasis on harmonious interpersonal relationships. . . . The typical principal is quite distant from curriculum or instructional decisions and initiates few changes in the school's program. Emphasis is placed on the existing professional competence of teachers and the value of "leaving teachers alone to teach. . . . [I]n strong contrast to the orientation of the effective principal, there is a lack of achievement orientation."(322)

Similarly, Hord and Hall (1987) describe three types of principal styles: responder, manager, and initiator. They found that effectiveness in facilitating change increases with movement from responder to manager to initiator. Rosenholtz (1985) reports that "principals or their administrative assistants in effective schools are ubiquitous in their efforts to monitor classroom affairs" (369). Some research even suggests that they are quite assertive and put pressure on teachers. "One of the principal and clearly controversial findings in this study," says Hubermann (1983), "was that successful implementation often occurred at places where administrators exerted strong and continuous pressure on teachers" (24) (see also Rosenholtz 1985, 361, 363).

On the other hand, Rossmiller's (1987) reading of the research on effective schools emphasizes the role of principals in building consensus and a team approach. He is in agreement with Rosenholtz's (1985) assessment of the literature, which stresses teacher participation in decision making and consensus building regarding shared goals. Moreover, as Deal reminds us, principals cannot focus just on instructional improvement. They can't risk neglecting any of four major domains to which leaders must attend: They must not only get things done, but also meet human needs, manage conflict, and create shared meanings (Deal 1987). Similarly, Cuban (1986) argues that there are three *interrelated* core roles in principaling: instructional, managerial, and political.

It is important to note, however, a strong dissenting view (Rallis and Highsmith 1986)—favorably discussed by Shanker (1988) in a column aimed at the National Association of Elementary School Principals convention—that management and instructional/educational leadership more realistically should be viewed as two *different* jobs that should be divided. This view underlies the increasing tensions between leaders in teachers and principals associations over the respective role each group should play in instructional leadership.[10] Reflecting this problem, Bossert (1988) notes that effective schools have not only strong principals but also teachers with high levels of autonomy, and he asks, "How are strong leadership and autonomy managed simultaneously?" (346). This key question is now a central issue in the evolution of the current school reform movement in the United States.

WHY DON'T SCHOOL ADMINISTRATORS DO MORE TO PROMOTE PRODUCTIVITY?

The discussion so far raises a number of questions about the motivations of school administrators. What are the principal incentives and constraints influencing their behavior? What are their goals, and among these, which are they trying to maximize or optimize? To what extent, and under what circumstances, are they merely trying to "satisfice," both in terms of their own behavior and in terms of organizational outcomes? These generic kinds of questions really apply to managers in general, in all kinds of organizations, public and private. The more germane questions here are, What accounts for the traditional deemphasis of productivity in American public schools? and How are school administrators drawn into the ambit of this tradition?

There are a variety of interesting answers to these questions to be found in the literature. Our brief survey of this subject is divided into three categories of explanations: economic-financial, sociological, and political. Our review is suggestive rather than exhaustive, but we believe that each of the explanations we discuss contributes something toward the construction of a comprehensive answer. Thus, we argue in conclusion that just as it would be absurd to disregard well-documented sociological and technological factors inhibiting educational productivity—such as ambiguous goals and a poorly understood technology—it also is no longer possible to disregard the influence of well-documented factors associated with the political economy of public schools, however unpalatable these may be to friends of public education who cling to the idea that the enterprise is essentially an altruistic crusade championed by disinterested public servants.

Economic and Financial Factors

To the extent that our knowledge about the education production function is weak or nonexistent, as some claim, apathy about educational productivity is understandable. As we noted at the outset, economists have directed a great deal of attention to the shortcomings of our knowledge in this arena. But, as Brown and Saks (1980) and others have shown, for all their sophistication economists still have been unable to develop models of the production function that are fully appropriate for education. Though the deficiencies of our knowledge in this area represent a major constraint on our ability to operate schools more efficiently, research on systematic instruction, effective schools, use of school time and time on-task, and cost-effectiveness (Levin 1983) has provided a basis for far more than random or "superstitious" behavior. Consequently, ignorance about the technology of education cannot be used as an excuse for doing nothing to improve the effectiveness of schools and teaching.

Thanks to scholars such as Hanushek, Murnane, Levin, and Brown and Saks, the search goes on among economists for better models of the education production function. For example, in "The Microeconomics of Schooling" Brown and Saks (1981) discuss the complexity of modeling teaching and learning situations. Among other things, they note the problem of assuming optimizing behavior or effort in a classroom or school where the product is not sold at a market price. Here, they direct attention to the value of Leibenstein's (1980) "X-efficiency theory" as a means for dealing more realistically with situations in which optimization is unlikely. "When there is imperfect maximization, Leibenstein posits the existence of 'inert areas,' representing decisions that may not be optimal but from which people may be unwilling to move simply because it is costly to do so" (Brown and Saks 1981, 249). Leibenstein's X-efficiency theory suggests to Brown and Saks (1981, 249–250) that what an effective school administrator may do is to provide the motivation for the extra efforts needed to break out of "inert areas" and, more generally, to perform in a less cybernetic and more responsive and efficient manner. In making this point, though, Brown and Saks (1981) touch on a key point influencing administrative behavior, one to which we shall have good reason to return: "Influencing the effort of lower levels requires some effort itself, *a cost that may not be less than the predicted benefits*" (249) (emphasis added).

Spending levels for the financial support for public schools constitute another issue associated with productivity. On one side are those who argue that contemporary "excellence" reforms are being erected on the sands of inadequately funded school systems in some states and locales (Fowler 1988). Overworked teachers in under-resourced schools scarcely provide a promising basis for improving the efficiency and effectiveness of public schools. As Kasten (1986) observes, "The prior condition for any effort at redesigning teachers' work is adequate resources in the form of salaries, reasonable class sizes, and supplies and materials. The accountability movement in education has focused on outputs and shown little interest in [such] resources" (281). On the other side are critics, such as Brimelow (1986, 1987), who castigate public educators for a "productivity collapse." They note that spending per K-12 pupil has nearly quadrupled in the United States since 1945 and output quality seems to have declined. Generally speaking, the critics have been winning the political debate over productivity. Their argument has been bolstered by findings such as those of Walberg and Fowler (1987), who conclude from their statewide analysis in New Jersey that "it appears that it is the educational policies of districts and the instructional practices in classrooms rather than expenditures that consistently determine achievement and efficiency. Thus, changes in educational policies and practices rather than expenditures may offer the best chance of improving efficiency" (13). Similarly, Ginsburg, Noell, and Plisko (1988) observe that the federally sponsored Wall Chart comparisons "reinforced findings that the level of resources in schools—in other words, money spent on education—is not strongly associated with school outcomes. Many high-achieving states had relatively modest expenditures.... The news media have publicized these low correlations and questioned whether school systems are using funds to maximum efficiency."

Sociological Factors

Perhaps the most comprehensive sociological explanation for the de-emphasis of productivity in schools is found in Meyer and Rowan's (1977, 1978) discussion of schools as "institutionalized organizations." Their starting point is the idea—supported by considerable evidence—that educational institutions tend to be "loosely coupled" organizations (March and Olsen 1976; Weick 1976; Meyer and associates 1978;

Hannaway and Sproull 1979). As they put it, this means that "structure is disconnected from technical (work) activity, and activity is disconnected from its effects" (Meyer and Rowan 1978, 79). This loose coupling is manifested in schools by such characteristics as the strong tendency to "leave instructional activities and outcomes uncontrolled and uninspected" (79). Despite this pattern, Meyer and Rowan argue that schools manage to command legitimacy and support by means of the use of standardized categories of students, teachers, and curriculum topics that "give meaning and definition to the internal activities of schools" (79). These "ritual classifications" are "institutionalized in the legal and normative rules of the wider society" (79). Meyer and Rowan (1978) conclude:

> In the American situation, attempts to tightly link the prescriptions of the central theory of education to the activities of instruction would create conflict and inconsistency and discredit and devalue the meaning of ritual classifications in society. Educators (and their social environments) therefore decouple their ritual structure from instructional activities and outcomes and resort to a "logic of confidence": Higher levels of the system organize on the *assumption* that what is going on at lower levels makes sense and conforms to rules, but they avoid inspecting it to discover or assume responsibility for inconsistencies and ineffectiveness. In this fashion, educational organizations work more smoothly than is commonly supposed, obtain high levels of external support from divergent community and state sources, and maximize the meaning and prestige of the ritual categories of people they employ and produce. (80)

To the extent that Meyer and Rowan's analysis is correct, it helps us understand the behavior of school administrators. "Ritual classification" and a "logic of confidence" are useful tools for people operating in loosely coupled organizations characterized by ambiguous goals and unclear technologies. In the absence of a well-understood production function, administrators and society generally may come to rely heavily on "myth and ceremonies" to structure activities in sensitive institutions like schools. Even if there were a better understood technology for effective education, disagreement and shifting priorities about the various goals of public schools can make continuity and effective planning and management quite difficult to achieve (McPherson, Crowson, and Pitner 1986, 80). This is especially a problem within the political structure of decision making for public education, because it lends itself to interest group activity and contestation. Cuban (1975) provides a vivid depiction of what can result in his account of the decision-making process in a turbulent period in the Washington, D.C., school district.

This point brings us to the question of what society or the governing segments of it really expect schools to be accomplishing. On the one hand, American schools are supposed to be promoting social mobility and a democratic, egalitarian society, with a strong emphasis on the civic and collective as well as private benefits of schooling. Yet, at the same time, many people, including some educators, continue to believe that students from lower social class backgrounds rarely are capable of much learning or social advancement. Schools and administrators often are caught in the middle of this tension, which manifests itself particularly through patterns of curriculum tracking for students of differing social classes. Many critics of these arrangements agree with Oakes's (1986) assessment: "Even as they voice commitment to equality and excellence, schools organize and deliver curriculum in ways that advance neither" (13).

Murphy and Hallinger's (1989) analysis of "equity as access to learning" underscores the problem. They show that evidence "is growing for the position that pupils in lower ability clusters and tracks not only often fail to receive the putative benefits of grouping, but receive less of many of the important alterable learning resources that promote such important outcomes as achievement and goal aspirations." Murphy and Hallinger conclude that "the lack of rewards gained by teachers working with low groups . . . the perceived need to trade academic expectations for student goodwill [and] a lack of inspection of learning conditions within and among groups and tracks has contributed to the problem, as has a generally reduced sense of accountability for outcomes of non-academic track students." Thus, to the extent that administrators adhere to the old notion of educational opportunity as merely access to schooling (with students shouldering full responsibility for the outcomes) and perceive (rightly or wrongly) that society expects little learning from disadvantaged children, their lack of accountability for results frees them from the burden of worrying about productivity.

This analysis, of course, connects with the Marxist critique of class bias in capitalist schooling systems (for example, Bowles and Gintis 1976). In this interpretation, schools are constrained to be instruments for social control and the reproduction of an unjust structure of social stratification. Schooling maintains inequality by fostering and reinforcing different skills and attitudes that divide people from one another. Because this is done in the name of "meritocratic" competition among students, the process is perceived to be fair, which legitimizes and maintains the system. It follows, in this view, that educational administration becomes far more a "technology of control" than anything to do with genuine education (Bates 1983).

Even if one does not accept this view, one is still left with the disturbing problem of the performance and functions of the tracking system. And, there is also the troublesome question of whether the public schools in America really have been expected to provide efficient, high-quality intellectual training. Jill Conway (1987) calls attention to the historic tension between elitism and egalitarianism in American schooling and its resolution toward anti-intellectual egalitarianism. In a provocative interpretation, she argues that this resolution was tacitly abetted by the feminization of teaching and stereotypes about women teachers' limited intellectual capacities and tendencies toward the maternal and emotional rather than the rational and critical mind-set necessary for intellectual education. Again, to the extent that society and school administrators have accepted an anti-intellectual form of egalitarianism, this orientation reduces expectations for academic productivity on the part of schools.

If public schools were as loosely coupled and anarchic as some have claimed (for example, Meyer and associates 1978; March and Olsen 1976), school administrators would face nearly insurmountable obstacles in trying to manage them efficiently and productively, even if they were strongly inclined to do so. However, recent research, such as Crowson and Morris's (1985) analysis of administrative control within the Chicago school system, supports Willower's (1979) contention that school systems are neither as loosely coupled nor as tightly bureaucratic as some earlier research indicated (for example, Hannaway and Sproull 1979; Rogers 1968).

Two sociological theories help to flesh out the arrangements that facilitate the functioning of loosely coupled organizations. "Negotiated order" theory is concerned with how order is established and maintained in organizations through a process of interaction among members who negotiate a variety of rules, agreements, arrangements, and understandings, most of which are informal and unofficial (Day and Day 1977; Strauss et al. 1963). Much of the informal bargaining that occurs in this interaction and negotiation can be understood in terms of "exchange theory," developed most notably by Homans (1958) and Blau (1964). Based on an economic calculus of benefits, and the need for mutually beneficial accommodations among groups and actors, exchange theory emphasizes the need for reciprocity and quid pro quo arrangements in social relationships (that is, "You scratch my back and I scratch yours.").

Crowson and Morris (1985) found that such negotiations and exchanges were among the key factors promoting coordination and control in the Chicago school system. Moreover, as we have noted earlier, recent scholarship on the problems facing school reformers is replete with evidence of the pervasiveness, throughout the entire hierarchy of school systems, of informal bargaining, "treaties" (Sedlak et al. 1986; Powell, Farrar, and Cohen 1985; Rosenholtz 1985), "mutual non-interference pacts" (LaRocque and Coleman 1985), and the like. Thus, Hubermann (1983) found that "much of the innovation process is taken up with bargaining, both explicit and implicit. One person's 'strategy' for school improvement collides with another person's 'strategy' for avoiding a loss of status or freedom or benefits" (23).

Political Factors

With the salience of bargaining behavior in exchange theory, negotiated order, and "organized anarchy" theory (March and Olsen 1976), we have entered the domain of theories that are political as well as sociological. It is but a short jump directly into the realm of "micropolitics" in organizations, with its focus on the strategic use of influence, manipulation, bargaining, and coalitions (Bacharach and Lawler 1980; Bacharach and Mitchell 1987; Hoyle 1985, 1986; Pfeffer 1978). But even without leaving the bounds of exchange theory, we can begin to see why school administrators frequently are reluctant to push for more-productive behavior: *The costs of working out such exchanges with subordinates often are perceived to be greater than the benefits received.*

To see why this is the case, one must look at the constraints on the ability of school administrators to direct or motivate teachers. As Hoyle (1986) observes in his evocative discussion of the micropolitics of schools in the British context:

> The problem for heads [i.e., principals] is that they have a high degree of authority but the legal sanctions which underpin this authority will only be invoked relatively infrequently. Moreover, teachers have a relatively high degree of autonomy supported by professional norms which inhibit the exercise of legally-based authority of the head. Thus the head's administrative control must depend to a considerable degree on the exercise of latent power and on influence. This would seem to be likely to encourage the head's deployment of micropolitical strategies in the somewhat gaping interstices within the management structure. (135)

In the American context, the power and authority of school principals seem even more limited. Based on interviews with 113 principals in fifty-nine elementary school districts in suburban Chicago, Dan Lortie concluded:

> The relationships principals find most valuable are not with their superiors [or with parents], but those with teachers. . . . Principals are dependent in many ways for their personal satisfaction and their ability to advance in their careers on their ability to get along well with the teachers in their buildings. . . . This dependency on teachers creates peculiar tensions for principals, largely because of the ambiguous nature of principals' authority. Central offices often possess final authority on many important matters and the principal's autonomy depends on his ability to gain the trust of

more highly placed administrators. That relationship is fragile and is often tested. Unhappy teachers can complicate the relationship. As a result, many principals take few risks with new programs and seek to build strong personal relationships with teachers. . . . The strong impression is of persons relying more on their ability to win influence and good relationships than on the assertion of powers being built into the office they hold. It is also consistent with a reality in which formal powers are indeed weak. Principals adapt to those realities in ways that are understandably rooted in interpersonal skills rather than use of powerful rewards and punishments. (*Education News* 1988, 10)

Given the conditions in which teachers typically work—as modestly compensated solo practitioners, heavily dependent for occupational survival and personal satisfaction on the cooperative attitudes and academic ability and success of their students (Lortie 1975)—the maintenance of a favorable balance between organizational inducements and their personal contributions is often problematic (Rosenholtz 1985). In particular, the psychic costs teachers face frequently threaten to overwhelm the psychic rewards or "earnings" they receive (Rosenholtz 1985). Thus, it is not surprising that teachers in typical schools are apprehensive about being "supervised" or evaluated and are reluctant to ask for help or advice (Rosenholtz 1985).[11] Consistent with exchange theory, they behave like Blau's (1955) government agents who were reluctant to ask for help and advice for fear of being thought incompetent or because they didn't want to become indebted to those from whom they sought help.

In this context, Hoyle (1986, 125–149) observes that both principals and teachers must be creative in exploiting the limited "goods" they have available for purposes of bargaining and exchange. Thus, a principal may swap lax application of rules and autonomy for a teacher's support and opinion leadership among peers. When the going gets tough, though, a principal may have to resort to bolder micropolitical strategies, such as dividing and ruling, co-optation, displacement, controlling information, and controlling meetings (Hoyle 1986, 140–148). Although concerned about the ethical issues involved, Hoyle notes that administrators sometimes use such tactics as 'rigging' agendas, 'losing' recommendations, 'interpreting' consensus, and 'massaging' the minutes of meetings (145–146).

Because playing politics or even exerting strong leadership can be risky for school administrators, we need to know more about incentives and disincentives that may foster or discourage more-venturesome behavior on their part. Here, theory and research (for example, Barry and Hardin 1982; Niskanen 1971) on rational choice behavior and the political economy of public sector organizations add considerably to the insights of exchange theory and micropolitics. Interpretations in this body of knowledge range along a continuum that runs from reasonable to strident versions of the same logic. Unfortunately, the more extreme versions—which unfairly contrast public sector organizations with idealized versions of efficient, profit-seeking firms—cause many people to dismiss the logic of the whole argument, which is quite consonant with the precepts of exchange theory discussed so far.

Rational choice theory begins with the reasonable assumption that individuals seek to maximize their welfare and, accordingly, make rational choices or decisions toward this end. In assessing the costs and benefits of alternative courses of action, they are sensitive to the incentive or reward structures in which they find themselves. Because public, nonprofit organizations lack a profit motive, this leads to questions about the nature of the incentives that operate in its absence. For instance, given the tenuous nature of principals' authority in public schools and their dependence on the good will of teachers, why should principals risk trying to change and improve things? What are the rewards for doing these kinds of things? As one of our practitioner/graduate students remarked, "How many principals are willing to stir things up and possibly have to move to another job as a result? How often will even risk-takers be willing to do this? And how many times will the superintendent or central office be willing to 'go to the wall' for principals when they stir things up?"

Of course, if there were keen incentives in the school district for improving performance, then one could envision the central office strongly supporting and rewarding principals who 'stirred things up' or, better, were able to improve productivity by more-harmonious interpersonal and group processes. Note, however, that even the latter approach involves changing things, which can be risky. The question remains, then, about how strong the incentives are likely to be for better productivity. A closer examination of the political economy of public schools provides a disturbing view of this matter.

Analysts using the perspective of market-oriented political economy contend that the nonprofit, government-supported character of public human services organizations tends to create a perverse structure of incentives for employees (Michaelsen 1977, 1981). In the quasi-monopolistic, consumer-insensitive setting of such organizations, the reward structure often is not oriented toward performance. "Public choice" theorists emphasize the profound effects of two features of public-sector organizations. First, public managers lack property rights or a profit motive in the successful performance of the organization. Second, the organization receives a tax-supplied budget independent of satisfying individual consumers. From these starting points, much of the behavior of public school personnel that might otherwise appear irrational or "loosely coupled" can be explained. For instance, because there are no profits in public schools to motivate and reward managers (and teachers' salaries are based on seniority rather than performance), educators—as rational, self-interested people seeking to maximize their own welfare—may be inclined to maximize their nonpecuniary benefits. This means that in place of profits (which would depend on satisfied customers) public educators may seek to maximize such things as the size of their budget, the scope of their activities, the ease of their work, and their power and prestige. On the other hand, they will try to minimize their psychic costs by avoiding risks and conflict insofar as possible.

In short, the personal goals of employees in public schools often will take precedence over the official goals of the schools because the costs of inefficient behavior, in terms of the official goals (such as student outcomes or consumer satisfaction), are low. Indeed, in the argot of economists, this state of affairs creates a "demand for inefficiency," because the "law of demand" postulates that demand for various "goods" increases as their cost decreases (Chambers 1975). Thus the discrepancy between personal and official goals that is accentuated by the reward structure in public-sector organizations creates the basis for the distinctive "bureaucratic politics" that characterize such organizations and their relationships with clients and sponsors (Boyd and Crowson 1981; Michaelsen, 1977, 1981; Ostrom and Ostrom 1971). From the point of view of productivity, Chubb and Moe's (1988) analysis comparing the attitudes of public and private school teachers and administrators suggests that the political preoccupations set in motion by public education's governance structure have negative consequences for school effectiveness.

Even if one rejects the "public choice" interpretation outlined here, Shapiro and Crowson's (1985) analysis of the supervisory behavior of twenty-four Chicago public school principals shows the value of rational choice theory. This study explored why these principals, on the average, spent only 7 percent of their time in classrooms, even though the observation and improvement of teaching are supposed to be among their most important roles. Although principals themselves were inclined to say that they were "just too busy" to be able to find the time, and that it was neither necessary nor very useful to observe teachers, the ethnographic data in this study suggested a more basic explanation to Shapiro and Crowson (1985): "It is just *not in the best interests* of building principals to engage in classroom observation" (17, emphasis in original).

In support of this conclusion and consistent with Lortie's observations reported earlier, Shapiro and Crowson note, first, that "principals intrude infrequently into the classroom teacher's private educational domain because principals need and depend upon the cooperation of teachers, a cooperation endangered by close supervision" (17). Thus, they found that "teachers may actively sabotage overly close supervision of effort" (17) with such micropolitical tactics as

> forgetting to bring requested materials to conferences, overloading a principal with trivial requests or decisions, constantly arriving late at meetings, neglecting personal duties (e.g., hall monitoring) and exhibiting a general slowdown in report preparation; these are among the subtle cues (plus some not so subtle such as increased numbers of grievances) delivered to principals by teachers to suggest that all is not well in the superior-subordinate relationship. (18)

As a result of these sorts of cues, "principals typically downplay the classroom observation element in the supervisory role in favor of a tacit understanding that teachers owe them something in return" (19).

A second reason why principals didn't observe teachers more in the Chicago school system is that such behavior was not rewarded by the system. Indeed, Shapiro and Crowson (1985) present evidence showing that sometimes principals were punished rather than rewarded for rigorous evaluations of teachers or efforts to get rid of true incompetents. Moreover, *the operative values in the system really emphasized control rather than instruction* as the purpose of classroom observation:

> Although conceivably a mechanism for the improvement of instruction . . . the observation of classroom activity serves the principal more as a mechanism for "keeping the lid on" in the school. Principals are more likely to be punished organizationally (e.g. transferred to less desirable schools) for their failure to keep their buildings devoid of visible conflict, away from damaging publicity and generally free of vocalized parental displeasure than for a failure to be instructionally effective. (22)

In sum, school administrators are not irrational. Like most people, they calculate the benefits and costs of different courses of action in light of the reward structure that prevails around them. Superintendents and central office administrators, as well as school principals, are sensitive to the likely consequences of their behavior. They try to anticipate the reactions and consequences of their acts and seek to optimize their welfare. Because of the significance of the feelings and attitudes of teachers, particularly due to the potential power of their unions, principals and even superintendents may be inclined to be more solicitous to their concerns than to those of (generally unorganized) parents. Given a reward system for teachers that is insensitive to performance—and teachers unions' resistance to reforms that would change this, such as merit pay and career ladders—those with the most interest in better productivity (parents and citizens) are in a weak position to pursue that interest.

As we noted at the outset of this section, a complete explanation of the tendency to de-emphasize concerns for school productivity would most likely combine and integrate the various themes we have covered under several headings. Thus, economic-financial, sociological, and political explanations would be united in a balanced and theoretically integrated fashion. We presently lack such a framework, but recent developments in the relatively new field of the economics of organizations (for example, Barney and Ouchi 1986; Moe 1984; Zald 1987) suggest that we are getting closer to a body of theory capable of handling many of the relevant concerns. Combining a "contractual perspective on organizational relationships, a theoretical focus on hierarchical control, and formal analysis via principal-agent models" (Moe 1984, 739), the new economics of organizations is moving toward a positive theory of hierarchy that illuminates the classical concern for balancing inducements and contributions in organizations (Barnard 1938; Simon 1947). In so doing, it aids the investigation of questions of personal goals, information asymmetry, shirking, monitoring devices, and incentive structures that range up and down a complex, multistage hierarchy of institution and environment (Crowson and Boyd 1987).

POLICY IMPLICATIONS: BREAKING THE PRODUCTIVITY LOGJAM IN EDUCATION

The picture of public education we have sketched out is one in which there is a strong tendency toward "treaties" and "peaceful," but unproductive, "co-existence" throughout the hierarchy, from superintendents down to students. Although there are effective schools and pockets of excellence here and there, these seem to be exceptions within the general framework. Insofar as productivity is concerned, school administrators and teachers too often seem to operate as fairly detached actors within loosely coupled systems. With students distancing themselves from schooling, through bargaining and "choosing" what they will learn (McKenzie 1979); teachers generally performing as isolated, solo practitioners; principals walking a delicate line vis-à-vis their ambiguous authority; and superintendents and central office administrators often rather detached about curricular and instructional matters, the actors within the system seem lonely, not only "at the top" but also the bottom and middle (cf. Jackson 1977).

The contemporary need to diagnose and cure what ails public education has created a virtual growth industry. Depending upon one's diagnosis, cures range from "hard" to "soft" prescriptions. If one accepts an unadulterated version of the diagnosis by "public choice" theorists, then the implications argue strongly for healthy doses of market competition, that is, merit pay, voucher plans, and the like. Though not necessarily connected logically, this approach is superficially compatible with hard-nosed recommendations to "get tough," raise standards, root out incompetents, and apply "no-nonsense" business methods. On the other hand, if one is drawn toward more-sociological diagnoses, then the prescription is more likely to involve ways to break down the detachment and isolation in school systems that foster unproductive exchange relationships, and replace them with more-collaborative professional arrangements (Rosenholtz 1985). When the problem is seen in this light, competition—which may exacerbate isolated individualism—seems just the opposite of the medicine that is needed (Bacharach, Bauer, and Shedd 1986; Cohen 1983; Johnson 1986; Kasten 1986). Indeed, in some of the most thoughtful analyses of the problem, Murnane (1981, 1985) and Cohen and Murnane (1985) have shown why, in the context of school teaching, merit pay tends not to work as intended.

What both schools of thought agree about, though, is that there is a strong need to "restructure" public schools so that their internal dynamics and incentives are more conducive to productive relationships. What is at issue, essentially, is how to achieve a more productive balance of control or integration (via markets or hierarchies or a mix of both?) and professional autonomy in school systems (cf. Lortie 1969; Boyd 1988; Elmore 1988; Kasten 1986).[12] The policy recommendations of the so-called "first" and "second wave" of the current reform movement are at odds on this matter. In a nutshell, the first wave reforms emphasized centralized control and standards for schools and teachers, but the second wave has emphasized restructuring schools and professionalizing and enhancing teaching as a career, goals that conflict with the first wave's emphasis (Boyd 1987). So far, our states have adopted much more of the first wave's agenda than that of the second wave. Significantly, with the exception of Minnesota and a few other places, proposals to promote competition (for example, merit pay, parental choice of schools) have not garnered substantial political support in either wave of the reform effort (Boyd and Kerchner 1988).

Critics of the first wave's tendency to try to "legislate learning" call attention to a vicious circle connecting school governance and school performance (Chubb 1988; McNeil 1986). Schools having problems attract more attention from reformers who impose additional outside mandates upon them, further eroding the organizational autonomy necessary to foster a climate for effective teaching and learning. Thus, Chubb (1988) notes that "schools have not been granted more autonomy; they have had it taken away. . . . Improvement is being pursued teacher by teacher through testing, credentialling, and evaluation, and not through efforts to foster consensus, collegiality, or collective responsibility" (47).

The tension between control and autonomy seen in the first and second waves also lurks in many policy proposals, even those calling for decentralization and restructuring. For example, Cuban (1988, 572) notes that David Kearns (1988), in his "Education Recovery Plan for America," calls for increased parental choice and teacher autonomy but couples these with a somewhat contradictory set of mandates regarding the length of the school year, required core courses, and the linking of student promotion and teacher pay to student achievement. Rather than being a fault, what this point illustrates is that optimal organizational arrangements may be characterized by what Peters and Waterman (1982) saw in their excellent companies as "simultaneous loose-tight properties." That is, they were "both centralized and decentralized" (15) and distinguished by "the co-existence of firm central direction and maximum individual autonomy" (318). The firm central direction sets the key values and parameters that guide activity, but the sphere of activity has an openness that encourages individual initiative and creativity. Analysis of the recent literature on educational policy and management suggests that the optimum approach in school reform also would be characterized by "simultaneous loose-tight properties" (Boyd 1987).

Thus, school-site management plans, school improvement efforts, and the restructuring of schools and the teaching profession must inevitably be conducted within the parameters of state and national goals, equity considerations, and legal requirements (Caldwell and Spinks 1988). We may wish to free schools and educators from bureaucratic regulations and release creativity, but as Albert Shanker's proposal (Olson 1988) to do this illustrates, it is very difficult to escape the need, within the framework of public schools, to attach a number of conditions constraining this very freedom. Though complete freedom is not possible, it is possible to reduce bureaucratic rigidity and provide—at the same time—both more professional autonomy and more emphasis on student learning outcomes. Through judicious combinations of accountability for achievement goals, professionalization, and incentive systems that promote teamwork and reward group efforts, public schools can become more productive. The challenge is to move the politics of educational productivity toward the achievement of such delicate combinations of "loose-tight" properties.

EPILOGUE—SPRING 1997

During the decade that has passed since this paper was written, many school administrators have become more concerned about their role and responsibility in improving both the overall performance of their organizations and student learning outcomes. Also, rather than relying on observations and evaluations of teachers by school administrators, many educators prefer to use "peer coaching" approaches to improve the performance of teachers. Finally, agreement continues to grow that "cooperative performance incentives" are more functional and effective than individualistic rewards and incentives.

NOTES

1. Baumol (1967) sees more complexity than Brimelow does. Noting the difficulties of increasing the efficiency of labor-intensive services such as education, he observes that public sector providers, such as public schools, must compete with the private sector for labor, with the consequence that public sector labor costs are likely to increase even without gains in economic efficiency.

2. Summarizing his *Forbes* article (Brimelow 1986), Brimelow (1987) says:

> [It] argued that the American education industry, like the Soviet agricultural industry, has the systemic flaws of all socialized enterprises operating outside the discipline of market forces. For example: it demands resources to the limit of its political capacity; it allocates them in the interest of its controlling bureaucracies without any particular regard for the result; its productivity is catastrophic; it is continually swept by top-down panaceas (open classrooms, virgin lands, longer school years) peddled to its political masters by assorted hustlers. (201)

3. In his generally supportive response to Kearns (1988), Cuban (1988) notes that increased productivity comes from three sources: labor, management, and technology. "By focusing on labor (and the role of the schools in helping to shape attitudes and skills), you ignore the crucial decision-making role that management plays in deciding whether to develop or apply technologies to production; you also ignore the strategic errors that corporate management has made over the decades. These decisions have had much to do with enhancing or hindering productivity" (572).

4. Address to the National Press Club in Washington, D.C., September 8, 1987.

5. Ibid.

6. Ibid.

7. Indeed, as discussed later, an argument has even been advanced that there may be a legal basis for a case of "educational malpractice" if educators fail to provide documented "effective schools" practices (Ratner 1985).

8. See the extensive review of research supporting these conclusions in Boyd and Crowson (1981, 336–361).

9. Given the increasing concern for school effectiveness, more-recent research might show more attention toward instructional improvement on the part of central office administrators.

10. On the issue of dividing the principal's responsibilities, see Donaldson's (1988) discussion of the principal's moral authority and the need for integrated leadership in the "just school."

11. As Rosenholtz (1985) stresses, "While the product of exchange in isolated settings is often sympathy, the product of exchange in collegial settings is often ideas" (378).

12. Whatever is done, a preliminary step is to expect schools to produce acceptable results with all children so that they must operate beyond a "logic of confidence" and mere access to schooling.

REFERENCES

Bacharach, Samuel B., and E. J. Lawler. 1980. *Power and Politics in Organizations.* San Francisco: Jossey-Bass.

Bacharach, Samuel B., and Stephen M. Mitchell. 1987. "The Generation of Practical Theory: Schools as Political Organizations." In *Handbook of Organizational Behavior,* edited by Jay Lorsch. Englewood Cliffs, N.J.: Prentice Hall.

Bacharach, Samuel B., Scott C. Bauer, and Joseph B. Shedd. 1986. "The Work Environment and School Reform." *Teachers College Record* 88, no. 2 (Winter): 241–256.

Barnard, Chester I. 1938. *The Functions of the Executive.* Cambridge, Mass.: Harvard University Press.

Barney, Jay B., and William G. Ouchi, eds. 1986. *Organizational Economics.* San Francisco: Jossey-Bass.

Barry, Brian, and Russell Hardin, eds. 1982. *Rational Man and Irrational Society? An Introduction and Source Book.* Beverly Hills, Calif.: Sage.

Bastian, Ann, N. Fruchter, M. Gittell, C. Greer, and K. Haskins. 1985. *Choosing Equality: The Case for Democratic Schooling.* New York: The New World Foundation.

Bates, Richard. 1983. *Educational Administration and the Management of Knowledge.* Victoria, Australia: Deakin University Press.

Baumol, William. 1967. "Macroeconomics of Unbalanced Growth: The Anatomy of Urban Crisis." *American Economic Review* (June).

Bickel, Robert. 1986. "Educational Reform and the Equivalence of Schools." *Issues in Education* 4, no. 3 (Winter): 179–197.

Blau, Peter M. 1955. *The Dynamics of Bureaucracy.* Chicago: University of Chicago Press.

——. 1964. *Exchange and Power in Social Life.* New York: John Wiley and Sons.

Bossert, Steven T. 1988. "School Effects." In *Handbook of Research on Educational Administration,* edited by Norman J. Boyan, pp. 341–352. New York: Longman.

Bowles, Samuel, and Herbert Gintis. 1976. *Schooling in Capitalist America: Educational Reform and the Contradictions of Economic Life.* New York: Basic Books.

Boyd, William L. 1987. "Public Education's Last Hurrah? Schizophrenia, Amnesia, and Ignorance in School Politics." *Educational Evaluation and Policy Analysis* 9, no. 2 (Summer): 85–100.

——. 1988. "Balancing Control and Autonomy in School Reform: Competing Trends and Policy Issues." Paper presented at American Educational Research Association Annual Meeting, New Orleans, April.

Boyd, William L., and Robert L. Crowson. 1981. "The Changing Conception and Practice of Public School Administration." In *Review of Research in Education,* Vol. 9, edited by David C. Berliner. Washington, D.C.: American Educational Research Association.

Boyd, William L., and Charles T. Kerchner, eds. 1988. *The Politics of Excellence and Choice in Education.* New York: Falmer Press.

Bridges, Edwin M. 1982. "Research on the School Administrator: The State of the Art, 1967–1980." *Educational Administration Quarterly* 18, no. 3 (Summer): 12–33.

———. 1986. *The Incompetent Teacher.* New York: Falmer Press.

Brimelow, Peter. 1986. "Are We Spending Too Much on Education?" *Forbes* (December 29).

———. 1987. "Victorian in Style or Substance? A Comment on Hickrod." *Journal of Educational Finance* 13, no. 2 (Fall): 198–201.

Brown, Byron W., and Daniel H. Saks. 1980. "Production Technologies and Resource Allocations within Classrooms and Schools: Theory and Measurement." In *The Analysis of Educational Productivity: Volume I, Issues in Microanalysis,* edited by Robert Dreeben and J. Alan Thomas, pp. 53–117. Cambridge, Mass.: Ballinger.

———. 1981. "The Microeconomics of Schooling." In *Review of Research in Education,* Vol. 9, edited by David C. Berliner, pp. 217–254. Washington, D. C.: American Educational Research Association.

Caldwell, Brian J., and J. M. Spinks. 1988. *The Self-Managing School.* New York: Falmer Press.

Chambers, Jay G. 1975. "An Economic Analysis of Decision-Making in Public School Districts." Unpublished paper. Graduate School of Education and Human Development, University of Rochester.

Chubb, John E. 1988. "Why the Current Wave of School Reform Will Fail." *The Public Interest* (Winter): 28–49.

Chubb, John E., and Terry M. Moe. 1988. "No School Is an Island: Politics, Markets, and Education." In *The Politics of Excellence and Choice in Education,* edited by William L. Boyd and Charles T. Kerchner. New York: Falmer Press.

Clark, David L., L. Lotto, and T. Astuto. 1984. "Effective Schools and School Improvement: A Comparative Analysis of Two Lines of Inquiry." *Educational Administration Quarterly* 20 (3): 41–68.

Cohen, Michael. 1983. "Instructional, Management, and Social Conditions in Effective Schools." In *School Finance and School Improvement Linkages for the 1980s,* edited by Allan Odden and L. Dean Webb, pp. 17–50. Cambridge, Mass.: Ballinger.

Cohen, David K., and Richard J. Murnane. 1985. "The Merits of Merit Pay." *The Public Interest* 80: 3–30.

Coleman, James S., T. Hoffer, and S. Kilgore. (March) 1981. *Public and Private Schools: A Report to the National Center for Education Statistics by the National Opinion Research Center.* Chicago: University of Chicago.

Coleman, James S., E. Q. Campbell, C. Hobson, J. McPartland, A. Mood, F. Weinfeld, and R. York. 1966. *Equality of Educational Opportunity.* Washington, D.C.: U.S. Government Printing Office.

Coleman, Peter. 1986. "School Districts and Student Achievement in British Columbia: A Preliminary Analysis." *Canadian Journal of Education* 11 (4): 509–521.

Conway, Jill K. 1987. "Politics, Pedagogy, and Gender." *Daedalus* 116, no. 4 (Fall): 137–152.

Crowson, Robert L., and William L. Boyd. 1987. "Rational Choice Theory and the School Administrator." Unpublished paper. University of Illinois at Chicago, Fall.

Crowson, Robert L., and Van Cleve Morris. 1985. "Administrative Control in Large-City School Systems: An Investigation in Chicago." *Educational Administration Quarterly* 21, no. 4 (Fall): 51–70.

Cuban, Larry. 1975. "Hobson v. Hansen: A Study in Organizational Response." *Educational Administration Quarterly* 11, no. 2 (Spring): 15–37.

———. 1986. "Principaling: Images and Roles." *Peabody Journal of Education* 63: 107–119.

———. 1988. "You're on the Right Track, David." *Phi Delta Kappan* 69, no. 8 (April): 571–572.

Day, Robert, and JoAnne V. Day. 1977. "A Review of the Current State of Negotiated Order Theory: An Appreciation and a Critique." *The Sociological Quarterly* 18 (Winter): 126–142.

Deal, Terrence E. 1987. "Effective School Principals: Counselors, Engineers, Pawnbrokers, Poets . . . or Instructional Leaders?" In *Instructional Leadership: Concepts, Issues, and Controversies*, edited by William Greenfield, pp. 230–245. Boston: Allyn and Bacon.

Donaldson, Gordon A., Jr. 1988. "Management Is Not a Four-Letter Word: On the Principal's Moral Authority." *Reflections* 1988, pp. 36–39. National Network of Principals' Centers. Cambridge, Mass.: Harvard Graduate School of Education.

Education News. 1988. "Studying the Work of Principals." Newsletter of the Department of Education, University of Chicago: 10–11.

Elmore, Richard F. 1988. "Choice in Public Education." In *The Politics of Excellence and Choice in Education*, edited by W. L. Boyd and C. T. Kerchner. New York: Falmer Press.

Erickson, Donald A. 1979. "Research on Educational Administration: The State-of-the-Art." *Educational Researcher* 8, no. 3: 9–14.

Erickson, Donald A., ed. 1977. *Educational Organization and Administration*. Berkeley, Calif.: McCutchan.

Fowler, Frances C. 1988. "The Politics of School Reform in Tennessee." In *The Politics of Excellence and Choice in Education*, edited by W. L. Boyd and C. T. Kerchner. New York: Falmer Press.

Fullan, Michael. 1982. *The Meaning of Educational Change*. New York: Teachers College Press.

Ginsburg, Alan, Jay Noell, and Valena White Plisko. 1988. "Lessons from the Wall Chart." *Educational Evaluation and Policy Analysis* 10, no. 1 (Spring).

Griffiths, Daniel E. 1966. *The School Superintendent*. New York: Center for Applied Research in Education.

Gron, Peter C. 1982. "Neo-Taylorism in Educational Administration?" *Educational Administration Quarterly* 18, no. 4 (Fall): 17–35.

Guthrie, James W., W. I. Garms, and L. C. Pierce. 1988. *School Finance and Education Policy*, 2nd ed. Englewood Cliffs, N.J.: Prentice-Hall.

Hannaway, Jane, and Lee S. Sproull. 1978–79. "Who's Running the Show? Coordination and Control in Educational Organizations." *Administrator's Notebook* 27 (9): 1–4.

Hanushek, Eric A. 1972. *Education and Race.* Lexington, Mass.: D. C. Heath.
———. 1979. "Conceptual and Empirical Issues in the Estimation of Educational Production Functions." *The Journal of Human Resources* 14, no. 3 (Summer): 351–388.
———. 1981. "Throwing Money at Schools." *Journal of Policy Analysis and Management* 1 (1): 19–42.
———. 1986. "The Economics of Schooling: Production and Efficiency in Public Schools." *Journal of Economic Literature* 24, no. 3 (September): 1141–1177.
Hartman, William T. 1988a. *School District Budgeting.* Englewood Cliffs, N.J.: Prentice Hall.
———. 1988b. "Understanding Resource Allocation in High Schools." Unpublished paper. University Park, Pa.: Pennsylvania State University (February).
Hodgkinson, Harold L. 1985. *All One System: Demographics of Education—Kindergarten through Graduate School.* Washington, D.C.: Institute of Educational Leadership.
Homans, George C. 1958. "Social Behavior as Exchange." *American Journal of Sociology* 63 (6): 597–606.
Hord, Shirley M., and Gene E. Hall. 1987. "Three Images: What Principals Do in Curriculum Implementation." *Curriculum Inquiry* 17 (1): 55–89.
Hoyle, Eric. 1985. "Educational Organizations: Micropolitics." In *International Encyclopedia of Education,* edited by T. Husen and T. N. Postlethwaite, Vol. 3, pp. 1575–1582. Oxford: Pergamon Press.
———. 1986. *The Politics of School Management.* London: Hodder and Stoughton.
Hubermann, A. Michael. 1983. "School Improvement Strategies That Work: Some Scenarios." *Educational Leadership* (November): 23–27.
Jackson, Philip. 1977. "Lonely at the Top: Observations on the Genesis of Administrative Isolation." *School Review* 85 (May): 425–432.
Jencks, Christopher, Marshall Smith, Henry Acland, Mary Jo Bane, David Cohen, Herbert Gintis, Barbara Heyns, and Stephan Michelson. 1972. *Inequality: A Reassessment of the Effect of Family and Schooling in America.* New York: Basic Books.
Jennings, John F. 1987. "The Sputnik of the Eighties." *Phi Delta Kappan* (October): 104–109.
Johnson, Susan Moore. 1986. "Incentives for Teachers: What Motivates, What Matters." *Educational Administration Quarterly* 22 (3): 54–79.
Jones, L. B., and K. A. Leithwood. 1988. "Draining the Swamp: A Case Study of School System Design." Unpublished paper. Toronto, Canada: Ontario Institute for Studies in Education.
Kasten, Katherine. 1986. "Redesigning Teachers' Work." *Issues in Education* 4, no. 3 (Winter): 272–286.
Katzman, Martin. 1971. *The Political Economy of Urban Schools.* Cambridge: Harvard University Press.
Kearns, David T. 1988. "An Education Recovery Plan for America." *Phi Delta Kappan* 69, no. 8 (April): 565–570.
Kirst, Michael W. 1983. "A New School Finance for a New Era of Fiscal Constraint." In *School Finance and School Improvement Linkages for the 1980s,* edited by Allan Odden and L. Dean Webb, pp. 1–15. Cambridge, Mass.: Ballinger.

———. 1984. *Who Controls Ours Schools?* New York: W. H. Freeman and Co.

LaRocque, Linda, and Peter Coleman. 1985. "The Elusive Link: School-Level Responses to School Board Policies." *Alberta Journal of Educational Research* 31, no. 2 (June): 149–167.

Leibenstein, Harvey. 1980. *Beyond Economic Man: A New Foundation for Microeconomics.* Cambridge, Mass.: Harvard University Press.

Leithwood, Kenneth A. 1988. "School System Policies for Effective School Administration." Unpublished paper. Toronto, Canada: Ontario Institute for Studies in Education.

Leithwood, Kenneth A., and D. J. Montgomery. 1982. "The Role of the Elementary School Principal in Program Improvement." *Review of Educational Research* 52 (3): 309–339.

Levin, Henry M. 1974. "Measuring Efficiency in Educational Production." *Public Finance Quarterly* 2 (January): 3–24.

———. 1983. *Cost-Effectiveness: A Primer.* Beverly Hills, Calif.: Sage.

Levine, Donald M., and Mary Jo Bane, eds. 1975. *The "Inequality" Controversy: Schooling and Distributive Justice.* New York: Basic Books.

Levy, Frank S., A. J. Meltsner, and A. Wildavsky. 1974. *Urban Outcomes: Schools, Streets, and Libraries.* Berkeley, Calif.: University of California Press.

Lortie, Dan C. 1969. "The Balance of Control and Autonomy in Elementary School Teaching." In *The Semi-Professionals and Their Organizations,* edited by A. Etzioni. New York: Free Press.

———. 1975. *Schoolteacher.* Chicago: University of Chicago Press.

Magnet, Myron. 1988. "How to Smarten Up the Schools." *Fortune* (February): 86–94.

Mann, Dale. 1981. "Education Policy Analysis and the Rent-A-Troika Business." Paper presented at the American Educational Research Association Annual Meeting, Los Angeles (April).

Mann, Dale, and Deborah Inman. 1984. "Improving Education within Existing Resources: The Instructionally Effective Schools' Approach." *Journal of Education Finance* 10 (Fall): 256–269.

March, James G., and Johan P. Olsen. 1976. *Ambiguity and Choice in Organizations.* Bergen, Norway: Universitetsforlaget.

Martin, William T., and Donald Willower. 1981. "The Managerial Behavior of High School Principals." *Educational Administration Quarterly* 17: 69–90.

McKenzie, Richard B. 1979. *The Political Economy of the Educational Process.* Boston: Martinus Nijhoff Publishing.

McNeil, Linda M. 1986. *Contradictions of Control.* London: Metheun/Routledge & Kegan Paul.

McPherson, R. Bruce, Robert L. Crowson, and Nancy J. Pitner. 1986. *Managing Uncertainty: Administrative Theory and Practice in Education.* Columbus, Ohio: Charles E. Merrill Publishing Co.

Meyer, John W., and Brian Rowan. 1977. "Institutionalized Organizations: Formal Structure as Myth and Ceremony." *American Journal of Sociology* 83: 340-363.

———. 1978. "The Structure of Educational Organizations." In *Environments and Organizations,* by Marshall W. Meyer and associates, pp. 78–109. San Francisco: Jossey-Bass.

Meyer, Marshall W., and associates. 1978. *Environments and Organizations*. San Francisco: Jossey-Bass.

Michaelsen, Jacob B. 1977. "Revision, Bureaucracy, and School Reform." *School Review* 85 (February): 229–246.

———. 1981. "A Theory of Decision Making in the Public Schools: A Public Choice Approach." In *Organizational Behavior in Schools and School Districts*, edited by Samuel B. Bacharach. New York: Praeger.

Mintzberg, Henry. 1973. *The Nature of Managerial Work*. New York: Harper & Row.

Moe, Terry M. 1984. "The New Economics of Organization." *American Journal of Political Science* 28, no. 4 (November): 739–777.

Murnane, Richard J. 1981. "Seniority Rules and Educational Productivity: Understanding the Consequences of a Mandate for Equality." *American Journal of Education* 90, no. 1 (November): 14–38.

———. 1985. "The Rhetoric and Reality of Merit Pay: Why Are They Different?" In *Merit, Money and Teachers' Careers*, edited by Henry C. Johnson, Jr. Lanham, Md.: University Press of America.

Murphy, Joseph. 1988. "Methodological, Measurement, and Conceptual Problems in the Study of Instructional Leadership." *Educational Evaluation and Policy Analysis* 10, no. 2 (Summer): 117.

Murphy, Joseph, and Philip Hallinger. 1989. "Equity as Access to Learning: Curricular and Instructional Treatment Differentials." *Journal of Curriculum Studies* 21, no. 2 (March): 129.

———. 1987. "New Directions in the Professional Development of School Administrators: A Synthesis and Suggestions for Improvement." In *Approaches to Administrative Training in Education*, edited by J. Murphy and P. Hallinger, pp. 245–281. Albany, N.Y.: State University of New York Press.

Natriello, Gary, and Sanford M. Dornbush. 1980–81. "Pitfalls in the Evaluation of Teachers by Principals." *Administrator's Notebook* 29 (6): 1–4.

Newsweek. 1981. "Why Public Schools Fail." (April 20): 62–65.

Niskanen, William A. 1971. *Bureaucracy and Representative Government*. Chicago: Aldine.

Oakes, Jeannie. 1986. "Keeping Track, Part 1: The Policy and Practice of Curriculum Inequality." *Phi Delta Kappan* (September): 12–17.

Olson, Lynn. 1987a. "Chiefs Urge That States 'Guarantee' School Quality to Those 'At Risk.'" *Education Week* 7, no. 11 (November 18): 1, 17.

———. 1987b. "Chiefs Unanimously Endorse School 'Guarantees' Policy" *Education Week* 7, no. 12 (November 25): 1, 16.

———. 1988. "Saying Reforms Fail Most Pupils, Shanker Argues for a 'New Type' of Teaching Unit." *Education Week* 7, 28 (April 6): 1, 26.

Ostrom, Vincent, and Eleanor Ostrom. 1971. "Public Choice: A Different Approach to Public Administration." *Public Administration Review* 31: 203-216.

Peters, Thomas J., and Robert H. Waterman, Jr. 1982. *In Search of Excellence: Lessons from America's Best-Run Companies*. New York: Harper & Row.

Peterson, Kent. 1978. "The Principal's Tasks." *Administrator's Notebook* 26 (8): 1–4.

Pfeffer, Jeffrey. 1978. "The Micropolitics of Organizations." In *Environments and Organizations*, by Marshall W. Meyer and associates, pp. 29–50. San Francisco: Jossey-Bass.

Pitner, Nancy J., and R. T. Ogawa. 1981. "Organizational Leadership: The Case of the Superintendent." *Educational Administration Quarterly* 17 (1): 45–65.

Powell, Arthur G., Eleanor Farrar, and David K. Cohen. 1985. *The Shopping Mall High School: Winners and Losers in the Educational Marketplace.* Boston: Houghton Mifflin Co.

Purkey, S. C., and M. S. Smith. 1983. "Effective Schools: A Review." *Elementary School Journal* 83 (4): 427–452.

———. 1985. "School Reform: The District Policy Implications of the Effective Schools Literature." *Elementary School Journal* 85 (3): 353–389.

Rallis, Sharon F., and Martha C. Highsmith. 1986. "The Myth of the 'Great Principal': Questions of School Management and Instructional Leadership." *Phi Delta Kappan* 68, no. 4 (December): 300–304.

Ratner, Gershon M. 1985. "A New Legal Duty for Urban Public Schools: Effective Education in Basic Skills." *Texas Law Review* 63: 777–864.

Rodman, Blake. 1988. "Administrators Seen to Be out of Step with General Public." *Education Week* 7, no. 17 (January 20): 1, 23.

Rogers, David. 1968. *110 Livingston Street.* New York: Vintage Books.

Rosenholtz, Susan J. 1985. "Effective Schools: Interpreting the Evidence." *American Journal of Education* 93, no. 3 (May): 352–388.

Rossmiller, Richard A. 1987. "Achieving Equity and Effectiveness in Schooling." *Journal of Education Finance* 12 (Spring): 561–577.

Salley, C. 1979–80. "Superintendents' Job Priorities." *Administrator's Notebook* 28: 1–4.

Sedlak, Michael W., Christopher Wheeler, Diana Pullin, and Philip Cusick. 1986. *Selling Students Short: Classroom Bargains and Academic Reform in the American High School.* New York: Teachers College Press.

Shanker, Albert. 1988. "Teachers Have Leadership Role: Principals' Dual Task Questioned." *Education Week, Conventions in Print* (March 30): 4.

Shapiro, Jonathan Z., and Robert L. Crowson. 1985. "Rational Choice Theory and Administrative Decision Making: Implications for Research in Educational Administration." Paper presented at the American Educational Research Association Annual Meeting, Chicago (April). [Forthcoming in *Advances in Research and Theories of School Management*, edited by Samuel Bacharach. Greenwich, Conn.: JAI Press.]

Simon, Herbert. 1947. *Administrative Behavior.* New York: Macmillan.

Sirkin, J. R. 1985. "West Virginia: Epic Mandate, Historic Conflict." *Education Week* 4, no. 39 (June 19): 1, 18–21.

Strauss, Anselm, L. Schatzman, R. Bucher, D. Ehrlich, and M. Sabshin. 1963. "The Hospital and Its Negotiated Order." In *The Hospital in Modern Society*, edited by Eliot Freidson. New York: Free Press.

U. S. Department of Education. 1987a. *Schools That Work: Educating Disadvantaged Children.* Washington, D.C.: U.S. Government Printing Office.

———. 1987b. *What Works: Research about Teaching and Learning*, 2nd edition. Washington, D.C.: U.S. Government Printing Office.

Urbanski, Adam. 1986. "Lessons Learned from Evaluating Administrators." *Education Week* 5, no. 24 (February 26): 24.

van Geel, Tyll. 1973. "PPBS and District Resource Allocation." *Administrator's Notebook* 22 (1).

――. 1987. *The Courts and American Education Law*. Buffalo, N.Y.: Prometheus Books.

Walberg, Herbert J. 1984. "Improving the Productivity of America's Schools." *Educational Leadership* 41, no. 8 (May): 19–27.

Walberg, Herbert J., and William J. Fowler, Jr. 1987. "Expenditure and Size Efficiencies of Public School Districts." *Educational Researcher* 16, no. 7 (October): 5–13.

Weick, Karl. 1976. "Educational Organizations as Loosely Coupled Systems." *Administrative Science Quarterly* 21 (March): 1–19.

Willower, Donald J. 1979. "Ideology and Science in Organizational Theory." *Educational Administration Quarterly* 15 (3): 20–42.

Wimpelberg, Robert K. 1988. "Instructional Leadership and Ignorance: Guidelines for the New Studies of District Administrators." *Education and Urban Society* 20 (3).

Zald, Mayer N. 1987. "Review Essay: The New Institutional Economics." *American Journal of Sociology* 93, no. 3 (November): 701–708.

3

The New Politics of Information in Education

Five Dimensions of the Change from District-Level to School-Site Financial Analysis

E. Vance Randall, Bruce S. Cooper, Sheree T. Speakman, and Deborah Rosenfield

If politics is about the authoritative allocation of values—with money being a key "value" in making most policy happen—then it is no wonder that those who understand, control access to, and make the best use of financial data are in strong positions of authority. Information is truly power, particularly when it comes to funding, allocating, and managing the resources of America's public schools, some $318 billion annually (National Center for Education Statistics, 1997). Public education is the nation's largest public service operation and the second most expensive, right behind the health-care system.

The power that results from data is alluring, even though information itself can be fairly neutral, even dull. When information is placed into an organizational and thus a political context, it threatens regimes, sells Edsel automobiles, leads to violence as with the anti-Semitic propaganda during the Holocaust, or frees nations (Paul Revere's call, "The British are coming!"). Data on education finance can bolster the control of district leadership or free up individual educators and separate schools to pursue an informed, autonomous path to meet the specified needs of local children and communities. Information is the lifeblood of organizations, and schools and school systems are no different. However, the cognitive dissonance between data and reality at the organization level creates tensions and conflict, both within the system and outside the system among the "publics" who pay for public schools and use their services (Bass, 1983). The resolution of the ontological conflict is achieved through two basic means: either by organizational change and adaptation or by playing the politics of information.

When a school system adopts a new operating reality that is the result of new information, then the system will ultimately modify the means and/or the ends to eliminate the epistemological inconsistencies. The "feedback loop" of systems theory, the "learning organization" of management theory (see Senge, 1990), and the "responsiveness to clients"— a central tenet of the quality management movement—all depend heavily on information theory to make things work and to adapt the organization to new conditions and realities. Consultants, propagandists, and politicians realize that information has the ability to transform reality and organizations, such as schools, often without elaborate regulation (Knight & McDaniel, 1979).

The alternative organizational reaction is to sustain the current method of operation using the politics of information. Several tactics, applied to shape and control information, help to maintain the status quo or to create the desired reality, thus controlling public perception and reaction of any number of stakeholder groups. In the great struggle between authoritarianism and autonomy, between central control and decentralized responsiveness, the regulation of information determines what kind, how much, and when information should be given and to whom.

In their earlier work on the "politics of productivity," Boyd and Hartman (Chapter 2) describe the paradox of the "loose-tight properties" of school reform (see also Boyd, 1987; Peters & Waterman, 1982). Nowhere is this simultaneous centralizing-decentralizing condition more obvious than in the processes of the information systems. Centralized, authoritarian systems may horde, obscure, contrive, construe, or misconstrue data. Or, they may elect, through the democratization and dissemination of vital information, to share what they know with subordinates in exchange for loyalty and commitment to "maximize individual autonomy" (Peters & Waterman, 1982, p. 318). In return, those working in the organization may feed information "up the chain of command" to keep their bosses informed and to help top strategists adjust to changing conditions in the trenches, or the system's "workers" may keep ideas and innovations to themselves. These "up-down," "top-down/bottom-up," and "centralized/decentralized" control issues ("loose/tight properties") take on expanded meanings when information flows within organizations are evaluated, well understood, and coordinated with the reforms in place.

Thus, in all organizations, the gatekeepers of the flow of information wield immense power "by opening and closing channels of communications and filtering, summarizing, analyzing and thus shaping knowledge in accordance with a view of the world that favors their interests" (Morgan, 1986, p. 167). The control, shaping, and channeling of information—the process of "shaping definitions of organizational realities"—is an important tool used not only in private organizations but also in totalitarian regimes (Morgan, 1986, p. 168; Owens, 1991).

Information may be differently politicized by making subordinates rely on the largess of those in command of such data. Thus, informational dissonance is reduced by weaving "patterns of dependence" (Morgan, 1986, p. 168), granting inordinate power to those who either have sole access to the right information or who possess superior analytical skills to process and derive meaning from information already available (see Herrington, 1996). Monopolistic possession and expert status together create a critical dependency, blocking or obviating factions with whom conflicts of interest exist.

Public education is a ubiquitous arena for witnessing the politics of information. Schooling is a high-stakes enterprise, a process where human identity is greatly shaped, where worldviews are created, and where social relationships and political relationships are justified. Operating as a near monopoly in many communities (because the vast majority of families cannot afford private schooling), public education creates a natural dependency on professionals for information and expertise, establishing school officials as information gatekeepers.

Accessibility is further complicated because education data are still typically designed and collected for reporting that meets federal and state mandates. The result is information that is neither user-friendly nor managerially relevant for decision makers at the district and school (see Speakman et al., 1996). Whatever the shortcomings of today's school-site financial and pupil performance information, however, clear signs are emerging that the demands by stakeholders for more and better data are being heard. These demands mean that the once routine provision of education information for compliance is rapidly becoming a high-stakes game of provision for performance.

The new politics of information in education comprises five dimensions:

1. *The Politics of Agency*: The initial issue in the politics of information is that of ownership and access. Who has access to "relevant" data, easily or otherwise obtained? Who is then to take control of the relevant data and to frame the problem for stakeholders? The

political conflict seems to emerge from contests waged in the course of establishing the participants in the situation being examined and the naming of the parties who will access data for defining, diagnosing, and communicating the issue identified.

2. *The Politics of Method*: Information is embedded in a framework, a model, and a method. Because education data are varied, of mixed quality, and abundant, those who control the politics of means and methodology are in an advantageous position. Which research models, measures, and techniques, not to mention technology, should be applied to the gathering and analyzing of data? Whose agenda do the chosen methods and models reflect? As information becomes more and more technical, the control over these methodologies will dominate the politics of education.

3. *The Politics of Meaning*: Information is subject to analysis and interpretation because the facts rarely speak for themselves. Parties can and will use the same data sets in totally different ways. With more-sophisticated methods emerging, school finance information taken from actual expenditures becomes more reliable as facts. Yet, opinions based on these facts will proliferate. Answers as to whose opinion is heard and how accessible information is to those who would form and present alternative options will be important.

   Disagreements over the meaning of school finance data will accelerate as this type of data becomes more accessible and democratically distributed. Whereas parties may be more likely to accept school-level data as correct and legitimate, participants may simultaneously disagree about the effectiveness of its use, for example, whether costs for administration are too high or low, whether enough money is being spent on student support services, or whether special education expenditures are increasing to the detriment of the regular education child. The politics of meaning may be a critical step supporting the politics of information.

4. *The Politics of Parity*: With expanded information available on school-level finance, it is important to readdress the degree to which equity should exist between levels of schools, types of pupils, locations of districts, and individual schools themselves. An outgrowth of the politics of meaning, the politics of parity emphasizes the value judgments to be placed on the disparities in spending, creating heroes and villains in a highly charged political atmosphere. Should district leadership, for example, cut back funding to a "gifted and talented" program in order to fulfill a court mandated requirement to spend more money on special and challenged students? Furthermore, with the equity of funding in education long a concern at the district level, equity is certain to

become an equally visible concern at the school site as school-level governance and school-level data (and their associated politics) become more widely available.

5. *The Politics of Action*: In the private sector, information is the prelude to decision making, effective or otherwise. In education, financial information communicated in a more transparent manner may lead initially to greater conflict as people decide to confront their lack of knowledge and, at the same time, set a course of action (Beach, 1993). Case data show the incredible ability of information to mobilize, unite, and focus public attention and interest. But whose solution is selected and why? This dimension of the politics of information is a convergence of the politics of ownership, method, meaning, and parity, which creates action or inaction.

The following sections address these five dimensions of information politics as seen in education, presenting four case examples and the implications of each.

DIMENSION 1: WHOSE PROBLEM, WHOSE DATA? *THE POLITICS OF PROBLEM OWNERSHIP AND DATA ACCESS*

A first source of conflict in the politics of information is that of problem definition and ownership, thus determining who will access the necessary information. Access and ownership often pit the traditional controllers of information against newly empowered school-site and community leaders, as well as against branches of local and state government. Since World War II, the fifty states have assumed an increasingly important role in funding education and have thus been major arenas for policy-making and the politics of education. Further, the states, spurred into action by the courts, were forced to craft plans to equalize local district spending. In *Serrano v. Priest* in 1971, the California high court ruled that the state bore major responsibility to ensure equal educational opportunity through the equitable financing of school districts. Subsequently, in thirty other states, public interest groups representing children living in poor districts pressed suits against their states for inequitable funding. Remedies to the inequalities identified in fifteen states with successful litigation further required increased state involvement in the funding of local education.

As a result of state-level activity, those fighting the great political battles over interdistrict equity were less likely to be the school, and its teachers and parents. Instead, finance experts, policy wonks, and advocates for the poor with a command of arcane technical language—including terms such as mill levy, assessed valuation, flat grants, equal yield, and fiscal neutrality—left the average parent, taxpayer, and local consumer unable to understand the esoteric language and to participate in the emerging debate. Even had these "outsiders" understood the technical discussion, the data needed by these newcomers to express informed opinions were held tightly out of reach by state and, occasionally, local officials. In contrast, with today's accelerating shift to school governance and shared decision making, issues of data ownership and access are again on the table. This democratization of education access by its practitioners has not been a comfortable one for the information managers with heretofore virtual hegemony over financial information and its interpretation.

Recent reforms—including school-site accountability, school-level report cards, local "town meetings" with parents, and school-site decision making—are having a strong effect in eroding the information dominance of state and district officials. This shift in governance and associated information is demanding more and better school-site data. Moving control from one level or agency to another energizes political conflict. Yet even with traditional groups resisting the sharing of control over information, information is being democratized alongside the dispersion of power and control.

Furthermore, in fiscally "dependent" school districts—those districts without taxing authority that are funded instead by other local agencies such as city hall or the town/county council—educational leaders want greater flexibility and control over their budgets. At the same time, city hall mayors and county or city councils in the 1990s are under increasing pressure to grasp more control of these same dollars in order to balance their budgets. The complicating factor is a dual level of fiscal and policy accountability vested in to two separate bodies, the city and the school board, making it difficult for some funding agencies to hold districts accountable.

Case 1: A Political Conundrum

New York City's Mayor Rudolph Giuliani found himself in 1994 facing a citywide budgetary shortfall, holding major fiduciary responsibility for public education, obligated to regulatory requirements for a balanced city budget, and with limited control over matters of cost, spending, and accountability in the New York City public school system. In contrast, for the city's other service agencies (for example, police, fire, parks and recreation, health, transportation, and welfare), not only did the mayor appoint each agency's top manager (the police, fire, and housing commissioners, for example), but he could readily access and analyze agency spending through the city's Office of Management and Budget (OMB).

Not so with the largest single city agency, the New York City Board of Education. Even though the mayor was expected to raise and allocate tax money to the board—over $8 billion in 1993–94—he was allowed to appoint only two of the seven board members (the five borough presidents name the remaining five board representatives). Further, the district's Chancellor, Raymond Cortines, did not report to the mayor. This left Cortines, at times, to foster a contentious operating relationship with Mayor Giuliani on issues important to Cortines because the chancellor was directly accountable to the seven-member board of education who hired him. This separation of power was the result of the 1969 "decentralization law" passed by the New York legislature to give greater control to the minority communities. However, it is ironic that this law, in turn, left the chancellor (the head superintendent), hired by the central board of education, with little effective control over the board's thirty-two Community School Districts' boards and superintendents.

An Information Void: The division in powers meant that the mayor put up the money for schools and was held accountable to the state but could not control school expenditures. In fact, the mayor believed that he could not even *obtain basic information about how money was being expended* in the largest and most costly agency in NYC. (The public school system in NYC is also, incidentally, the nation's largest local education authority with over a million pupils, 147,000 employees, and 1,116 public schools.) When the state legislature cut its allocation to New York City, pressure mounted in the spring of 1994 to reduce city spending against a total New York City budget of $32.4 billion. Desperate to understand the board of education's finances, Mayor Giuliani looked outside the system for direction. He appointed a trusted colleague, lawyer, and certified public accountant, Herman Badillo, as Special Counsel for Fiscal Oversight of Education to obtain information on costs and, ultimately, to bring spending in line with state mandates. Well known and respected, Mr. Badillo was Deputy Mayor under Koch, was a four-time U.S. Congressman, created the bilingual education legislation, and was a former Bronx Borough President and city housing commissioner.

Mr. Badillo's task was not an easy one. The Board of Education was a labyrinth of information—for example, data were residing on five separate computer systems for human resource and finance alone. Further, management information necessary for the performance of individual schools was limited, and even then, prepared in large part by the central board, popularly called 110 Livingston Street. And, staff numbers and the location of these same employees were largely unavailable. The tales of "management bloat" were rampant. Neither the chancellor nor the school board was able to dispel these doubts in the minds of the mayor, Mr. Badillo, or the public-at-large.

Operating without a common base of information, the parties (the chancellor, mayor, teachers unions, administrators union, and business community) were unable to discuss the "facts of the facts" in finance, a critical platform for discussions of efficiency, balancing the budget, and school effectiveness. By example, at one meeting to which all the parties had been invited to discuss the proposed analysis of annual spending, the union president, Sandra Feldman of the United Federation of Teachers, reached into her briefcase and presented the AFT's *own* analysis of school expenditures that was not congruent with the board's reports filed with the state and OMB. This was not surprising given the fact that the union maintains its own personnel, salary, benefits, and dues data, but it made the discussion difficult nonetheless without an ability to agree on a baseline of information from which additional analysis would be undertaken. Equally important, without common ownership, mutual trust, and ready access to data, the problems of the budget crisis showed little chance of being resolved while looking at educational spending alone.

On behalf of the mayor, Herman Badillo took responsibility for the data crisis and turned over the challenge of producing the data set on the 1993–1994 annual budget to Coopers & Lybrand L.L.P., an independent professional services firm with an extensive accounting and auditing practice. In July 1994, Herman Badillo commissioned an extended analysis of the school board's budget, using a new financial analysis methodology for detailing spending by function, program, and school type or level. The need for outside review was obvious. No one trusted anyone's data. Spending in one area rarely agreed or cross-footed with spending data from other sources. And the city's schools confused cuts in "budgeted" funds with real cuts in "actuals."

On October 4, 1994, and after months of working with detailed financial information drawn from the board's computer systems, the mayor, Mr. Badillo, and Sheree T. Speakman of Coopers & Lybrand, L.L.P., held a press conference to release the first comprehensive analysis of the city schools' spending meant to be read and understood by all the stakeholders of education in the city. Using more than four million financial transactions categorized into the NYCPS's 311,000 line-item general ledger, the study applied the methodology known as the School District Budget Model (SDBM) to the board's own data for an analysis of every dollar of spending, by function, by program, and by school versus central usage.

Release of the report considerably disarmed the politics of access and ownership. So, too, were the politics of method disarmed because of the rigorously consistent methodology of the definitions supporting the cost categories used in the Coopers & Lybrand model. Table 3.1 shows the six frames by which the board of education's $8.050 billion budget for 1993–94 could be analyzed, tracing resources from the central administration down to instruction in the classroom. These frames set the stage upon which the politics of meaning is played out among the different interest groups, political ideologies, and potential areas of conflict.

As shown in Table 3.1, **Frame 1** aggregates 100 percent of costs, showing that the New York City Board of Education was spending $8.050 billion or some $7,918 per pupil in 1993–1994. **Frame 2** differentiates the costs between Central and School sites, indicating the resources that are used by the Board of Education ($1.5 billion), leaving 81.4 percent at the school site or $6,442 per student ($6.550 billion). This finding did much to dispel the myth of "administrative bloat," although Cortines and his successor, Dr. Rudolph F. Crew, have been able to reduce the central office staff costs still more as the mayor had requested.

In New York City, the contentious issue of the centralization/decentralization of authority was finally addressed by the New York state legislature, which just passed the most dramatic overhaul of the NYC schools' balance of powers since 1969 when the state legislature enacted the Community Control laws, breaking NYC schools up into thirty-two separate self-governing "communities" and their representative Community School Districts across the city. In January 1997, the governor signed the reorganization bill into law, a new arrangement that greatly enhanced the "centralized" power of the chancellor and weakened the local boards. The chancellor can now (a) appoint the thirty-two community school district superintendents from lists provided by the boards, (b) determine the school principals in these districts who previously were selected by the community boards and superintendents, and (c) unseat a duly elected school board member if improprieties

Table 3.1.
Systemic Cost Structure by Frame: NYC Public Schools, 1993–94

		I Percent	II Per Pupil	III Dollars (in Billions)
Frame 1. Aggregation	Systemic	100.0%	$7,918	$8.050
Frame 2. Structural	School Site	81.4%	$6,442	$6.660
Frame 3. Functional	Instructional	47.8%	$3,787	$3.850
Frame 4. By Type	High Schools	39.5%	$3,126	$0.951
Frame 5. Program	Regular/Special	29.2%	$2,308	$2.176
Frame 6. Contractual	6/8 Time	21.9%	$1,734	$1.763
Teacher Time	5/8 Time	18.2%	$1,441	$1.465

occur. Thus, the chancellor and now the mayor have more of a voice in how the thirty-two school districts spend money. Already, the two leaders are sharing information, thus reducing political conflict over access, methods, and the meaning of financial data.

Frame 3 considers the functions or "use" of the resources. How much of the 81.4 percent that is spent in schools is expended on direct classroom instruction of students? Of that amount, 47.8 percent of total district per pupil spending, or $3,787 per pupil, was actually reaching the school and classroom to support direct teaching and learning. Here, the politics revolve around the size, level, and pay of the teacher force, because most of the 48 percent went to pay teachers (salary and fringe benefits). Much of the structure, salaries, benefits, stipends, and the like, of this 48 percent is derived from the results of the collective bargaining process. Thus, the parties will battle over the appropriate level of investment (for example, How much of a teacher raise can the district afford?)—placing a continuous demand on quality results from the board's information system.

Frame 4 then separates costs by type or level of school. Because the High School Division is directly controlled by the chancellor (the elementary and middle schools come under the thirty-two Community School Districts in 1994), we can assume direct political control over secondary schools by the top authorities. This frame shows the effects of direct control; the chancellor has authority to cut costs in secondary schools, whereas the previously decentralized lower schools were more autonomously-run under community-elected school boards. Thus, it comes as no surprise to find that high schools spent 39.5 percent on direct instruction in the classroom (which is $3,126 per pupil), compared to the overall system average of $3,787 per pupil (47.8 percent) for instruction. In contrast, this tends not to be the pattern in the nation's schools as a whole.

Frame 5 then separates costs by special and regular education programs. Although the overall average for all students is 48 percent of total district per pupil expenditures in the classroom for instruction, with the special education costs removed, the regular education classroom resources drop to 29.2 percent, a number that declines still more when the actual teaching time of teachers is considered. Here, the politics revolve around those lobbying for special education services versus other groups.

Finally, **Frame 6** traces the effects of the teachers' contract on costs. For teachers instructing six-eighths of a day, as do the elementary teachers, the percent of elementary teacher costs actually dedicated to instruction is 21.9 percent ($1,734 per pupil out of the system average of $7,918 per pupil). Because high school teachers, by contract, teach five periods daily of about fifty minutes each, high schools dedicated

18.2 percent or $1,441 per pupil to direct instruction out of the system per pupil total of $7,918. The remaining three to four periods of a high school teacher's time are spent on planning, meeting with colleagues, having lunch, and/or supervising students in the halls and lunchrooms.

The politics of Frame 6 involve the power and authority of the teachers' union and other groups to influence personnel policies and the number of "contact hours" teachers put in. Here we see the shifting foci of school politics using a system that tracks the dollars from the system to the child. The structural decisions made will be accompanied by public opinion, whether derived from central office administrators, school-site educators, high school teachers and parents, special education parents and advocates, or unions and other groups concerned about the number of working hours and days spent by teachers.

As the analysis of the 1993–1994 education spending in New York City schools became known, the politics began to heat up. Ultimately, acrimonious public debate triggered the resignation of Chancellor Ray Cortines, who was then replaced by Dr. Rudolph F. Crew, a selection preagreed with the mayor. During the six-month transition process, Beverly Donohue, formerly assistant director of the NYC Office of Management and Budget (OMB), became the board of education's chief financial officer. Using the October 1994 report on the SDBM as a foundation, she developed and refined a similar model to analyze the 1995-1996 costs at every school in the New York City Public Schools. A forty-one-volume report was released in the fall of 1996 that presented vital information on spending for the 1,116 schools, individually, by type, and by jurisdiction (community school board).

DIMENSION 2: WHOSE MODELS? *THE POLITICS OF METHODS, MEASURES, AND TECHNIQUES*

After the fundamental issues of legitimacy, ownership of, and access to data are at least partially resolved, the next area of political conflict surrounds the "means" for measuring and analyzing education allocations, efficiency, and equity. Traditionally, the states have used only the most basic information on issues of compliance, rarely venturing into the complex world of measuring efficiency and productivity (Hanushek, 1994). In fact, basic benchmarks on costs and spending are only now emerging. Little useful information, therefore, is available to districts and schools on how best to use resources.

We know, first of all, that the "unit of analysis" in school finance research can have a major effect on results and public policy decisions. If a state court were to compare spending per pupil between schools, instead of between districts, the findings would be very different.

Recent analysis of expenditures at the school site indicates much greater inequalities in spending among schools than among districts within the same state (Cooper, et al., 1994; Farland, 1997; Picus, 1996, 1997).

The metric used to determine cost-per-unit may affect outcomes of financial research. Districts that report Average Daily Attendance instead of Average Daily Membership may be disadvantaged in state aid and may appear different in terms of the spending levels and percentages devoted to students and instruction. Third, financial models may vary as to their inclusiveness and comprehensiveness—for example, whether to include all district expenditures or just those costs from the general fund or the operating funds—which will influence the size of the budget and thus the perception of spending. Typically, districts do not include in their totals their capital spending, their pass-through dollars, and tuition payments to other districts to provide special services for some children. Thus, their costs appear different because the size of their pie is different. Fourth, models may aggregate costs at the district level without providing the underlying detail by school. The effect is to gloss over the differences by school sites and programs by using only averages across schools instead of actuals within each site (Busch & Odden, 1997).

Other battles may occur over (a) formulas for allocating costs to districts, schools, and programs because revenues to districts are based on the cost metrics; (b) whether to portray the real or average cost of teachers, with the middle-class schools preferring the use of "average teacher salary" and the schools in poorer communities, the actual—because apparently schools in poor neighborhoods cannot easily hold the more experienced, more highly-paid teachers; and (c) means of determining the cost of maintenance and upkeep, with more-dilapidated, high-use schools in rougher neighborhoods favoring an "as-needed formula," with other schools wanting their "fair share" of renovations and improvements.

In general, then, the modernization of school financial information carries with it the usual supporters and resisters, as does any move to design a "better mouse trap." Resistance comes from those wedded to the extant system of data collection and reporting. The new models—in this case, school-site specific, efficiency-, and equity-related approaches—are usually evaluated in terms of which system benefits our district and school financially. Potential embarrassment over resulting data may lead districts to focus political debate on questions of method rather than on questions of facts.

The enlightened use of information in the Information Age depends on participants constructing a common frame of reference regarding what data mean. This cooperation is built almost entirely from a unanimous acceptance of the methodology used to generate the data. Much like New York City, where the politics of method divided the mayor and the chancellor until better methods and data were available, other districts, too, have found that the politics of method significantly color the entire debate. As this next example illustrates, continued focus on the politics of method has enormous implications for the politics of meaning and parity and, ultimately, on the politics of action.

DIMENSION 3: FIGHTING FOR UNDERSTANDING: *THE POLITICS OF MEANING*

Life in the Information Age depends on participants constructing a common meaning about data and trends. It is one thing to build complex models and to generate data—tons of data. It is quite another to determine what various user groups understand and the nature of the politics at arriving at these understandings. We have a useful example: a school district that volunteered to join a statewide study on school-site equity and then struggled to understand and come to grips with the "meanings" of the information (Randall et al., 1996; Hertert, Busch, & Odden, 1994).

Case 2: Equity and Effectiveness in the Blue Mountain School District

In the late fall of 1994, the state superintendent of public instruction authorized the formation of the Task Force for Educational Equity and commissioned it to investigate a variety of issues, including fiscal equity for individual schools in the state. The task force was comprised of school finance experts in the state office of education, school board members, former superintendents, representatives from the various ethnic groups in the community, and research consultants.

A particular school district, Blue Mountain School District (pseudonym), was invited to participate in this study for two reasons. First, it was a large district in a state with a diverse student population. Second, the Blue Mountain School District (BMSD) was recommended as having exemplary financial records and procedures. BMSD agreed to participate on the condition of anonymity. The expenditure data were analyzed for the 1994–1995 school year. A representative from the BMSD was invited to attend all task force meetings, had access to all task force reports, and was designated by the district as its liaison.

Fiscal and enrollment data were collected with the support and assistance of district and state education office personnel. A beta-test version of In$ite, a methodology developed by Coopers & Lybrand starting in New York City, was used to account for the total expenditures in the district for 1994–1995 and to analyze and report the data by school site, function, and program (three categorical programs were examined: Chapters 1 and 2, Bilingual Education, and Special Education). Teacher and student demographic data were compared with student achievement scores and school-site expenditures. Also, two dividing lines, creating two sets of less-affluent and two more-affluent areas of Blue Mountain, were used to examine the issue of fiscal neutrality—or the equity principle of equal education opportunity for all. In addition, data about nontraditional resources—for example, funds raised by schools from athletic and social events—were collected to determine whether these "private" sources of revenue had any impact on the calculated determination of interschool equity.

The report documented several key findings with respect to equitable distribution of district financial resources. On a positive note, the report found that total expenditures, as well as general education funding, were made in an equitable fashion. Expenditures for classroom instruction had the greatest degree of equity, followed by leadership, operations, and instructional support.

Expenditures for leadership were not excessive and, in fact, were below the national average of about 9 percent (see Cooper, Bloomfield, & Speakman, 1997). A substantial portion of the budget was being spent directly on classroom instruction. Junior high schools, as a type, were the most equitably funded, followed by high schools and then elementary schools. Nontraditional (off-the-books) sources of revenue did not have a significant impact on fiscal equity.

On the negative side, the research found that moderate to severe inequities between schools appeared in spending for Special Education, Titles 1 and 2 (except for junior high schools), and Bilingual Education (i.e., Alternative Language Services). Greater variation was also found in expenditures across the In$ite functions (instruction, instructional support, operations, and leadership) for all schools combined than among the three types (elementary, junior high, and high schools).

When the financial information was coupled with demographic and achievement information, other inequities emerged: (a) Schools on one side of the school district spent slightly more per student than schools on the other side; (b) Schools with lower standardized test scores tended to have teachers with fewer overall years of experience, shorter service in their schools, less formal training and degree hours, lower salaries, and were younger on average. This was a significant finding, given that the characteristics most highly correlated with student achievement were teachers' years of experience and formal training.

The range of expenditures between highest and lowest outlier schools created too much organizational dissonance. Education expenditures did not meet standards of equity for the three categorical programs. Furthermore, the data showed that schools in the less affluent areas of

Table 3.2.
Teacher Characteristics and Student Achievement:
Blue Mountain Public Schools, 1994–95

Teacher Characteristics	1st Quartile 0–25th Percentile	2nd Quartile 26th–50th Percentile	3rd Quartile 51st–75th Percentile	4th Quartile 76th–100th Percentile
Years of Experience	11.9	13.5	14.3	15.4
Years in Assignment	7.2	7.4	7.9	8.0
Teachers Age (years)	44.8	45.1	45.6	47.0
Grad. Credit Hours	4.4	4.6	4.7	4.8
Percent Ethnic Minority	4%	5%	4%	2%
Salary (annual)	$30,422	$31,583	$32,302	$32,980

the district had lower per-pupil expenditures than schools in the more affluent areas of the district. When schools were grouped into quartiles by student achievement, as presented in Table 3.2, the teachers in the highest performing schools were slightly more experienced (15.4 years in the highest quartile to 11.9 years in the lowest quartile); had longer service in their schools (8.0 years versus 7.2 years), were older (47 years compared to 44.8 years), had a few more graduate credit hours of training (4.8 credits to 4.4), were less ethnically diverse (4 percent minority students in the lowest-achieving schools compared to 2 percent in the highest), and were paid less well as teachers ($30,422 annually in the lowest quartile versus $32,980 for those in the highest quartile).

As shown in Table 3.3, spending on instruction went from $1,272 per pupil in the 1st Quartile (lowest performing) to $1,522 per pupil in the 4th Quartile, a difference of $250. Total general-education spending by school also varied systematically by quartile with $168 per pupil separating the 4th Quartile (high performing) schools at $2,322 per pupil and $2,154 per student in the 1st Quartile.

And Table 3.4 shows student demographics and achievement, again organized by the performance quartiles of the students to test neutrality. The 1st (low-end) Quartile showed greater poverty (32% versus 7% on free lunch), more minority students (17% to 5%), higher student mobility among schools (55% for the 1st Quartile and 23% for the 4th Quartile), and a slightly higher drop-out rate (3.3% in the 1st Quartile and 3.1 in the 4th Quartile). The student/teacher ratio, however, remained fairly constant across all four quartiles with a ratio of 23.8 students to teacher in the 1st Quartile and 24.3 in the 4th Quartile.

A draft of the final task force report was presented to the district superintendent and senior staff members in the BMSD office. The range of spending depicted in the report among levels of schools and within

Table 3.3.
Expenditures and Student Achievement:
Blue Mountain Public Schools, 1994–95

Instructional Spending	1st Quartile 0–25th Percentile	2nd Quartile 26th–50th Percentile	3rd Quartile 51st–75th Percentile	4th Quartile 76th–100th Percentile	Difference between 1st & 4th Percentiles
General Education—Instruction	$1,272	$1,503	$1,505	$1,522	$250
General Education—Total	$2,154	$2,204	$2,172	$2,322	$168
Total Expenditures—Teaching	$1,922	$1,865	$1,802	$1,793	($129)
Total Expenditures	$2,928	$2,864	$2,740	$2,822	($106)
Difference between Total and General Education	$774	$660	$568	$500	

functions elicited comments of disbelief. How could such inequalities exist, the district wondered, given their commitment to equity? The researcher from the task force then reminded the BMSD representatives that the fiscal data were provided by the district with assistance from their own office of budgeting and accounting. The meeting ended with an admonition to the researcher that the BMSD did not accept the findings and that they should be altered. The researcher was never given any specifics as to what was in error nor what the corrected data would show. Any suggestion or indication of fiscal inequalities was simply unacceptable.

With help from BMSD representatives, the report went through several drafts; the data were checked, and revisions made. A final draft of the report was given to the district through its representative on the commission, asking for final feedback before the report was presented to the state board of education. Here a serious communications break-

Table 3.4.
Student/School Demographics and Student Achievement:
Blue Mountain Public Schools, 1994–95

Student Demographics	1st Quartile 0–25th Percentile	2nd Quartile 26th–50th Percentile	3rd Quartile 51st–75th Percentile	4th Quartile 76th–100th Percentile
Free Lunch SES	32%	23%	15%	7%
Minority Students	17%	13%	10%	5%
Mobility Rate (% ADM)	55%	39%	30%	23%
Drop-Out Rate	3.3%	2.4%	2.8%	3.1%
Student to Teacher Ratio	23.8 to 1	23.5 to 1	24.2 to 1	24.3 to 1

down within the BMSD occurred, and the superintendent never saw the report before it was presented to the state board of education.

Despite fairly positive findings in the study, the district's response was anything but accepting. BMSD issued a press release several days after the report was issued, declaring that the equity study was "seriously flawed from beginning to end" and that the report was an "outrage." A good portion of the district's hasty and visceral response was due probably to three major causes. First, an employee of the district revealed the identity of the sample district (BMSD) to the news media. Second, as is usually the case, the media ignored the overall findings— that the district had met the equity standards—and released comments almost totally focused on those areas of spending that needed improvement. Third, a state legislator who lived in the district had submitted a bill that would allow residents in school districts with over fifty thousand pupils to vote whether to divide their district. The bill seemed to be targeted at Blue Mountain School District, and the BMSD superintendent and school board felt that the equity study could be used by the lawmaker to gain support for the partitioning law. Clearly, even though the task force had one set of interpretations, the district's agenda influenced it (the district) to develop a wholly different interpretation of the same data. Because the district officials were not in control of the methodology, they stymied the work of the task force by attempting to discredit the methodology and the data. The district maintained that the task force used "simplistic and misleading concepts of equity, untested software, and inappropriate, emotionally-charged terminology," and that the "broadly-stated conclusions were not supported by the data."

The district was able to convince the state board of education to rescind its acceptance of the task force report because of alleged "factual errors." The state board agreed and asked the district to submit a list of specific objections to the task force and asked the group to report to the state board. The district's objections were more issues of interpretation and definition of terms than questions about the validity of the data. As of now, the task force has not reported to the state board of education, and the official status of the report remains unresolved.

DIMENSION 4: WHOSE SCHOOLS, WHOSE KIDS?
THE POLITICS OF PARITY

After issues of information ownership, access, method, and meaning are considered and dealt with, the next area for political activity is an analysis and comparison of results among schools and programs. Public schools and their educators are not used to being compared. In fact, education prides itself on being "unique" and highly "child-centered," meeting the individual needs of students, and working in a "caring" rather than a competitive environment. Though parents as consumers have long "shopped around" for the right school district for their family (see Teibout, 1956), states and districts have been hesitant to engage in politics of all-out competition for resources and results at each school.

Yet, the new Information Age is sure to bring with it more-advanced means for comparing schools, classrooms, and students (see Bock, Wolfe, & Fisher, 1996 for an evaluation of the Tennessee "value-added assessment system"). Already, the development of In$ite™—the Finance Analysis Model for Education™—enhances the capacity to compare individual school spending by function and program. Issues of equity, once confined to interdistrict analysis, are now possible at the school site. Preliminary data gathered in a number of schools across districts using In$ite indicate several potential areas of political concern: the underfunding of elementary school classrooms, in comparison to middle and high schools; the differences in resources to individual schools; and the different levels of spending on students by their needs and conditions.

Case 3: The Power of Parity Analysis

With data from *School Based Budget Reports of the Board of Education of the City of New York* (November 1996), Table 3.5 shows the analytical power of information that explains school-site costs by function and program—focusing on the distribution of spending among a school population. This "outlier" analysis compares schools that are spending one standard deviation or more above and below the mean on (in this case) the direct instruction of children in the classroom—the core technology of education. The first two rows of Table 3.5 show data on all-system spending at the school level of which 80.7 percent or $6,728 per student—out of the New York Public Schools' overall per pupil average of $8,342—was reaching the school site. (This amount—$8,342 per pupil—is arrived at by dividing the total $8.840 billion budget for school-year 1995–1996 by the total pupil enrollment of 1,059,642.) The NYC Board of Education also did calculations using just the dollars spent on children within the system (removing "pass-through" funds that went to children in nonpublic schools and special education out-of-district placements: These totals were therefore lower, a total of $7,717 per pupil, instead of the full cost of $8,342 per pupil, reducing the denominator and therefore increasing the ratio going to schools: $6,728 divided by $7,717 per pupil equals 87.2 percent.

Further, systemwide instructional costs comprised 51.1 percent ($4,260 per pupil) of which $3,260 per pupil was general state and local money and $1,000 was from categorical funds: federal, state, and private; instructional support reached 7.8 percent ($653 per pupil), school-site operations was 15.4 percent ($1,288 per pupil), and school-level leadership was $527 per pupil or 6.3 percent of total system per pupil costs. A single New York City Community School District (#32) was then selected as a management unit for further equity analysis. In Table 3.5, rows 3 and 4 present all school costs in District 32 which is comprised of elementary- and middle-level schools only, because the high schools are run centrally.

Data indicate in District 32 in the New York City Public Schools that 77.2 percent (or $6,442 per pupil) reached the schools as a group and that 50.0 percent ($4,174 per pupil or $3,163 general funds and $1,011 categorical dollars) was expended in the classrooms for instruction, slightly below the systemwide average. Six percent was spent on instructional support, 15.4 percent on operations, and 5.8 percent on leadership (costs of school principals, assistant principals, and school offices). When, however, we remove the categorical aid for special education, bilingual, and Titles 1 and 2 (see Table 3.5, rows 5 and 6), the general aid expenditures per pupil overall went to $5,314 or 63.7 percent of the systemwide per pupil cost of $8,342. Instructional costs similarly were reduced from 50 percent to 45.3 percent ($3,781 per pupil). Most dramatically, instructional support (guidance, librarians, coaches, extracurriculum, computer, and media) went from 6 percent to 0.6 percent (from $499 per pupil to $51)—indicating that most of the extra services given to students in NYC District 32 came under federal and state categorical programs, not from local tax levy (General Education) funds. Operations and leadership under general education were much

Table 3.5.
"Outlier" Elementary Schools by Function: Comparison Analysis at the School Site, NYC Public Schools, 1995–96
(Total District = $8,342 per pupil)

			I Total School	II Instruction	III Instructional Support	IV Operations	V Leadership
SYSTEMWIDE	All Schools	1. Per Pupil $	$6,728	$4,260	$653	$1,288	$527
		2. % Distr. Total	80.7%	51.1%	7.8%	15.4%	6.3%
DISTRICT 32 SCHOOLS	District 32 All Education	3. Per Pupil $	$6,642	$4,174	$499	$1,285	$486
		4. % Distr. Total	77.2%	50.0%	6.0%	15.4%	5.8%
	General Education	5. Per Pupil $	$5,314	$3,781	$51	$1,044	$438
		6. % Distr. Total	63.7%	45.3%	0.6%	12.5%	5.3%
OUTLIERS	PS 116 HIGH Elem. School	7. Per Pupil $	$6,001	$4,424	$39	$1,067	$471
		8. % Distr. Total	71.9%	53.0%	0.5%	12.7%	5.7%
	PS 376 LOW Elem. School	9. Per Pupil $	$3,808	$2,305	$8	$893	$602
		10. % Distr. Total	45.7%	27.6%	0.1%	10.7%	7.2%
DIFFERENCES	Between HIGH and LOW	11. Per Pupil $	$2,193	$2,119	$31	$174	($131)
		12. % Distr. Total	26.3%	25.4%	0.4%	2.1%	(1.5)%

the same as reported for all schools/all programs (rows 3 and 4), because operations and administration are most often from the general fund anyway.

The power of school-site information is the ability to compare each and every school by function. In the case of District 32 schools, we took the highest and lowest (outliers) elementary schools in the distribution because teaching and learning are the core technology of education and are a useful way of categorizing spending differences—concentrating on general education costs because special and categorical aid are unevenly distributed. As shown in Table 3.5, rows 7 through 12, of the twelve elementary schools in the district, Public School 116 (PS 116) was the highest spending on direct instruction at $4,424 per pupil or 53.0 percent, while Public School 376 (PS 376) was the "low" outlier at 27.6 percent for instruction ($2,305 per pupil)—with 25.4 percent separating the two ends of the distribution (a $2,119 per pupil difference). Overall, too, PS 116 spent $6,001 per pupil (71.9%), whereas PS 376 expended a total of only $3,808 per pupil or 45.7 percent, for a difference of 26.3 percent or $2,193 per student between the top and bottom of total school-site general education spending. (We removed categorical programs because they are not evenly distributed across the district.) The remaining variables were not very different for instructional support, operations, and leadership.

Hence, school-site information moves analysis from the state and district level to the instructional function in each school, the level where students, teachers, and parents are located. We learned from this limited example of parity analysis in one district in NYC (a) that special education and other categorical programs absorb most of the instructional support resources in NYC, where spending went from 6 percent to less than 1 percent (0.6 percent) or $39 per student at PS 116 and only $8 per general education student at PS 376; (b) that spending on classroom instruction ranged from 53 percent to only 27.6 percent; and (c) that using system averages may obscure variation between general and all-education and between high and low outliers.

DIMENSION 5: PRAXIS OR PARALYSIS?
THE POLITICS OF ACTION

The last dimension in the new politics of information is action: "What to do with the findings?" Though parties may fight over access, methods, equity, meaning, they might really go to war over the use of the information and its meaning. In Blue Mountain School District, for example, the process led to violent inaction, as the school district refused even to "accept," much less to use, the In$ite data (although they later purchased a copy of the software, perhaps to implement it themselves because their relationship with the state task force was strained). In New York City, until the parties could agree on the school expenditure data, Mayor Guiliani and Chancellor Cortines were at a near standstill. Thus, data and politics can come together through "actionable information."

The politics of action takes two forms. First, key actors may take strategic steps to use the data, starting to reallocate funds to needed agencies within the system. Second, the information itself, when made public, may motivate the community and other interested parties to bring pressure and to reexamine policies and practices. The "invisible hand" of information—after it's defined, analyzed, and made handy to users—may have a more powerful effect on schools than a whole set of requirements, mandates, and rules.

Case 4: The Politics of Information Comes to Suburbia

A case in the state of New York is informative. Since the 1996 arrival of the New York Commissioner of Education, Dr. Richard Mills, a new statewide, grade-specific examination has been used, one based *not* on "minimum" basic skills but on actual grade-level achievement. The target has also changed. Because minimum competencies were often aimed at low-income and inner-city students (middle-class schools were less worried because most of their students met the minimums), the power of the information has also been changed. Now, suddenly, 99 percent of middle-class students who previously passed a minimum competency test (normed to detect students operating a grade level or more *below* the norm) did not fare as well on the grade level test. Parents in upper-class communities such as Scarsdale and Irvington in suburban Westchester County, New York, and Oyster Bay on Long Island, found that 30–40 percent of their third-grade children were *not*, in fact, reading on the third-grade level (Berger, 1997, pp. B33–34).

These school- and district-specific data rang an alarm bell in the suburbs, where self-esteem and housing values are geared to high test scores. Realtors immediately lost sales. Parents went into orbit. And superintendents held special public meetings to explain the realities of the achievement of students. School boards began to reexamine past practices: Scarsdale, New York, had a policy of no homework until the fourth grade. Teachers had blithely used so-called "whole language" approaches to reading and writing—which encouraged creativity but not always accuracy, spelling, grammar, and other testable standards (see Manzo, 1997). And parents wondered where all their tax money was going if as many as 40 percent of their children were not performing at grade level.

The state used a simple means for disseminating these test results; they sent each newspaper, radio station, and television station in the state a disk with the performance of students in their region. The data just appeared in the local media, and schools were suddenly concerned and accountable about real information at each school level. The politics shifted from school boards, state agencies, and state and federal legislatures to each and every school and student. Though conflict had not dissipated, it had focused on learning, results, and the use of resources by school.

Action followed knowledge. Though school superintendents, defending their districts and jobs, tended to criticize the easy public access, the methodology, testing, and sampling, the public read the results in the local paper and acted. Perhaps one method of bypassing the control of bureaucracies over their data is to deliver the outcomes to the press and let the power of information take over. Certainly, as this case shows, school districts can move quickly to reexamine practices, the use of funds and time, and policies on such things as assigning homework. Public opinion is more powerful than bureaucratic good intentions.

CONCLUSIONS

The politics of school finance is changing. No longer do issues, conflicts, and negotiations occur only "up there" somewhere in the state courts, legislatures, or even school boards. With the need and demand for—and the availability of—more accurate, timely, and reliable school-site and classroom data, we can expect an initial rise in the micropolitics of schools around costs, measurement, problems, meaning, and change.

Part of this political activity will be an adjustment to new information and accountability, its interpretations, and its focus. After school-site data are accessible and understood, we assume that the politics of change will give way to the politics of related interest groups. This change in the level of analysis affects the nature of accountability and personalizes the new developments. In effect, changes in the level of analysis alter the accountability and personalize the process. No longer are problems in school finance some esoteric issues far away at the district or state level, done by faceless participants. Instead, the new politics of information starts with local information, affecting the lives of identifiable students. As other data are related to costs—such as teacher behaviors and student achievement as in the twin cases of Blue Mountain School District and Scarsdale, New York—the stakes rise and the constituents become engaged. It is then that the five dimensions of the new politics of information come together:

- **Ownership:** Citizens take an interest and control over their own lives and can obtain the data they need, thus ending the major problem of the issues of ownership and access, as shown in the NYC suburban case study.
- **Methods:** Participants understand enough concerning the "models" and "methods" used for analyzing the financial and academic data to get involved (the SAT is perhaps the nation's most scrutinized and best-understood test because parents and students can examine their results and prepare for the examination). In the Blue Mountain case, the district leadership did not accept the methods of the task force, distrusted the results, and refused to change. Here, the politics of information became negative, and the process was stopped. In suburban districts in New York, the parents and school board members were likewise dazzled and confused by the new third-grade test results—but accepted the outcomes and began to change policies in terms of the scores.
- **Parity:** At the heart of the political future is the setting of benchmarks, making comparisons, and motivating schools to improve opportunity and performance based on a more efficient use of resources. In all three cases—NYC, Blue Mountain, and the New York state districts—the power of information was its ability to give participants ways of finding out "How are we doing?" and then to make comparisons possible. Under the new NYC school-site reporting model, administrators, parents, and teachers are able to trace resources to their own schools by categories, programs, and locations. These developments will allow for both more accountability at the "top" and greater involvement at the "bottom."
- **Meaning:** The politics of meaning is perhaps the most difficult to predict. It is the ability of better data, in a known and concerned context, to help constituents to construct meaning and to motivate reformers to restructure the enterprise. In all four case examples, participants struggled to deal with new data, new comparisons, and new ways of knowing.
- **Action:** The praxis of open access, greater ownership, better data, increased parity, and clearer meaning may shape a new politics of information in education. The issues are now perceived by parents as facts and figures about their schools, the schools their children attend. This connection of data and action (praxis) will require a different kind of scrutiny of decisions that few school officials have previously known and a commensurate shift and dispersion in power and control. Thus, the democratization of information democratizes power. This change is healthy, bringing the politics, decision making, control, and data all to the same level. Thus, everyone is accountable—teachers to instruct effectively, managers

to help make decisions that increase efficiency, parents to support schools and children, and politicians to report on the progress of our education system.

In a paraphrase of Chairman Mao's garden metaphor, Berne, Stiefel, and Moser (1997) recently explained that "school-level analysis is a relatively new area and as such it is worthwhile to let a thousand flowers bloom; while many weeds will grow as well, it is too early to cut off potentially productive ways to gather and analyze data" (253). But without state-of-the art information systems and a political structure that takes ownership, understands, shares, and uses the educational and financial data, we cannot hope to sow and harvest the benefits of the Information Age for the betterment of schools and students.

REFERENCES

Bass, B. M. (1983). *Organizational Decision Making*. Homewood, Ill.: Richard D. Irwin.

Beach, L. R. (1993). *Making the Right Decision*. Englewood Cliffs, N.J.: Prentice-Hall.

Berne, R., Stiefel, L., & Moser, M. (1997). "The Coming Age of School-Level Finance Data," *Journal of Education Finance*, 22(3), 246–254.

Berger, J. (1997, February 23). "State's Rating of Schools Hackles in the Suburbs," *New York Times*, Metro Section, pp. B33–34.

Bock, R. D., Wolfe, R., & Fisher, T. H. (1996). "A Review and Analysis of the Tennessee Value-Added Assessment System," Nashville, Tenn.: Comptroller of the Treasury.

Boyd, William Lowe. (1987). "Public Education's Last Hurrah?: Schizophrenia, Amnesia, and Ignorance in School Policy," *Educational Evaluation and Policy Analysis 9*, no. 2 (Summer): 85–100.

Busch, C., & Odden, A. (1997, Winter). "Introduction to the Special Issue: Improving Educational Policy and Results with School-level Data: A Synthesis of Multiple Perspectives," *Journal of Education Finance*, 22 (3), 225–246.

Cooper, B. S. and Associates (1994). "Making Money Matter in Education: A Micro-Financial Model for Determining School Level Allocations, Efficiency, and Productivity," *Journal of Education Finance*, 20(1), 66–87.

Cooper, B. S., Bloomfield, D. C., & Speakman, S. T. (1997, February). "School-Site Finance and Urban Education Equity: New Legal Arguments, New Reform Opportunities," *Education and Urban Society*, 29(2), 149–161.

Farland, G. (1997, Winter). "Collection of Fiscal and Staffing Data at the School-Site Level," *Journal of Education Finance*, 22, 280–290.

Hanushek, E. (1994). *Making Schools Work*. Washington, D.C.: The Brookings Institution.

Herrington, C. D. (1996). "The Politics of School-Level Finance Data and State Policy-Making." In L. O. Picus and J. L. Wattenbarger (Eds.), *Where Does the Money Go? Resource Allocation in Elementary and Secondary Schools* (15th Annual Yearbook of the American Education Finance Association), pp. 236–252. Thousand Oaks, Calif.: Corwin Press, Inc.

Hertert, L., Busch, C., & Odden, A. (1994). "School Financing Inequalities among the States: The Problem from a National Perspective," *Journal of Education Finance, 19* (3), 231–255.

Knight, K. E., & McDaniel, R. R., Jr. (1979). *Organizations: An Information Systems Perspective*. Belmont, Calif.: Wadsworth Publishing Co.

Manzo, K. K. (1997, March 12). "Study Stresses Role of Early Phonics Instruction," *Education Week, 16*(24), 1, 24.

Morgan, G. (1986). *Images of Organizations*. Newbury Park, Calif.: Sage Publications, Inc.

National Center for Education Statistics. (1997). *Mini-Digest of Education Statistics, 1996*. Washington, D.C.: NCES (February 1997).

Owens, R. G. (1991). *Organizational Behavior in Education*, 4th ed. Englewood Cliffs, N.J.: Prentice-Hall.

Peters, T. J., & Waterman, R. H., Jr. (1982). *In Search of Excellence: Lessons from America's Best-Run Companies*. New York: Harper & Row.

Picus, Lawrence O. (1996). "Are Productivity and Equity Compatible? A Case Study of Texas School Finance," in Bruce S. Cooper and Sheree T. Speakman (Eds.), *Optimizing Education Resources*, Vol. 6 in the Series, "Advances in Educational Productivity," Herbert J. Walberg (Series Editor), pp. 217–242. Greenwich, Conn.: JAI Press, Inc.

Picus, L. O. (1997). "Using School-Level Finance Data: Endless Opportunity or Bottomless Pit?" *Journal of Education Finance, 22*(3), 317–330.

Randall, E. V., Hite, S. J., Norcott, B., Wilson, C., & Anderson, L. (1996). *Intradistrict Fiscal Equity. A Case Study of One Utah District*. (Utah Educational Equity Task Force Report). Salt Lake City, Utah: Utah State Office of Education.

Senge, P. M. (1990). *The Fifth Discipline: The Art and Practice of the Learning Organization*. New York: Currency Doubleday.

Speakman, S. T., Cooper, B. S. et al. (1996). "Bringing Money to the Classroom: A Systemic Resource Allocations Model Applied to the New York City Public Schools." In L. O. Picus & J. L. Wattenbarger (Eds.), *Where Does the Money Go? Resource Allocations in Elementary and Secondary Schools* (15th Annual Yearbook of the American Educational Finance Association), pp. 106–132. Thousand Oaks, Calif.: Corwin Press.

Teibout, C. M. (1956, October). "A Pure Theory of Local Expenditures," *Journal of Political Economy, 65*, 416–424.

4

The Role of the School Board in Resource Allocation

Elaine M. Chichura and William T. Hartman

> Allocation of resources among different programs in the district budget is a critical function of the budget. If funding were unlimited, there would be no need to make any choices among district programs, and each program would receive all the requested resources. However, resources are limited and choices have to be made on how the monies will be spent.
>
> (Hartman 1988, 4)

PURPOSE OF THE STUDY

Central to the concept of resource allocation are the decision-making process utilized to distribute the resources and an understanding of the organizational structures and the overall constraints within which the allocation decisions are made.

Public schools as formal organizations have broad-based goals, limited access to resources with which to achieve those goals, and a formal hierarchy with which to manage the process of goal achievement. The local board of education has the unique function of combining the economic and the political dimensions of this formal organization in an effort to provide and maintain a thorough and an efficient education for all children of the state.

Of particular interest to the study was the examination of how school boards make resource allocation decisions. More specifically, we investigated the extent to which resource allocation decisions were based on the formal goals of the organization, on the structure of the organization, or on the self-interests of the individuals associated with the organization. Results of this study provide a basis for understanding the decision-making process as it currently exists, which can enable the board of education to meet the goals of public education in a better fashion, thus improving the educational process through more-effective resource allocations.

CONCEPTUAL–THEORETICAL FRAMEWORK

This study investigated the role of the board of education in the process of resource allocation for public schools. To provide the conceptual framework for conducting the study and analyzing the results, several related research areas were drawn upon. First, the role of school boards as governing units—their legal basis, their composition, and their responsibilities—was examined. Because school boards make budgetary decisions within the fiscal capacity of their districts, an understanding of the economic environment within which boards operate was required. To analyze specific school board behaviors in terms of the decision-making process three theoretical perspectives—the rational, the bureaucratic, and the political models—were utilized. They represent a range of possible explanations of the role that school boards play in the process of resource allocations for public schools.

The actual levels of funding for education contributed by the local school district have been related to four sets of interacting variables (Jones, 1985, p. 201). One set of variables, generally titled governmental, involved the amount and the type of federal and state aid made available to local districts. A second set of variables, termed the economic variables, dealt with the economic conditions of the local district and included the property wealth of the district and how that wealth was distributed (that is, residential, commercial, industrial); in addition, they also included the personal income of residents and the number of unemployed residents. A third set of variables was the demographic and social composition of the district and included the size of the district; the population density; the educational levels of voters; the occupational status of voters; and the racial, ethnic, and religious composition of the local school district. The fourth and final set of variables was referred to as the political and the administrative variables. These variables included descriptors of the members of the board of education and the district administration, particularly the superintendent.

The rational model approach to decision making emphasized knowledge and understanding on the part of the decision maker concerning inputs, outputs, and processes of implementing decisions. Inputs referred to the necessary resources, the ingredients, or the elements needed to carry out a particular decision. Outputs represented the desired goals or the desired results anticipated from the implementation of a particular decision. Process referred to an essential link of knowledge, of understanding, and of efficiency between the inputs and the outputs of a decision (Cibulka, 1987, pp. 8–13). This model implied that decisions were based on logic and purposeful reasoning (Stokey & Zeckhauser, 1978, p. 3) and assumed that decision makers were aware of predetermined and prioritized goals of the organization. More importantly, it assumed that decision makers had an active desire to achieve those goals in the most efficient manner (Cibulka, 1987, p. 13).

Examples of budgeting approaches based on the rational model were the planning-program-budgeting system (PPBS), performance budgeting, and zero-based budgeting (Cibulka, 1987, p. 8). These systems of budgeting represented attempts to improve school productivity and were based on the following assumptions:

- One or more agreed-upon "products" or learning outcomes
- A "scientific" instrument for measuring student progress toward those outcomes
- Research techniques that make it possible to separate schooling effects from out-of-school influences (such as home environment and individual IQ) upon student achievement (Garms, Guthrie, & Pierce, 1978, p. 249)

A board of education that utilized a rational model approach to decision making in the area of resource allocation would exhibit behavior, both purposeful and deliberate, directed toward improving student achievement. According to Peterson (1976, pp. 134–135), the usefulness of the rational model "depends on showing that board members agreed on certain objectives, that reference to these objectives was made during the course of policy making, and that policy outcomes were consistent with these objectives." Budgetary planning would be systematic, procedural, and goal-directed with little if any responsiveness shown to short-term or external pressures (Cibulka, 1987, pp. 8, 12–13).

The bureaucratic model originated with a theory of organization based on the work of Max Weber. In defining an ideal bureaucracy, Weber cited the following characteristics as described by Hall and listed in Owens (1981, pp. 10–11):

1. A division of labor based on functional specialization
2. A well-defined hierarchy of authority
3. A system of rules covering the rights and duties of employees
4. A system of procedures for dealing with work situations
5. Impersonality of interpersonal relations
6. Selection and promotion based only on technical competence

This type of organizational structure was intended to simplify the system of administration and the management of large and complex organizations that served a large clientele (Owens, 1981, p. 12). Behavior within these organizations was highly dependent on preestablished routines or standard operating procedures (Allison, 1971, pp. 81–83). The concepts of authority, responsibility, and policy development typically flowed from the top levels of the bureaucratic organization down through the lower levels of the organization. Standard operating procedures (SOPs), often developed by the upper levels of the organization, were defined by Allison (1971) as "rules according to which things are done" and as "routines for dealing with standard situations" (p. 68). The SOPs, structured in a simple manner, were easily understood and implemented on a regular basis by a large number of individuals (Allison, 1971, p. 83). Situations not dealt with through the utilization of SOPs appeared slow, formal, and often inappropriate. The functioning of large organizations on the basis of a routine means of operation was described as an inevitable feature of the exercise of public authority in modern society (Allison, 1971, p. 266).

A system of budgeting representative of the bureaucratic model was that of incrementalism. Incremental budgeting as described by Wildavsky (1975, pp. 5–6) was one in which the process of budget development was directly linked to and directly dependent on the previous year's budget. With this method of budgeting, a large portion of the budget was determined by previous decisions and long-term planning. Education examples of budgetary items included here would be mandatory curricular programs and negotiated salaries.

A school board utilizing a bureaucratic decision-making model for budgetary development would focus on maintaining the status quo within the organization and maintaining an atmosphere of stability by allowing few changes, which would act to minimize conflict within the organization (Meyer, 1971, p. 7). In this approach decisions would be made following predetermined rules and systems for action rather than being based on performance or organizational goal-directed criteria.

The political model approaches to decision making described the process of decision making in public schools from two different perspectives. These were power or control and the theory of public choice. Both of these perspectives centered on the concept of self-interest.

The power or control model of decision making is based on the concept of local control. This concept of control is supported by the governmental structure legally established to provide education as a service. Within this structure the local board of education was responsible for making decisions that reflected the larger school community. This larger school community included the administration, the teachers, the students, and the local citizens (McGivney & Moynihan, 1972). Often these segments of the larger school community organized to reflect interests concerning particular issues or to represent general group interests. These groups were referred to as special-interest groups.

Special-interest group activity was often aimed at influencing the decision-making processes and the policy formation of the board of education. In general, it was believed that the boards of education tended to be most responsive to interest groups that were internal to the school organization, particularly the local teachers' association. It was also found that the boards of education were most likely to be responsive to interest groups representing issues that were highly visible in the community and external to the school organization. Examples of these issues included taxation, finance, and building concerns (Zeigler, Jennings, & Peak, 1974, pp. 96–102). In this manner it was clear that the board of education was a political entity, making decisions of political consequence in the community (Garms, Guthrie, & Pierce, 1978, p. 327).

Though there was a multitude of research on politics in public schools, this study was particularly concerned with the research that examined specific influential forces and pressures on the board of education as the central decision-making body within school systems. An example of one such study was conducted by Kerr (1964). He argued, at least for suburban school districts, that the board of education functioned to legitimatize or "rubber stamp" policies of school systems as controlled by the superintendent and the professional educators.

In contrast, Vidich and Bensman (1969) described a different situation occurring in small, rural school districts. In the district described, the community appeared to have a greater impact on the functioning of the school system.

Other theories, such as the dissatisfaction theory as described by Lutz (1980), present still another view of influences on the functioning of the board of education. This theory, which focused on the rate of participation in governance, stated that participation in school governance increased when the public was dissatisfied.

School boards functioning under a political power or a control decision-making model for budget development would be strongly influenced by and responsive to their perceptions of the wants, needs, and self-interests of significant influential segments or special-interest groups within the larger community they had been elected to represent.

The public choice or political economy models, which represented alternative political approaches to decision making, viewed resource allocation decisions as a function of the behavior of self-interested individuals reflecting their personal needs, personal values, and personal goals. This concept, as described by Boyd (1982, pp. 113–115), involved the tension created through the interaction of the goals of the individual and the more formal goals of the organization. The costs and the benefits of action influenced behavior and ultimately affected the functioning of the organization.

A political economy view implied that members of the board of education may not have organizational goals in mind when making resource allocation decisions. The board of education, more strongly influenced and directed by their own need to avoid conflict, may be more responsive to their perceptions of the wants, needs, and self-interests of the school district employees. Under this decision-making model the board of education's responsiveness to teacher personal-need satisfaction would be shown through the fair and equitable treatment of all teachers within the school district, with special attention being paid to this group during district budget development.

Using the public choice model of decision making, the board of education would also be influenced by the recommendations of the school district administration, in terms of their own self-interests, to avoid conflict and maintain good relations with the teaching staff and the community. With this decision-making model the goal of satisfying the self-interests of the school district employees replaces the more formal goals of the school, such as meeting student needs and increasing student achievement levels.

DATA COLLECTION METHOD

A systematic case study approach that examined four school districts located in northeastern Pennsylvania was utilized to study the decision-making role of the board of education in resource allocation for public schools. The school districts were selected as a result of their size, their economic conditions, the length of superintendent tenure, and the predominant social class composition. Two districts were selected to represent smaller, more-rural schools reflecting traditional values. The other two school districts were selected to represent a larger, more-suburban type of community climate. Information concerning the actual identity of participating districts was held confidential for the reporting of the study. Results were reported by referring to the two rural districts as District "A" and District "B"; the two larger districts were designated District "C" and District "D."

The descriptive component of the study resulted from data collected through the review of state and district documents, through direct observations of board of education behavior at formal public meetings, and also through personal interviews with selected individuals. With data collected during the 1987–1988 school year, the study focused on the role of the board of education in the planning and the adoption of school district budgets for the 1988–1989 school year.

Meetings pertaining to the planning and the adoption of the budget were attended and tape-recorded. The budget meetings reported in the research included both public and closed executive sessions conducted by the four boards of education. Observations included the presentation of the budget to the board, documentation of questions asked by the board members, documentation of the community response to the budget presentation, documentation of any apparent conflict, documentation of any board reaction or response to conflict, and documentation of reasons given publicly by the board members to justify their particular vote on both the tentative and the final budgets. In total, the research reported on thirty-two meetings or approximately seventy-four hours of meeting time in the four school districts involving the boards of education budgetary planning and decision making.

The interview process involved a total of thirty-seven personal interviews with representative members from the four school districts. The personal interviews alone provided a total of approximately fifty hours of tape-recorded data. In order to obtain a more complete and varied description of the role that the board of education plays in the budgetary decision-making process, interview subjects representing different segments of the larger school community were selected to participate in the research. The participants selected to be interviewed in each school district included three individuals representing the board of education, the superintendent, the business manager, two members of the teachers' association, and two members of the community. In one of the districts, four board members were interviewed because of the interest each had expressed by personally volunteering to participate in the research.

The analytical component of this study involved the examination of the descriptive data in terms of conceptual models of the rational, the bureaucratic, and the political approaches to the process of decision making. Data from the descriptive portion of this study were compared and contrasted in terms of the theoretical perspectives presented in the review of selected literature. This comparison was done to determine which theoretical model or combination of models best described the role of the board of education in the process of resource allocation for public schools.

FINDINGS

Specific questions posed by the research and the resultant answers to those questions found by the study follow.

1. What Procedures Do School Boards Use for the Development of District Budgets?

In all four school districts involved in the research, the board of education was involved in the budget development process as a committee of the whole. Even though Districts A, C, and D each utilized a type of subcommittee structure to conduct the duties and the responsibilities assigned to the board of education, none of the districts assigned the specific duties associated with the process of budget development to a select subcommittee. At the time of the research, all the districts, except District B, were in the initial stages of developing long-range financial planning committees, which were expected to become involved in the development of the budget for the 1989–1990 school year. All of the proposed planning committees were expected to involve members of the board of education, the administration, and interested members of the community.

All four school districts examined followed timelines for board participation in the development of the budget, but those timelines varied with each district. Although over half of the members of the board of education had indicated that they have informal input into the budget development process on a continual, year-round basis, they also identified more-specific timelines for their formal participation in the process. For example, in District A the board of education had only one meeting where members specifically reviewed the proposed budget prior to the actual vote for preliminary adoption of the budget. In contrast, members of the board of education in District D held seven meetings directly pertaining to budget development.

Areas of the district budget directly determined as a result of decisions made by the board of education centered primarily on educational programs or offerings that were not mandated by the state or the federal government and areas that were of special interest to the community. Examples of these budget items found in the research were projects concerning buildings and facilities, athletics, the band, and special curricula, such as the family life curriculum in District D and the advanced levels of language classes offered in Districts C and D.

Areas of the district budget not directly determined as a result of decisions of the board of education represented the largest portion of the total district budget in each of the four school districts examined. Estimates found in the research that indicated the portion of the district budget that was not directly controlled by the board of education ranged from 60 to 95 percent. The largest portion of these uncontrollable expenditures was associated with professional employees' salaries and benefits. In District A the board of education did participate in contract negotiations with the professional staff. However, the research indicated that the board had experienced only a limited amount of control over salaries through that process, primarily related to the use of multiyear contracts, which were implemented on an annual basis. As one superintendent had stated, "The board has no control over eighty percent of the budget once the contract decision is made." New members of the board of education experienced a total lack of control over this area of the budget because they had not even been members of the board during the time that contracts were negotiated.

The board of education was found to participate to varying degrees in different areas of the district budget. In each of the four school districts studied, the boards participated to a greater extent in the areas of the budget where they demonstrated personal experience and familiarity. For example, decisions affecting the educational programs, such as textbook selection and purchase, were made as a direct result of the input received from professional educators, and decisions concerning buildings and facilities were often made as a direct result of input from specific members of the board of education.

2. Which Theoretical Model or Combination of Models Best Describes the Role of the Board of Education in the Process of Resource Allocation for Public Schools?

The data describing the role of the decision-making models are summarized and presented in Tables 4.1 and 4.2. Table 4.1 summarizes findings from all four school districts that supported the existence of the theoretical decision-making models. Concepts pertaining to each of the four decision-making models are listed in order of the frequency of their occurrence in the four school districts examined. The frequency of occurrence refers to the number of school districts in which a specific concept was found. A frequency of "4" indicates that the concept was found in each of the school districts that had participated in the study. This frequency is listed to the right of each concept listed in the table.

Table 4.2 represents a similar method to summarize findings from all four school districts that argued against the existence of the theoretical

Table 4.1.
Concepts Supportive of Decision-Making Models.

RATIONAL MODEL		BUREAUCRACTIC MODEL		POLITICAL—POWER OR CONTROL MODEL		POLITICAL—PUBLIC CHOICE MODEL	
goals	4	use of SOPs	4	special interests	4	wants and needs of staff	3
zero-based budgeting	2	previous decisions	3	avoidance of dissatisfaction	4	fair and equitable to staff	3
outputs	2	fixed costs	2	rubber stamp	3	wants and needs of public	1
performance budgeting	1	comparison of budgets	2	central role of school	2	reward and motivate staff	1
production-function	1	status quo to minimize conflict	2	trustee vs. representative	1	participative management	1
priorities	1	chain of command	2			conflict avoidance	1
board control-curriculum	1	long-range financial planning	1				
program budgeting	1	span of control	1				
willingness to spend money	1	policies and procedures	1				
efficiency	1	incremental budgeting	1				

decision-making models. Again, the frequency of occurrence of each concept is listed to the right of each concept.

As can be seen when reviewing Table 4.1, the goals of education were present in the budgetary decision-making process within each of the four school districts studied. However, those goals were often stated in terms of "providing for the needs of students." As indicated by Table 4.2, specific student needs were left undefined in each district. Budget-

Table 4.2.
Concepts Arguing Against the Existence
of Decision-Making Models.

RATIONAL MODEL		BUREAUCRACTIC MODEL		POLITICAL—POWER OR CONTROL MODEL		POLITICAL—PUBLIC CHOICE MODEL	
undefined student "needs"	4	no formal budget comparison	4	absence of rubber stamp	4	unequitable to staff	2
noneducational goals	2	budget changes were dependent	3	cmmunity apathy	2	limited control	2
educational process unclear	2	no long-range financial planning	3	lack of community involvement	2	lack of control	1
lack of control over budget	2	LRFPC not functional	1			limited concern for staff	1
unclear measure of outputs	1	elimination of allotment system	1				
reverse production-function	1						
no link of inputs and outputs	1						
no measure of outputs	1						
absence of zero-based budget	1						
limited control over inputs	1						
lack of efficiency	1						

ary planning that followed a true rational model of decision-making was described as being systematic and procedural and was directed toward increasing student achievement. The rational model was based on the assumptions of control over inputs, a measure of outputs, and an understanding of the process of education. Data presented indicated a desire on the part of the board to make decisions in a rational manner, but at the same time clearly indicated their inability to function in this manner. The board of education simply did not know how to directly link the district budget with student achievement in spite of their concern for providing for student needs. A general comparison of data from all four school districts indicated that of the four theoretical perspectives examined, the rational model of decision making was the only model that was found to have had more concepts occurring, which argued against its own existence.

In each of the four school districts, resources were often allocated on the basis of utilization of standard operating procedures, as indicated in Table 4.1. These procedures, based on previous decisions, were often implemented in order to avoid conflict and to simplify the decision-making process. However, as indicated in Table 4.2, methods used to make budgetary decisions were dependent on individual budget categories and were not made based on a formal comparison with or link to the previous year's budget. Comparison of budgets by members of the board were on an informal and individual basis. As with the rational model of decision making, members of the board expressed a desire and a belief that they should function in a bureaucratic manner when making budgetary decisions, but they were often unable to function in that manner.

In each of the four school districts examined, the board of education was keenly aware of the special interests of the larger school community and expressed a concern for satisfying those interests. In addition, each board exhibited behaviors that expressed its desire to avoid community dissatisfaction. Although often indicating a desire to function in a more rational or bureaucratic manner, the boards in each of the four school districts recognized their responsibility to protect the public interests in the local system of education.

Concern for the self-interests of school employees also played a somewhat limited role in the board's budgetary decision-making process. This concern for employees was observed to varying degrees in the different districts involved in the research. For example, in Districts C and D there was even a lack of reference to the needs, values, or goals of individuals in the school organization when district budgetary decisions were made. District A exhibited a stronger concern for employee self-interests, but to a large extent the board was unable to act on that concern because of the legal constraints within which they were forced to function.

The source and the amount of revenues available for education had a direct impact on the resource allocation decisions of the board of education. Federal funds were found to have only a limited impact on the board's resource allocation decisions because those funds were often in the form of categorical funding that limited the flexibility of their use at the local school district level.

In terms of total resources available to school districts, the flexibility of the board to determine the level of local funding available was vital to the budgetary decision-making process. For example, District D had a strictly limited total amount of funding available for the 1988–1989 school year because of a number of factors that were unique to that district: the county's reassessment of property values, which placed a legally determined limit of 10 percent on property tax increases; unsettled lawsuit in which the district was involved; and a much smaller than expected increase in state subsidies. These combined factors placed a severe limitation on the spending capacity of the school district. The frustration experienced by the board of education in trying to make budgetary decisions when members were faced with such constraints was directly observed in the number of budgetary meetings conducted by the board of education in District D. Whereas another district conducted only one official budgetary planning session prior to the preliminary adoption of the budget, District D conducted seven sessions for that particular purpose. Another example of this frustration was observed in the final vote to adopt the budget. In District D the final vote to adopt the budget formally was five "yes" and four "no" votes. In contrast, the strongest opposition to the adoption of the final budget in other districts was witnessed in a final vote of seven "yes" and two "no" votes. This frustration was also directly voiced by one member of the board of education in District D when at the meeting that immediately followed the final adoption of the budget, this member submitted a formal letter of resignation to the board of education. In the letter, he explained that his resignation was directly related to his opposition to the budget that had just been adopted, a budget with an expenditure increase larger than the revenue increase for the upcoming school year.

RESOURCE ALLOCATION MODEL

As a result of the findings of the research, a model was developed. This model depicts the board of education as utilizing a combination of all four decision-making models in resource allocation decisions. The research clearly indicated that an interaction of all four models was present in the school districts that were examined. The model is presented in Figure 4.1.

At the center of this model is the rational model of decision making. As was described, a desire to make decisions in a rational manner and a concern for student needs were present in each of the four school districts studied. The size and the location of the rational model in Figure 4.1 indicates that this model plays a minor role in the overall process of budget development, but it still represents the ultimate or central concern of the board of education.

The bureaucratic model is also shown to be a feature in the overall process of resource allocation. This model, depicted as slightly larger, is located just above the rational model in the figure. The larger size of the bureaucratic model indicated its more frequent application to various areas of the process of budget development. The interaction between the bureaucratic model and the rational model represented instances in the budget development process when the board of education made resource allocation decisions by using bureaucratic methods to achieve rational goals. An example of this use of bureaucratic methods is the use of a purchasing cycle for textbook replacement. The interaction of the bureaucratic model and the public choice model indicates a similar situation where bureaucratic methods were utilized to deal with employees in a fair and equitable manner to avoid conflict at this level.

The public choice model is depicted as having a minor interaction with the rational model. This interaction of these two models appeared in the research but only to a limited extent. In addition, the motives for this interaction were not clearly defined in the research. The location of public choice at the bottom of the model indicates that this model played a role that was secondary to that of the other three models examined.

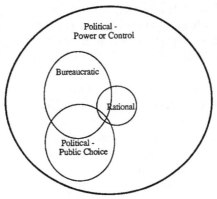

Figure 4.1. Resource Allocation Model.

The power or control model is presented as the dominant model of decision making used by the board of education in making resource allocation decisions. In all areas of budget development, the power or control model appeared to be a factor interacting with the other models of decision making. The circular representation of the resource allocation model suggests that the process is cyclical and never ending, in addition to interacting constantly with the component parts of the overall process.

The Resource Allocation Model contains elements that appeared to be somewhat similar to the Garbage Can Model of organizational choice as described by Cohen, March, and Olsen (1986, pp. 311–314). The Garbage Can Model described the decision-making process in organizations that were characterized as organized anarchies. These organizations were defined as having unclear and/or unspecified goals, unclear technology, and fluid participation. Educational organizations were identified as one type of organization that demonstrated these particular features (Cohen, March, & Olsen, pp. 311–312).

The Garbage Can Model described the process of decisionmaking as one that was resultant from the complicated interaction of problems, participants, solutions, and the opportunity for choice (Cohen, March, & Olsen, pp. 313–314). Problems were defined as the concerns of individuals from inside as well as from outside the organization. Participants were defined as individuals interacting with the problems of the organization on a somewhat temporary or fluid basis. Solutions referred to actual decisions that were made by the organization's participants. The opportunity for choice referred to the specific times or occasions when an organization was expected to make decisions (Cohen, March, & Olsen, pp. 313–314).

Rather than describe the decision-making process of educational organizations as a rational and/or systematic process, both the Resource Allocation Model and the Garbage Can Model were based on the complicated interaction of organizational components. This complicated interaction offers a possible explanation for the apparent contradictions, chaos, and imprecision found in the data collected as a result of this research.

Examples of the interaction described in the resource allocation model were presented throughout the study. Specific statements follow to support the assumptions upon which the model was developed.

The examination of District A suggests that no one model of decision making was used exclusively by the board of education to make resource allocation decisions for the district. This conclusion was most appropriately described by a veteran member of the board when he said, "Looking at the school as a business, I have to look at three things. Personally, you have to think about the education of the kids, you have to think about the taxpayers who are directly or indirectly footing the bill, and you have to think about all of your employees. And I don't know which one of those is most important. I think they are all equally important. If you rukey-duke one of them, boy, does it drastically affect the rest. If you are not fair with your employees, they know about it right away. That is the cruelest thing you can do—not be fair with your employees. By the same token you need to be fair and responsible to the taxpayers and the kids."

In District B a similar conclusion was described by a member of the board of education during his interview when he said, "We [the board] have to listen to what the teachers have to say and to what the public has to say. And we have to sit in the middle and try to make a decision that benefits all sides, but mainly the student. You have to ask, 'How is it going to benefit the students?'" He continued, "You have to ask what the public wants and what are your needs [educationally]." Another member of the board of education showed agreement with this statement when he said, "Everyone is always worried about a tax increase. How many mills will this cost? How many mills will that cost? And we try to arrive at a happy medium, without knocking out any programs that are worthwhile and still adding programs that are worthwhile and doing things that are worthwhile. The board is concerned about tax increases, but increases are program by program."

Another example of this interaction was also described by one member of the board of education from District C. During his interview he said, "It is going to cost us so much to educate the students. I have to be aware of that cost versus the people that are going to pay for that, and I have to judge it accordingly. The goals of education in the policy manual are met in the budget process. Overall, we consider the students, the staff, and the facilities in the budget process."

A balanced approach was described in District D, when once again this same interaction of decision-making models was expressed. The process was described as being one that reflected the idea that the board of education was forced to act as a balancing agent in making resource allocation decisions. This balance of models was described by various individuals who had been interviewed for the research. For example, the business manager said, "They [the board] are in a precarious position. They have to balance two sides. They have to look at education and at what is needed for the district, and they have to look at the taxpayer. They get the influence from both sides." She also explained that the board itself represents a balance of interests when she described the board as being divided into three groups, each group having a different area of expertise. The three groups that she identified were those members who had a strong educational orientation, those who had a strong financial orientation, and those who had a strong maintenance orientation. She said, "All of these factions have to interact. It's a give-and-take. All three have to compromise." When asked whether community groups affect the budgetary decisions of the board, she again referred to the different factions of the board. She said, "It depends. With certain board members it will have more of an impact than with others. If it is a board member that's looking at the fiscal portion of the budget, he will ask, 'Is it economically sound to have a teacher for three children?' They will definitely look at that situation and say, 'No, it's not.' If you are looking at those board members with an educational orientation, they will say, 'These children plan to go on to further their education, and they will need these courses.' So it ends up to be a discussion, a give-and-take that the board has to go through."

A member of the board said, "The allocation of total resources for education is the main duty of the board. It's the board's responsibility to keep pressure on the system to run efficiently, especially when we are faced with limited resources. We need to keep the purse strings tight enough to encourage the professional staff to be efficient. We try to make the superintendent and the business manager justify their numbers. Our goal is to keep staff morale up and the cost to the community down. It's a factor of good management." He continued, "The board is a balancing force. If we keep our thumb on expenses too strongly, we discourage the educational process. We discourage our professional staff. Our staff needs a good atmosphere and a good feeling. If not, some of the good teachers will leave, and we already employ too many mediocre teachers." He also explained another type of balance when he said, "We all want the budget to decrease, but the special interests want it to increase. The board and the superintendent are responsible for keeping it in balance."

A member of the community summarized the same concept of balance when he said, "The board is in a tough position. It's not easy for a lay member of the community to take a budget and adopt it. After all, it was put together by a full-time professional educator, and then the board has to try to trim it. So they look at things like stoves for the home economics room. They don't want to pare education. It's very difficult. I think the board does the best job that they can."

The data presented clearly support the idea described that not one, but instead a combination of decision-making models, was utilized by the boards of education in the four school districts studied. The extent to which each model was used varied with the different situations encountered in the districts. However, board members were aware of the necessity to balance the sometimes competing concerns for students, staff, and taxpayers. Overemphasis on one to the detriment of the others would upset the equilibrium among educational goals, maintenance of organizational morale and effort, and community support sought by board members.

REFERENCES

Allison, G. T. (1971). *Essence of decisions*. Boston: Little, Brown and Company.

Boyd, W. L. (1982, Summer). The political economy of public schools. *Educational Administration Quarterly, 18*, 111–130.

Cibulka, J. G. (1987, February). Theories of education budgeting: Lessons from the management of decline. *Educational Administration Quarterly, 23*(l), 7–40.

Cohen, M. D., March, J. G., & Olsen, J. P. (1986). A garbage can model of organizational choice. In J. G. March & R. Weissinger-Baylon (Eds.), *Ambiguity and Command* (pp. 311–336). Boston: Pitman Publishing.

Garms, W. I., Guthrie, J. W., & Pierce, L. C. (1978). *School Finance: The Economics and Politics of Public Education*. Englewood Cliffs, N.J.: Prentice Hall.

Hartman, W. T. (1988). *School District Budgeting*. Englewood Cliffs, N.J.: Prentice Hall.

Jones, T. H. (1985). *Introduction to School Finance Techniques and Social Policy*. New York: Macmillan Publishing Company.

Kerr, N. D. (1964, Fall). The school board as an agency of legitimation. In A. Rosenthal (Ed.). (1969). *Governing Education: A Reader on Politics, Power, and Public School Policy* (pp. 137–172). New York: Anchor Books Doubleday & Company.

Lutz, F. W. (1980, August). Local school board decision-making: A political anthropological analysis. *Education and Urban Society, 12*(4), 452–465.

McGivney, J. H., & Moynihan, W. (1972, December). School and community. *Teacher's College Record, 74*(2), 209–224.

Meyer, M. W. (Ed.). (1971). *Structures, Symbols, and Systems: Readings on Organizational Behavior*. Boston: Little, Brown, and Company.

Owens, R. G. (1981). *Organizational Behavior in Education*, 2nd ed. Englewood Cliffs, N.J.: Prentice Hall.

Peterson, P. E. (1976). *School Politics Chicago Style*. Chicago: The University of Chicago Press.

Stokey, E., & Zeckhauser, R. (1978). *A Primer for Policy Analysis*. New York: W. W. Norton and Company.

Vidich, A. J., & Bensman, J. The clash of class interests in school politics. In A. Rosenthal. (Ed.). (1969). *Governing Education: A Reader on Politics, Power, and Public School Policy* (pp. 225–252). New York: Anchor Books Doubleday and Company.

Wildavsky, A. (1975). *Budgeting: A Comparative Theory of Budgetary Processes*. Boston: Little, Brown and Company.

Zeigler, H. L., Jennings, M. K., & Peak, G. W. (1974). *Governing American Schools: Political Interaction in Local School Districts*. North Scituate, Mass.: Duxbury Press.

5

Reconciling Equity and Excellence

Resource Allocation in School Districts

Peter Coleman, Stephen Easton, and
Linda LaRocque

He is well paid that is well satisfied . . . .
Shakespeare, *The Merchant of Venice*, IV.i.415.

RESOURCE ALLOCATION PRACTICES IN SCHOOL DISTRICTS

At present, what little information we have about resource allocation practices in school districts suggests that they are random with respect to values such as equity and excellence (Goertz, 1989; Kirst, 1988). A careful examination of practice in a group of districts in British Columbia, Canada, suggests that this portrait is overgeneralized. There are important differences in allocation policies among districts, which are related both to differences in norms or beliefs and to differences in district quality.

With respect to resource allocation in public school education generally, equity and excellence are usually treated as competing policy goals, poles apart. Funding schemes seek an equatorial band, which yields some of each (Colvin, 1989). We argue below that equity and excellence are not polar opposites but rather are like parallels of latitude, which can never meet. Consequently districts require allocation policies that promote two separate policy purposes, to be judged by two sets of criteria.

We address in particular the district level of operation; unless otherwise noted, the discussion relates to that level. We write as Canadians who consider the similarities between educational issues in Canada and the United States far more important than the differences; we note instances in which the differences seem significant.

Our interest in the themes developed in this chapter arose from the findings of a study of ten British Columbia districts conducted by two of the authors (P. Coleman & LaRocque, 1990), and later work by Peter Coleman and colleagues on family contributions (P. Coleman, Collinge, & Tabin, 1995).

Coleman and LaRocque examined district administrative norms and practices with regard to academic emphases, school accountability, management of change, eliciting professional commitment, parental involvement, and parental integration in instruction. Resource allocation was not a major focus of the study, yet the respondents, district and school administrators, discussed resource allocation issues throughout the interviews. More- and less-successful districts[1] clearly differed in their approaches to resource allocation with respect to (a) the conceptualization of resources, (b) the decision-making process, and (c) the norms underlying resource allocation decisions.

Conceptualization of Resources

Our respondents referred to a resource as that which could be distributed or made available in some way to support the implementation of district goals, policies, and programs. They divided resources into two broad categories: fiscal and nonfiscal. We have labeled the latter "productive resources."

In the less successful districts, the availability of fiscal resources such as funding for teacher release time, for materials, and for travel to attend workshops was seen as the major determinant of the success of change initiatives. Thus in one district, administrators and teachers felt that it was necessary to examine the scope and sequence of core programs across grades and schools, but the committees established for this purpose stopped operating well before completion of their task because funds for release time were depleted. In the less successful districts educators believed that little could be attempted or accomplished without fiscal resources.

Although fiscal resources were also of concern in the more successful districts, much more attention was given to productive resources such as time, personnel, and information. District administrators advocated certain practices and deliberately made time for them: Principals' meetings were occasions for examining performance data and planning improvements; school visits were opportunities for monitoring school performance and improvement efforts, and for providing principals with guidance and support in these. Principals also patterned their utilization of time on this model. A number of schools in the more successful districts arranged their daily schedules to give the staffs one afternoon every second week for collaborative planning of change. Furthermore, implementation of new programs and practices was seen as a matter of learning, and thus as a process that required time. Months, even years, of lead time was allocated in order to give principals and teachers a chance to get used to the new program or practice, to develop appropriate knowledge and skills, and to gain an understanding of the purpose of the innovation and the improvements it represented for students and programs.

Another form of productive resource allocation was personnel assignment. Important initiatives were always made the responsibility of a particular district administrator. Principal appointments were based on such factors as willingness and ability to deal with change, the need to introduce new ways of thinking into the district, the needs of particular schools, the strengths and weaknesses of individuals, and the best principal-school match. District administrative positions were created or redefined so as to (a) emphasize instructional concerns; (b) ensure that district administrators left their offices to work with principals and teachers in their own environment, the school, as much as possible; and (c) facilitate the administrative team approach in the district.

A third kind of productive resource was information. District administrators ensured that a wide variety of school-specific performance data (achievement test results, client survey results, school assessments, goal reviews, program evaluations) were available to schools, and they encouraged the collaborative analysis of these data, both amongst school staffs and between district and school administrators, for the purposes of planning improvements. Information was also provided through ongoing (as opposed to one-shot) in-service programs, which were designed to support both these collaborative efforts and the initiatives resulting from them. The more-successful districts supported these programs over time, and encouraged and facilitated staff development programs at the school level.

Not once in the more successful districts was the success or failure of a district initiative directly attributed by a respondent to fiscal resources; but program and instructional improvements were frequently attributed to the allocation of the productive resources described earlier. This is not to deny the role, often symbolic, played by fiscal resources; fiscal allocations signaled the perceived importance of an activity, and hence usually preceded and stimulated the allocation of quite disproportionate levels of productive resources such as teacher time and attention.

What was particularly interesting about the allocation and use of such productive resources was that this resulted in shared working knowledge (Kennedy, 1984), an important feature of succcessful districts. Educators, within and across district and school levels, were encouraged to learn from one another and to acknowledge that they were mutually supportive. For example, discussions of performance data between district administrators and principals and between principals and their staffs contributed to their shared working knowledge about school performance and about monitoring in general. They had to learn together what constituted a meaningful goal, how many goals a staff could pursue actively during a year, how goals were derived from performance data, and how the degree of goal attainment could be determined. Collaborative analysis of achievement data resulted in an increased understanding of existing district and school achievement in various subject areas, of where additional effort was needed, and of the instructional uses of monitoring. The ongoing refinement of the school assessment process required district administrators, principals, and teachers to come to a progressive series of agreements on what aspects of school life should be examined, what kinds of information about these various aspects of school life should be collected, how they should be collected, and how and by whom they should be interpreted. Shared working knowledge provides an excellent illustration of the contribution of productive resources: vital to school improvement, yet almost impossible to enter into a production function. The allocation and use of productive resources increased shared working knowledge; these activities provided educators with *opportunities to learn*. This point will be taken up again later.

Resource Allocation and Decision Making

The more-successful districts were becoming increasingly decentralized; the less-successful, increasingly centralized. Interestingly, decentralization was associated *simultaneously* with the development of common purposes and of school autonomy. Because purposes were shared, resources could readily be allocated so as to support both district and school initiatives. Centralization, unsurprisingly, was accompanied by an increasing sense of powerlessness on the part of principals; it was not accompanied by an increased sense of district purpose. Consequently there was no agreed basis other than simple numerical equality on which to make resource allocation decisions.

Decentralization was associated with increasing principal involvement in district decision making. In the more successful districts principals were actively involved in all phases of the decision-making process: identifying problems, establishing priorities, proposing courses of action, and evaluating outcomes.

Higher principal involvement in district decision making was accompanied by increased school autonomy. Schools were encouraged to adapt, extend, and supplement district initiatives. For example, schools expanded district testing programs by increasing the number of times per year that the students were tested, by testing additional grade levels, or by using additional tests. District-required school assessment was modified by school staffs, who played a large role in designing the goal review and school assessment processes for their particular schools. They developed data-gathering instruments, collected and interpreted the data, and planned improvements. District administrators ensured that some reliable and comparable data were collected and utilized; but by encouraging school-level adaptation, they also ensured that the collection of data was meaningful to school staffs.

These linkages between principal involvement in decision making, a shared sense of direction, and school autonomy within a district framework of goals or priorities recurred throughout the interview data of principals in those districts moving towards decentralization. With common purpose, school autonomy to allow responsiveness to local needs and circumstances was possible without a return to what had existed before in these districts, an anarchy of largely independent fiefdoms paralleling the typical secondary school (Herriott & Firestone, 1984).

Less-successful districts tried to establish district directions through formal policy-making procedures that involved seeking feedback from those affected by the policy during the development stage. District administrators frequently cited problems with this approach; for example, that feedback took the form of negative reactions rather than problem solving or consensus building. Principals also were dissatisfied with this approach to decision making; they felt like a rather weak lobby group vying with others, especially the teachers' associations (the teacher union locals in British Columbia), for the ear of the board. In one district central office, administrators viewed the district's meta-policy on policy-making as a means of opening up the policy process, but the principals saw it as a means of centralizing decision-making power. They did not consider providing feedback on a draft of a policy as meaningful participation in decision making. It is revealing that the phrase "ran it by" was used by many of the respondents in these districts—"The Superintendent ran it by us at the Administrators' meeting"; "I ran it by my staff." This denotes superficiality of treatment. There was neither intensive discussion of issues nor any sense of commitment to district initiatives.

To summarize, the decentralization approach to principal involvement was based on concern for common goals, collaborative problem-solving, and the development of shared working knowledge. Both district- and school-level administrators in the more successful districts believed that shared leadership strengthened rather than weakened everyone's influence: They would have found Tannenbaum's (1962) formulation, "the total amount of control exercised in a group or organization can increase, and the various participants can acquire a share of this augmented power" (p. 247), acceptable. Efforts to establish a common purpose in the less successful districts centered on the policy process, in which the principals were only one of many groups whose feedback was sought. Principals became increasingly resistant; district initiatives became increasingly ineffective. In sum, both district- and school-level administrators experienced an increasing sense of powerlessness, although each thought the power was held elsewhere: "Conversely, the total amount of control can decrease, and all may share the loss" (Tannenbaum, 1962, p. 247).

In the more successful districts, resource decision-making allowed meaningful involvement of principals at district level and teachers at school level in decisions important to them. The professionals could influence the organization and felt efficacious. They possessed the *capacity to be heard*. This point will be revisited.

Resource Allocation Norms

The districts in our study adopted two different approaches to resource allocation. The first was driven by a norm of equality; the second, by a norm of excellence.

Resource allocation in the less successful districts, driven by a norm of equality, ensured that each school, and each professional, received an equal share of whatever was being distributed, whether it was personnel, supply budgets, or opportunities for professional development. The district administrators who made such decisions were guided largely by collective agreements, policy statements, and the like. The approach fostered a competitive atmosphere in which "winning" meant getting more than others. For example, in one district principals spent time and effort acquiring computers for their school and boasted about the number thay had accumulated. There was little concern about how or even whether the computers were used.

Resource allocation in the more successful districts was driven by the excellence norm. This was true even of such resources as district administrator time. District administrators spent most of their time on matters related to programs and instruction, and much of this work was done in schools rather than in the central office. The question guiding resource allocation decisions was "How and where will this do the most good with respect to student learning?" As we have seen, such decisions were made by district and school administrators and staffs in collaboration. Increasingly schools were being given more control over resources, most notably with respect to curriculum/instructional improvement projects and professional development. One district was also experimenting with a formal school-based budgeting system.

The fundamental difference between these two approaches was demonstrated by the way each handled professional development. In the equality approach, established procedures ensured that all professionals had equal access to travel funds; district professional development days offered a wide variety of sessions from which teachers could select those they wished to attend. These districts offered few in-service opportunities within the district and instead relied heavily on funding teachers to attend out-of-district conferences and workshops. This approach to district professional development was all consistent with the belief that instructional change was both the prerogative and the responsibility of the individual classroom teacher.

In the excellence approach, the districts made a long-term commitment to providing in-service programs in a broad area related to district priorities, and facilitated school-based staff development activities in this area. There was a clear and definite focus to district in-service programs, and an emphasis on both collaboration and shared working knowledge. School staff development projects received higher funding priority than did individual professional development activities; travel to attend out-of-district workshops was more likely to be funded if a direct connection to district and school priorities could be demonstrated. All this was consistent with a belief in shared responsibility for instructional and program improvement.

The two approaches were also associated with different norms with respect to fiscal resources. Principals in the "excellence" districts felt constrained to stay within their school budgets and to spend money wisely, in support of district and school priorities. These norms were not shared by counterparts in the "equality" districts.

To summarize, the equality approach to resource allocation was associated with a belief in individual responsibility for improvement, an emphasis on the potency of fiscal resources (with little concern for cost control), and a move towards centralization of decision making. In contrast, the excellence approach was associated with a belief in shared responsibility for improvement, an emphasis on the potency of productive resources, an acceptance of the need to control costs, and a move towards decentralization of decisions to school level. Shared working knowledge ("opportunity to learn") and meaningful collaboration ("capacity to be heard") were central to this approach. That is, the approach emphasized productive resources, not fiscal resources.

EQUITY AND EXCELLENCE

The analysis of the differing resource allocation systems of ten British Columbia school districts raises a number of issues concerning the distinction between fiscal and productive resources and the relationship of each to equity and excellence goals. We focus upon the emerging notion of productive resources in what follows.

Fiscal Resources and Equity

The use of fiscal resources (here simply that which money can buy—higher salaries for teachers, more teachers to reduce class size or PTR, more support services, longer school days and years, and so on) has been central to the pursuit of the policy goal of equity. This approach to resource allocation became popular after the Coleman Report (1966), despite the fact that J. S. Coleman et. al (1966) had shown that different service levels were not significant predictors of student achievement. Although accepting that "the relation between cost and quality" was unclear, Coons, Clune, and Sugarman (1970), in an influential book, argued that generous funding from the state level for poor districts was necessary, "If money is inadequate to improve education, the residents of poor districts should have at least an equal opportunity to be disappointed by its failures" (p. 30). This proved to be an expensive error, but a major part of the policy agenda of states (Guthrie, Garms, & Pierce, 1988, p. 130), and of Canadian provinces (Coleman & LaRocque, 1984) rested firmly on this proposition.

Together with this continued emphasis on funding, equity advocates shifted from a policy goal of *equality* of educational opportunity measured by inputs, to a policy goal of *equity* of opportunity through compensatory funding and programs, intended to equalize the outputs of the system. As Mosteller and Moynihan (1972) put it, "Henceforth the measurement of quality in education is output" (p. 28). This "vertical equity" (Guthrie, Garms, & Pierce, 1988, p. 302) case is usually argued at the student level. However, if some school districts have unusually high and uncontrollable costs due to such features as geography, student dispersion, or student family status, scholars have argued that they should be proportionately compensated for these by central funding allocations (Guthrie, Garms, & Pierce, 1988, p. 158; P. Coleman, 1987a).

Significant changes in state and provincial funding of districts have been driven by such equity concerns. But student achievement levels remain strongly associated with family background variables (Walberg & Shanahan, 1983). If equity is defined as achievement levels disassociated from family background, race, or ethnicity, there remain significant inequities in the United States (Guthrie, Garms, & Pierce, 1988) and in Canada (Coleman & LaRocque, 1984; Lawton, 1987a). However, when family contributions, labeled "social capital" by James Coleman (1987), are treated as alterable variables, and attention is fixed not on *who parents are* (status measures) but on *what they do*, the "curriculum of the home" (Walberg, 1984), it becomes clear that family contributions are themselves a productive resource (Monk, 1992, p. 311) and are part of the solution to inequity. We will return to this issue.

Some scholars have argued that inequities continue as a consequence of inadequate local implementation of federal mandates (Hargrove et al., 1981). However, the confusion between equality and equity (P. Coleman, 1987a) is also important: School districts continue to allocate resources internally on the basis of equality (Kirst, 1988, p. 317), without adequate measures of need, resulting in inequity. Even equality of allocation, although intended, is rare in practice: Goertz's (1989) detailed case study of seventeen U.S. districts shows that Chapter 1 staff were allocated to schools randomly with respect to achievement levels in fifteen of the districts; in the others there were *fewer* teachers in schools with achievement deficits.

Others have argued that policies intended to address the equity goal must be selective with respect to both types of intervention (Barnett & Escobar, 1987), and types of clients, as class and circumstance come to play a larger role, and ethnicity and race a smaller role, in defining the disadvantaged in the United States (Wilson, 1987).

The difficulties described in these empirical studies are instances of a general problem of targetting. The issue of classroom time illustrates this, for both the equity and excellence goals. Levin (1984) argues that a variety of approaches to more-efficient time utilization should be tested, and explicitly cautions policymakers that "each of these policies must be a sensitive and selective one rather than a broad brush approach to reform" (p. 162). Kirst (1988, p. 382) has advanced a very similar line of argument.

Yet broad-brush approaches, based on equality of allocation, continue to be adopted. These are not selective with respect to either purpose, type of intervention, or client need. The failure of such policies to redress inequities in achievement derive, we believe, from the assumption that costs and quality are tightly coupled, making careful targetting unnecessary. This is an expensive error (Odden, 1990).

Fiscal Resources and Excellence

Fiscal resources have been widely used in the United States to spur educational reform with respect to excellence (Odden, 1985; 1990). Educational expenditures in the United States rose by 21 percent after inflation between 1983 and 1988 (Odden & Marsh, 1987). Much of this money has gone to increasing teacher salaries (Sedlak et al., 1986, p. 131). In Canada, there is less conviction about the utility of additional expenditures (Easton, 1988), and education spending adjusted for inflation has been flat during roughly the same period (Lawton, 1987a). However, teacher salaries were about 15 percent higher in Canada (Lawton, 1987b) before the U.S. increases, which have roughly equalized average salaries between the two countries.

Yet the most-careful longitudinal analyses have been unable to demonstrate a significant relationship between overall spending and outcomes for individual students or for classes or schools (Rossmiller, 1986). Walberg and Fowler (1987) have shown that for at least one U.S. state, New Jersey, there is simply no relationship between district spending per student and the achievement of students. A meta-analysis of district-level studies has suggested that the cost-quality relationship has changed in the last two decades from positive to neutral (Childs & Shakeshaft, 1986). In British Columbia, there is a continuing significant *negative* relationship between spending and achievement in districts in the province (Coleman, Walsh, & LaRocque, 1988).

Many relatively poor districts have now had the opportunity to be disappointed by the failure of money to solve their problems of quality. Hanushek's view that "throwing money at schools" (1981; 1986; 1989) would not help to improve them seems now to be broadly accepted (Colvin, 1989; Odden, 1990). (Note that in low-spending U.S. states in the 1980s there was still evidence of resource inadequacy at the school level [Rosenholtz, 1989; McLaughlin & Yee, 1988], as there was in some British studies [Mortimore et al., 1988]).

Using allocation systems as incentives to increase educational productivity is currently popular. Such schemes tend to yield state-sponsored inequities (Colvin, 1989) such as merit pay. But there is little evidence that merit pay schemes in school districts work (Mitchell, Ortiz, & Mitchell, 1983; Johnson, 1990). Schemes either have rapidly been abandoned or have quickly lost any connection with classroom performance (Cohen & Murnane, 1985; Murnane & Cohen, 1986). This failure is rooted in a misconception about what motivates teachers (Mitchell, Ortiz, & Mitchell, 1983; Johnson, 1990) and particularly about the relative importance of fiscal and productive resources as levers to changing teacher behavior.

In sum, then, fiscal resources in the form of compensatory programs have largely failed to promote either equity or excellence. The failures seem to result from a lack of careful specification of targets, arising in part from the failure of production functions to yield good guidance (Monk, 1992) and from misunderstandings regarding teacher incentives or indeed the whole issue of productive resources, considered next. The overwhelming evidence (Hanushek, 1989) that in the past costs and quality have been unrelated suggests the need for a fundamental reconsideration of how various kinds of resources can be used in the promotion of educational quality.

Productive Resources and Excellence

This reconsideration should begin with a broader conception of resources (Kirst, 1988; Rossmiller, 1987; Monk, 1992), and analyses of what characteristics of districts, schools, and classrooms in fact promote equity and excellence.

The second wave of reform in the United States in the 1980s focused on teacher issues: Repopulating, retraining, and restructuring the teaching profession constitute the central themes (Mitchell, Ortiz, & Mitchell, 1983, p. 4). But proposals and programs for restructuring are often based on false conceptions of teacher careers (Johnson, 1990; McLaughlin & Yee, 1988) and the nature of incentives for teachers (Mitchell, Ortiz, & Mitchell, 1983; Sedlak et al., 1986, p. 135). As Lortie (1975) pointed out and others have confirmed (Rosenholtz, 1989), major rewards of teachers are largely controlled by students (Metz, 1993; Mitchell, Ortiz, & Mitchell, 1983). Classroom bargains are so pervasive in American high schools (Sedlak et al., 1986; Sizer, 1984) largely because of this mutual benefit feature of schooling.

Teacher variables are important "productive resources" that can help us to attain both the equity and excellence policy goals. The relationship between incentives for teachers, productive resources, and the excellence goal can be summarized thus:

1. Both extrinsic and intrinsic rewards are important to teachers, although variations in the former are not motivating (Stern, 1986). Intrinsic rewards become incentives in the workplace (Mitchell, Ortiz, & Mitchell, 1983, p. 188); incentives are culturally determined (p. 194) and operate effectively for teachers at individual, school, and district levels (p. 193).
2. Commitment and efficacy are alterable variables, affected particularly by workplace incentives such as autonomy, learning oppor-

tunities, and level of capacity to affect change (Rosenholtz, 1989; McLaughlin & Yee, 1988; Fuller et al., 1982), and by feedback of various kinds, particularly from students (Lortie, 1975; Rosenholtz, 1989; Smylie, 1988) and parents (Hoover-Dempsey, Bassler, & Brissie, 1987). Both commitment and efficacy have consequences for teacher performance (Rosenholtz, 1989; Ashton & Webb, 1986) and career satisfaction (McLaughlin & Yee, 1988).

3. Commitment and efficacy increments affect teacher performance and in turn student outcomes, themselves the most significant intrinsic rewards for teachers (Lortie, 1975; Rosenholtz, 1989). Thus the possibility of a positive spiral exists.

Productive resources of such kinds are critical to the attainment of excellence.

Furthermore, teacher practices are the key to enlisting the family as a productive resource. Parental contributions to student learning are amongst the most important of "proximal variables" (Wang, Haertel, & Walberg, 1993). Recent work in Canada suggests that these contributions are maximized when teachers engage in collaborative practices with students and parents (P. Coleman, Collinge, & Tabin, 1995; in press). Again, teacher efficacy seems to be a prerequisite to such collaboration (Hoover-Dempsey, Bassler, & Brissie, 1987).

Consideration of the family as a productive resource suggests yet another form of nonfiscal resource: the synergy arising from the treatment of school as community. Stevens and Slavin (1995) have demonstrated the contribution of cooperation as an organizing principle to test scores and other important outcomes. These elements necessarily rest upon school autonomy, or school-based management, and stronger notions of school as community, topics to which we will return.

Productive Resources and Equity

Murphy and Hallinger (1989) ask "how we may assess equality of access to knowledge within classrooms and schools" (p. 130). They argue, with Oakes (1985), that tracking is the device by which differentiated learning opportunities are provided to subgroups of the population of a classroom or school, resulting in inequities.

At the classroom level in elementary schools, ability-grouping studies have rarely found that streaming (that is, the assignment of students to classrooms by ability level) is either beneficial or disadvantageous for any student subgroup (Slavin, 1987, p. 307), despite the fact that low-ability classes tend to receive slower-paced instruction (p. 325) from teachers. Within-class ability grouping is often beneficial for all students, and particularly beneficial for low-ability students (p. 320), when (a) the grouping plan reduces student heterogeneity in the subject being taught, (b) assignments to groups are flexible, and (3) teachers adapt the level and pace of instruction for the various groups (p. 322). Slavin suggests that within-class grouping is likely to be perceived by students as an effort to help them (p. 324), and to result in teacher efforts to reduce achievement disparities (p. 325).

In high schools, assignment to track is not overtly based on socioeconomic, race, ethnic origin, or gender differences, but on previous achievement (Gamoran & Behrends, 1987; Oakes, 1985). However, early achievement is heavily influenced by such variables. Gamoran and Behrends (1987) review both large-scale quantitative studies and ethnographic studies. The former do not show any consistent impact of tracking on achievement (p. 419); in the ethnographic studies "the quantity and consistency of the findings clearly point to a pattern of instructional differences favoring high-track classes" (p. 424). These instructional differences are explicable with our model of teacher incentives. Working with unpromising students is avoided by teachers (p. 424). Working with such students lowers teacher efficacy and hence their expectations of students (Smylie, 1988).

Elementary schools differ in effectiveness (Mackenzie, 1983). In unusually effective schools a variety of linked characteristics that are mutually reinforcing combine to provide a global ethos (Mackenzie, 1983; Rutter et al., 1979; Goodlad, 1984). This most important quality of such schools is inherently not capable of deployment so as to affect some students or teachers more than others.

In secondary schools there are strong between-school variations in incentives. In inner-city schools, the incentives for students at the disposal of teachers are irrelevant to students (Metz, 1993). These students provide only limited incentives to teachers through academic achievement (Metz, 1993). Students and teachers in such schools agree that academic work is unimportant to the students. The "classroom bargains" literature on the high school (Sedlak et al., 1986; Sizer, 1984) represents the negative side of the "psychic rewards" element in teacher incentives. Such agreements are quite the reverse of those established in effective secondary schools, in which the centrality of academic matters and high expectations for learning are almost universal findings (Rutter et al., 1979; Goodlad, 1984).

In sum, productive resources differ in two major ways from fiscal resources: They are global in nature; positive ethos affects all (Monk, 1992). Further, they are not easily marshalled by policymakers or administrators: Important teacher incentives are controlled by students and colleagues rather than by administrators or policymakers. Other productive resources such as family contributions (the curriculum of the home) or cooperation/community are controlled by teachers and other participants rather than administrators. It is not surprising that centralized allocation systems are ineffective in enhancing productivity (Kirst, 1988) and that traditional production-function studies based on fiscal variables have been poor guides to policy (Monk, 1992).

The Ethics of Allocation Systems

Strike (1985) has argued that equity and excellence goals conflict, resulting from "a view of excellence dominated by human capital theory and a view of equity dominated by the Jeffersonian ideal. Such conflicting ideologies will manifest themselves in incompatible views of how educational resources ought to be allocated" (p. 415). He suggests that the ethical status of an allocation system is to be judged not by the goodness of the result (for example, benefits arising for clients) but by the legitimacy of the decision process and the justness or fairness of the allocation system. Strike (1988) argues that "justice claims trump both goodness claims and process claims" (p. 146) in the event of a dispute between the different kinds of rights.

Strike (1988, p. 174) assumes that the claims of goodness and fairness compete for scarce fiscal resources. But if the resources critical to the attainment of the policy goal of excellence are not fiscal resources, and hence neither inherently scarce nor targetable, then perhaps there is no competition. Productive resource allocation policies intended to promote excellence, to be judged by goodness of the result, need not necessarily be incompatible with fiscal resource allocation policies intended to promote equity, to be judged by justice as fairness, in which allocations of scarce and deployable resources reflect educational need.

The argument that equity and excellence goals are indeed on different parallels of latitude, and never meet, then rests on the decoupling of costs and quality, on the probability that fiscal and productive resources must by their nature be treated differently, and finally on the ethical argument that suggests that excellence and equity are to be judged by different standards.

AN ECONOMIC PERSPECTIVE ON RESOURCE ALLOCATION

Thus we focus on district-level policy. However, we adopt economic models to guide the policy proposals. School effectiveness studies seem to challenge economic theory because in general the schools described as unusually effective achieve their results by "maximizing the efforts of teachers and students" (Brown, 1988, p. 200), without fiscal incentives. However, this is illusory because "a nonmarket environment, such as the internal organization of a school, creates its own incentives and restraints within which people optimize choices" (Brown, 1988, p. 201). That is, in educational environments the resource allocation problem has different, nonfiscal content; the players play for different chips. The chips in this case are largely district- and school-level incentives.

Efficient Equity

The golden rule tells us "Do unto others as you would have them do unto you." But to economists a more appropriate apodictic reads "Do *not* do unto others as you would have them do unto you, their tastes may be different." This difference strikes to the heart of the apparent conflict between equity and excellence. The central notion of equity is equal access to resources; the central notion of excellence is performance. If people (students, teachers, administrators) differ in substantive ways, and provided that resource differentials translate directly into performance differentials, then equality of resource allocation guarantees unequal performance. Conversely, it is necessary to allocate resources unequally to equalize performance.

Efficiency in Educational Contexts

In general the notion of efficiency refers to the attainment of specific objectives, achieved subject to some constraints. In the case of public education, the constraint set is rich although not intrinsically different from those faced by the firm.[2] The prices of inputs are part of the constraint set. Thus districts exist in a particular geographical region; the price they must pay for teachers is a reflection of what teachers could obtain in some other line of work locally, or by remaining in the household, or by moving to another region.[3]

The objectives we choose to specify and the implicit relative weighting amongst these are also critical to the model. We may, for example, prize the differentiated performance of each individual, or we may wish all students to perform equally; we may wish individuals to improve their relative performance each year, or treat performance as a function of groups of students—a school system may choose within its set of objectives to weight the education of disadvantaged groups more heavily than others.

This list refers exclusively to the objectives of the process and suggests that what is required is an explicit weighting, or an operationally clear implicit weighting, of the objectives in education if we are to make any sense whatsoever of the notion of efficiency (Hanushek, 1986). In Conan Doyle's *Silver Blaze*, what is important is what the dog did *not* do in the night. Similarly what is important in understanding the relationship between objectives and efficiency is what is *not* in the specification of the objective function—the elements of the constraint set—and the process by which the efficient allocation of resources is achieved. These constitute two distinctly different ingredients in the alchemy of the efficient allocation of resources. The constraint set will bound what can be obtained, and the allocation of resources will reflect trade-offs among objectives that will be matched to the trade-offs available in the constraints. Our difficulty in determining the nature of the constraint set, in particular the technology of learning, makes it hard to solve some of the allocational questions that arise.

An Efficient Allocation System

The maximization of the objective function (set of objectives) is achieved when the value of the additional resources added to any part of the productive process relative to the costs of these resources is equated along all margins to which resources can be devoted.[4] This equalization is a characteristic of optimality. Consider an equal allocation of resources to all facets of production. There are gains to be had by withdrawing resources from those activities that yield a relatively low return per unit of resources invested and spending them on activities that yield a relatively high level of return per unit of resources.[5] It is difficult to imagine that an environment in which equal amounts of resources are devoted to all schools or classrooms will lead to an efficient allocation. Process, in this context, is a red herring. The efficient allocation of resources *is* the process that provides the matching of objectives to constraints. To try to require a particular allocation without specifying the objective function, and identifying the trade-offs it has with other possible objectives, is to confuse means and ends. This is not to prejudge the case for equal spending. If there are no other objectives that enter into the objective function being optimized, then it most certainly can be achieved efficiently. If, however, there are other objectives, such as performance levels, then equalization is inefficient.

Efficiency and Incentives

Economic approaches to studying behavior assume that remuneration is linked to performance. That is not to say that financial reward is all-important. Economists characterize the relevant kind of remuneration as the "equalization of net advantage." The full value of the "wage" paid includes both the financial and psychic income received by the participant. Observations of this kind help to explain why it is that unpleasant jobs, or jobs in unpleasant locations, require a higher wage. Thus it comes as no surprise that teachers find rewards both in the classroom and from their paychecks.

Pay thus generally conceived is the mechanism by which resources are induced to flow to their efficient locations in the production process. In the usual model of a firm's behavior, the matching of margins of (the valuation of) objectives and constraints is predicated on the assumption that incentives can be found to draw resources to their most desirable location. In the education business, this is a truly heroic assumption, and the conditions that lead to its violation help to explain why elementary and secondary education is frequently characterized as likely to be inefficient (Easton, 1988).

Constraints on Efficiency

Education is often described with the language of production theory. One input, a child, enters the system; other inputs, such as teachers, materials, instructional time, and peers, are combined in a process that produces an educated child, the output. The objectives of that process are frequently conflicting and differ from individual to individual. Let us suppose that we can specify some objectives so that we may focus our discussion on the kinds of constraints faced by policymakers seeking to meet these.

The first problem is that the nexus of education is still unclear. What proportion of the child's education, measured as the addition to knowledge, social skill, or other, is due to the classroom, the school, the district, the province? Within the classroom, how much of the value-added accrues because of the peer group, the teacher, the materials, the organization of the school, the press for accountability of the district? These are vital issues if our allocation of resources is going to be driven by some notion of efficiency.

Put most simply, consider the implications if the teacher is thought to provide 100 percent of the value-added in a child's education. The value-added refers to the value of the increment in output associated with an increment to an input. The implication for an efficient allocation is that the teacher should receive 100 percent of the resources devoted to education. Now, however, suppose that teachers and books combine to generate a child's education. Efficient allocation requires that now both productive inputs should be used. The efficient solution to the allocation suggests that the ratio of the (marginal) contribution to the value-added of the production process relative to the cost of the input should be matched in the two activities. This is an important choice, because a dollar to buy a book is a dollar less to pay another teacher. The valuation of the contribution of each, teachers and books, has two components. First, the valuation implied by the objective function, how much each increment to performance is weighted vis-à-vis the other performance measures; second, the technical datum: how much each additional teacher, and how much each additional book, contributes to the student's performance.

The same kind of scenario can be sketched for any number of inputs. If there is any deviation from the optimum rule, resources can be reallocated to increase the total benefit. What must be the case, however, is that the factors of production—the books, and teachers, and other productive inputs—each receive a reward that is related to their contribution. If a teacher's marginal product relative to wage is too high, this suggests that there are too few teachers, and efficiency could be enhanced by hiring additional teachers and reducing the amount spent on the other input, books. On the other hand, if the relationship between the marginal product and the wage is too low, this suggests that there are too many teachers relative to books.

The Rewards to Factors of Production

The vast majority of schools are not profit-maximizing entities, but the conditions that pertain to efficiency are still vitally relevant, given the resource constraints of the public sector. An integral part of the process of resource allocation is that the factors purchased are receiving what they are worth, their marginal products. What is essential in the process with respect to schools is first that we are able to identify the value-added to a student's performance induced by the teacher, *ceteris paribus*. We can then value and pay it appropriately.

But we cannot identify a teacher's contribution (Hanushek, 1986; Summers & Wolfe, 1977). The difficulty in identifying performance means that the rate of pay is likely to be inappropriate from the standpoint of optimization. We will tend to have too many or too few teachers relative to other factors of production (Eberts & Stone, 1986). The allocation will be determined on a basis that may have only a tenuous relationship to the optimal. In an environment in which teachers bargain collectively, we would expect there to be too many teachers, given an effective teacher union. Taxpayers are paying more for that particular resource than would be the case otherwise.

A high price usually reduces purchasing of the factor, that is, it results in fewer teachers (relative to books and other unorganized inputs). But in fact we observe more teachers per student now than in earlier, less-well-organized times. This can be explained by the notion of the "equalization of net advantage"; the value of nonpecuniary benefit makes up part of the true wage. One of the ways to raise the "salary" teachers receive has been to decrease the size of classes, provide for specialized classes and services, increase paid preparation time, and the like. These have been primary union bargaining targets. In the absence of a clear analysis of the teacher's contribution, such bargaining has been effective. Furthermore, if assessment of the marginal product is too difficult and resources are added in a way that does not contribute to efficiency, then we might also expect that teachers will be paid in too homogeneous a fashion.

The Role of Merit Pay

The point of merit pay is to encourage good teachers to do more of whatever they are doing so well, that is, to reward production. Merit pay schemes are seldom deemed to have been successful (Murnane & Cohen, 1986). In Canada, as in the United States, the criteria for teacher salary advancement remain time in service and the teacher's own education, with few exceptions. Merit pay schemes have failed, in part, because we are unable to identify the marginal product of teaching. Suppose it takes two teachers to "produce" output, not one, or suppose it takes a team of teachers, aides, volunteers, and administrators. Rewarding one of these factors of production to the exclusion of the others will not cause output to increase appreciably, and it may justifiably engender negative consequences from the unrewarded members of the team.

As an analogy, consider professional sport. Players receive both individual wage incentives and bonuses based on team performance. The key to such an approach is the ability (and desire) to identify both the marginal contribution of the individual and the contribution of the joint inputs, and then to pay the individual and the team proportionally to their joint contribution to performance. Similarly, if we are unable to identify the teacher contribution for a merit pay scheme and suspect that group contributions are important, then a proper "merit pay" scheme should reward the better teacher, the better team, the better school, the better district, in proportion to the better performance. We may want to reward the student for more learning if we are convinced that it is internal motivation, not teaching and books, that was most relevant to the valued product. In this way resources will be encouraged to flow to more-efficient locations. To the extent that a school can be identified as contributing more to students, merit pay should accrue to the school, and it should be allowed to expand to draw more resources and students.

In sum, the process of allocation following upon rewards depends importantly upon identifying the relevant nexus of production. To "fine-tune" the structure of rewards implies an understanding of who and what contributes to value-added. Until we understand the locale in which the objectives we value are produced, any merit pay scheme will be groping for success. Our efforts to discover the nature of the educational process are central to the task of moving toward more-efficient allocation of the hundreds of billions of dollars North America spends in educational production.

SUMMARY: RESOURCE ALLOCATION
IN SCHOOL DISTRICTS

Resource allocation activities at the district level to address equity and excellence goals are critical to goal attainment. Mitchell, Ortiz, and Mitchell (1983) conclude their discussion of teacher job performance by suggesting that "policies that give primary attention to strengthening organization-level, purposive incentives have the greatest chance of improving overall teacher work performance" (p. 209). School-level incentives are also likely to be important: "Policies that facilitate the development of appropriate group-level, solidarity incentives will also significantly improve teacher work performance" (p. 210). These fall within the purview of the district because principals are critical to such solidarity incentives (Blase, 1987). District-level allocation schemes, which in general treat the school as the recipient (Goertz, 1989; Hartman, 1988), rather than the classroom, the teacher, or the student, constitute the appropriate locus for policies addressing these objectives.

Three lines of argument have been established: from a study of high-performing school districts; from the literature on educational productivity; and from treatments of efficiency in economics. Each contributes to the emergence of two general conclusions. First, central prescriptions from the state (province) about the particular resource mix most likely to be productive in a particular school are *necessarily ill-informed and constrain the attainment of equity and excellence objectives.* They are ill-informed because we cannot specify even a general production function for public education; when school-level differences must be taken into account, the task is truly hopeless at present. They constrain the attainment of objectives because productive resources are vital, and resist deployment through state policies.

Second, high levels of school autonomy with respect to both fiscal and productive resources are desirable. Such autonomy with respect to resource decisions is generally labeled School-Based Management. It has a considerable history (P. Coleman, 1984; Caldwell, 1987) and is currently being implemented quite broadly in England and Australia (Caldwell & Spinks, 1988). The devolution in Australia is most advanced in the State of Victoria (Chapman & Boyd, 1986). School-Based Management has been advocated in the United States to allow more-efficient decisions and more-careful targeting of resource use (Kirst, 1988) and also because it corresponds best with existing governance models in North America (Clune, 1993). Community-based schools are also being advocated for other reasons including concerns with democracy (Kahne, 1994), with crisis management, and with parental choice (P. Coleman, 1994; Bauch & Goldring, 1995).

From our data on high-performing districts we argued that educator and other participant opportunities to learn and be heard are central to productive ethos. Given such an ethos, a commitment to more-careful targeting of resource allocations and the avoidance of wasteful practices are probable outcomes of participant responsibility for decisions about resource use (P. Coleman, 1987b; P. Coleman & LaRocque, 1990). These studies, read in conjunction with the considerable literature on teacher commitment and other kinds of productive resources, suggest the potential of school autonomy for helping in the attainment of both objectives.

We suggest then a kind of deregulation of schooling, somewhat resembling Kerchner and Boyd's (1988) "third policy cluster" in its public policy aspect, but with an emphasis upon school-level autonomy to maximize productive resources. We recommend pilot projects resembling that described by Stevens and Slavin (1995) within selected school districts in which a positive ethos exists. Schools engaged in these projects would receive broad resource entitlements, based on weighted pupil count (as much as 90 percent of district operating funds per student can be channeled to schools in an efficient district [P. Coleman, 1984]). These schools may require exemption from district and state regulations. They would be expected to use these freedoms to experiment with resource allocation and instructional arrangements. Much of the case for school autonomy with respect to curricular and instructional issues has already been made by Goodlad and associates (1987).

There are two major caveats, however. First, such devolution must occur within a normative context in which accountability to students and parents is strongly emphasized, and second, autonomy must be matched with careful monitoring of outcomes (P. Coleman, 1984; P. Coleman & LaRocque, 1992; Ferris, 1992). Without such a normative context, school autonomy can readily be abused. Although such scrutinized devolution may seem paradoxical, Coleman and LaRocque (1990) found that the most-decentralized districts had developed careful monitoring practices in which the freedom of schools to experiment in resource and instructional arrangements was constrained by the need to demonstrate the ways in which these experiments were beneficial to students.

The participating schools would necessarily agree to careful self-assessment and broad participation in school decision making. In particular, tracking practices and their impact on student progress and satisfaction must be carefully monitored. There is little doubt that some self-serving educational practices like classroom bargains would continue. However, given stronger teacher voice, the cynicism that underlies such practices may decline. The available evidence suggests that at least some of these pilot schools would develop a strong ethos in Rutter's (et al., 1979) sense, including relatively high levels of teacher and family commitment. If the pilot schools do improve in this way, then the lot of disadvantaged students within them must necessarily improve.

This caveat differentiates our proposal from those in Australia or the United Kingdom because it suggests a strong district presence in the schools, not as regulator but as assessor and guardian of accountability to clients. This role, for an organization headed by an elected school board, is both sensible and manageable; it is in fact performed by boards in our high-performing districts (LaRocque & Coleman, 1989). Our approach might be called "managed devolution" to reflect this critical element.

The second major caveat is that the policy responsibilities of the district must include decisions regarding the "mainstreaming" of disadvantaged students into desirable school locations. This process must be judged by "justness" criteria and could supplement and help to inform parental choice, presently a dubious advantage for some parents (Kerchner & Boyd, 1988, p. 106), although potentially important if parents make informed choices (P. Coleman, 1994).

Higher levels of equity and excellence may be joint products of more-autonomous schools that enjoy higher levels of teacher commitment and performance, higher levels of contributions from parents, and are carefully monitored.

Experiments in "managed devolution" will potentially provide a greater range of instructional arrangements, which will allow more-careful assessment of the strengths and weaknesses of various resource allocation patterns. The elusive general educational production function may emerge from this diversity of arrangements. This would allow more-efficient central allocation schemes to be developed. However, given the power of productive resources and the difficulty of capturing them in quantitative models, school-level autonomy will always be a better option than central control and allocation of resources to maximize the provision of both excellence and equity in the public schools.

NOTES

1. Successful districts were high-performing districts (district performance level was determined by student achievement and per pupil costs). We standardized and aggregrated student test scores, and calculated a residual using Community Education Level as a predictor. Similarly, we standardized and aggregated the 1982 per pupil costs, and residualized them with District Mean Grade Size, an important predictor of costs. A high-performing district was one with higher-than-predicted

residual achievement scores and lower-than-predicted residual costs; conversely, a low-performing district was one with a low residual achievement score and a high residual cost score. Administrative norms and practices, identified through analysis of interview data, differentiated between districts and constituted more or less positive district ethos (P. Coleman & LaRocque, 1990).

2. In general, some objective, like profit maximization for the firm, is accomplished in the face of a budget constraint. This may take the form of prices paid to factors of production and the technology of production. The latter point is most important here.

3. Imagine that we start off in a basic balance or equilibrium among the wages in different parts of the economy. Should teachers receive salary increases if there is no measured gain in productivity? The answer is that if wages do not rise, teachers may be drawn into manufacturing until the wage rates return to the initial parity. This may take place through a reduction in teaching staff or through the value of what is being taught rising with the general wealth of society as (even the same) educational output is able to offer access to higher income. The value of the teachers' product is a demand derived from the value it has to the student (parent, taxpayer), which depends in part on the personal or societal income that it can generate.

4. Hirshleifer (1980, p. 286) provides an explanation of why it is that an efficient allocation in a production process will reflect an allocation of resources so that additions to cost occasioned by additional output (marginal costs) will be equal to the ratio of the cost of the factor—p1 is the cost of factor 1, relative to its marginal product, mp1: $MC = (p1/mp1) = (p2/mp2) = ... = (pi/mpi)$. In the expression, the price of the factor is the wage for labor, the rental rate on equipment, or the cost per period of any other input. The marginal product (of say input 1) is the change in output per unit increment in input 1, for given levels of the other inputs.

5. We are assuming that the school functions in a way that does not allow it to act as a monopolist in providing educational services and that inputs are purchased in competitive markets. Both of these assumptions are open to dispute, but the details of the differences, and their consequences for the interpretation, are less important in this context than the general line of argument.

REFERENCES

Ashton, P., & Webb, R. (1986). *Making a difference: Teachers' sense of efficacy and student achievement*. New York: Longman.

Barnett, W. S., & Escobar, C. M. (1987). The economics of early educational intervention: A review. *Review of Educational Research, 57*(4), 387–412.

Bauch, P. A., & Goldring, E. B. (1995). Parent involvement and school responsiveness: Facilitating the home-school connection in schools of choice. *Educational Evaluation and Policy Analysis, 17*(1), 1–21.

Blase, J. J. (1987). Dimensions of effective school leadership: The teachers' perspective. *American Educational Research Journal, 24*(4), 589–610.

Brown, B. W. (1988). The microeconomics of learning: Students, teachers, and classrooms. In D. H. Monk & J. Underwood (Eds.), *Microlevel school finance: Issues and implications for policy*. The Ninth Annual Yearbook of the American Education Finance Association. Cambridge, Mass.: Ballinger.

Caldwell, B. J. (1987). *Educational reform through School-site management: An international perspective.* A paper presented at the 1987 Conference of the American Educational Finance Association, Arlington, Virginia.

Caldwell, B. J., & Spinks, J. M. (1988). *The self-managing school.* Philadelphia, Pa.: Falmer.

Chapman, J., & Boyd, W. L. (1986). Decentralization, devolution, and the school principal: Australian lessons on statewide educational reform. *Educational Administration Quarterly, 22*(4), 28–58.

Childs, T. S., & Shakeshaft, C. (1986). A meta-analysis of research on the relation between educational expenditures and student achievement. *Journal of Educational Finance, 12*(2), 249–263.

Clune, W. H. (1993). The best path to systemic educational policy: Standard/centralized or differentiated/decentralized? *Educational Evaluation and Policy Analysis, 15*(3), 233–254.

Cohen, D. K., & Murnane, R. J. (1985). The merits of merit pay. *Public Interest, 80*(1), 3–30.

Coleman, J. S. (1987). Families and schools. *Educational Researcher, 16*(6), 32–36.

Coleman, J. S., Campbell, E. A., Hobson, C. J., McPartland, J., Mood, A. M., Weinfeld, F. D., & York, R. L. (1966). *Equality of Educational Opportunity.* Washington. D.C.: U.S. Government Printing Office.

Coleman, P. (1984) Improving schools by school-based management. *McGill Journal of Education, 19*(1), 25–43.

Coleman, P. (1987a). Equal or equitable?: Fiscal equity and the problem of student dispersion. *Journal of Educational Finance, 13*(1), 71–96.

Coleman, P. (1987b) Implementing school based decision making. *The Canadian Administrator, 26*(7), 1–11.

Coleman, P. (1994). *Learning about schools: What parents need to know and how they can find out.* Montreal, Quebec: Institute for Research on Public Policy.

Coleman, P., & LaRocque, L. (1984). Economies of scale revisited: School district operating costs in British Columbia, 1972–1982. *Journal of Educational Finance, 10*(1), 22-35.

Coleman, P., & LaRocque, L. (1990). *Struggling to be 'good enough': Administrative practices and school district ethos.* London: Falmer Press.

Coleman, P., Collinge, J., & Tabin, Y. (1995). The coproduction of learning: Improving schools from the inside out. In B. Levin, W. J. Fowler, & H. J. Walberg. *Organizational influences on educational productivity* (pp. 95–113). Advances in Educational Productivity, Volume 5. Greenwich, Conn.: JAI Press.

Coleman, P., Collinge, J., & Tabin, Y. (in press). Learning Together: The Student/Parent/Teacher Triad. *School Effectiveness and School Improvement.*

Coleman, P., Walsh, J., & LaRocque, L. (1988). School district achievement and unit costs. *Canadian Journal of Education, 13*(1), 231–237.

Colvin, R. L. (1989). School finance: Equity concerns in an age of reforms. *Educational Researcher, 18*(1), 11–15.

Coons, J. E., Clune, W. H., & Sugarman, S. D. (1970). *Private wealth and public education.* Cambridge, Mass.: Harvard University Press.

Easton, S. T. (1988). *Education in Canada: An analysis of elementary, secondary and vocational training.* Vancouver: Fraser Institute.

Eberts, R. W., & Stone, J. A. (1986, January). On the contract curve: A test of alternative models of collective bargaining. *Journal of Labor Economics*, 66–81.

Ferris, J. M. (1992). School-based decision making: A principal-agent perspective. *Educational Evaluation and Policy Analysis, 14*(4), 333–346.

Fuller, B., Wood, K., Rapoport, T., & Dornbush, S. M. (1982). The organizational context of individual efficacy. *Review of Educational Research, 52*,(1), 7–30.

Gamoran, A., & Behrends, M. (1987). The effects of stratification in secondary schools: Synthesis of survey and ethnographic research. *Review of Educational Research, 57*(4), 415–437.

Goertz, M. (1989). *Sub-district allocation of education resources*. Paper presented at annual meeting of the American Educational Research Association, San Francisco, Calif.

Goodlad, J. I. (1984). *A place called school: Prospects for the future*. New York: McGraw-Hill.

Goodlad, J. and Associates (1987). Structure, process, and an agenda. In J. Goodlad (Ed.), *The ecology of school renewal*. The Eighty-sixth Yearbook of the National Society for the Study of Education, Part 1. Chicago, Ill.: University of Chicago Press.

Guthrie, J. W., Garms, W. I., & Pierce, L. C. (1988). *School finance and education policy: Enhancing educational efficiency, equality, and choice*. Englewood Cliffs, N.J.: Prentice Hall.

Hanushek, E. A. (1981). Throwing money at schools. *Journal of Policy Analysis and Management, 1*(1), 19–41.

Hanushek, E. A. (1986, September). The economics of schooling: Production and efficiency in public schools, *Journal of Economic Literature, 24*, 1141–1177.

Hanushek, E. A. (1989). The impact of differential expenditures on school performance. *Educational Researcher, 17*(3), 24–32.

Hargrove, E. C., Graham, S. G., Ward, L., Abernethy, V., Cunningham, J., & Vaughn, W. K. (1981). School systems and regulatory mandates: A case study of the implementation of the Education for All Handicapped Children Act. In S. Bacharach (Ed.), *Organizational behavior in schools and school districts*. New York, N.Y.: Praeger.

Hartman, W. T. (1988). *School district budgeting*. Englewood Cliffs, N.J.: Prentice Hall.

Herriott, R. E., & Firestone, W. A. (1984). Two images of schools as organizations: A refinement and elaboration. *Educational Administration Quarterly, 20*(40), 41–57.

Hirshleifer, J. (1980). *Price theory and applications*, 2nd ed. Englewood Cliffs, N.J.: Prentice Hall.

Hoover-Dempsey, K. V., Bassler, O. C., & Brissie, J. S. (1987). Parent involvement: Contributions of teacher efficacy, school socioeconomic status, and other school characteristics. *American Educational Research Journal, 24*(3), 417–435.

Johnson, S. M. (1990). Redesigning teachers' work. In R. Elmore & Associates (Eds.), *Restructuring schools: The next generation of educational reform*. San Francisco: Jossey-Bass.

Kahne, J. (1994). Democratic communities, equity, and excellence: A Deweyan reframing of educational policy analysis. *Educational Evaluation and Policy Analysis, 16*(3), 233–248.

Kennedy, M. M. (1984). How evidence alters understanding and decisions. *Educational Evaluation and Policy Analysis, 6*(3), 207–226.

Kerchner, C. T., & Boyd, W. L. (1988). What doesn't work: An analysis of market and bureaucratic failure in schooling. In W. L. Boyd & C. T. Kerchner (Eds.), *The Politics of Excellence and Choice in Education.* The 1987 Yearbook of the Politics of Education Association. New York: Falmer Press.

Kirst, M. W. (1988). The internal allocation of resources within U.S. school districts: Implications for policy-makers and practitioners. In D. H. Monk & J. Underwood (Eds.), *Microlevel school finance: Issues and implications for policy.* The Ninth Annual Yearbook of the American Education Finance Association. Cambridge, Mass.: Ballinger.

LaRocque, L., & Coleman, P. (1989). *The politics of excellence: Trustee leadership and school district ethos.* A paper presented at the Annual Meeting of the American Educational Research Association, April, San Francisco.

Lawton, S. (1987a). *The price of quality: The public finance of elementary and secondary education.* Toronto, Ontario: Canadian Education Association.

Lawton, S. (1987b). Teachers' salaries: An international perspective. In K. Alexander & D. H. Monk (Eds.), *Attracting and compensating America's teachers.* Eighth Annual Yearbook of the American Educational Finance Association. Cambridge, Mass.: Ballinger.

Levin, H. M. (1984). About time for educational reform. *Educational Evaluation and Policy Analysis, 6*(2), 151–164.

Lortie, D. C. (1975). *Schoolteacher.* Chicago, Ill.: University of Chicago Press.

McLaughlin, M. W., & Yee, S. M. (1988). School as a place to have a career. In A. Lieberman (Ed.), *Building a professional culture in schools.* New York: Teachers College Press.

Mackenzie, D. E. (1983). Research for school improvement: An appraisal of some recent trends. *Educational Researcher, 12*(4), 5–17.

Metz, M. H. (1993). Teachers' ultimate dependence on their students. In J. W. Little & M. W. McLaughlin (Eds.), *Teachers' work: Individuals, colleagues, and contexts* (pp. 104–136). New York: Teachers College Press.

Mitchell, D. E. , Ortiz, F. I., & Mitchell, T. K. (1983). *Work orientation and job performance: The cultural basis of teaching rewards.* Riverside, Calif.: University of California Press.

Monk, D. H. (1992). Education productivity research: An update and assessment of its role in education finance reform. *Educational Evaluation and Policy Analysis, 14*(4), 307–332.

Mortimore, P., Sammons, P., Stoll, L., Lewis, D., & Ecob, R. (1988). *School matters: The junior years.* Wells, Somerset, England: Open Books.

Mosteller, F., & Moynihan, D. (1972). *On equality of educational opportunity.* New York: Vintage Books.

Murnane, R. J., & Cohen, D. K. (1986). Merit pay and the evaluation problem: Why most merit pay plans fail and a few survive. *Harvard Educational Review, 56*, 1–17.

Murphy, J., & Hallinger, P. (1989). Equity as access to learning: Curricular and instructional treatment differences. *Journal of Curricular Studies, 21*(2), 129–149.

Oakes, J. (1985). *Keeping track: How schools structure inequality.* New Haven, Conn.: Yale University Press.

Odden, A. (1985). Education finance 1985: A rising tide or steady fiscal state? *Educational Evaluation and Policy Analysis, 7*(4), 395–408.

Odden, A. (1990). Class size and student achievement: Research-based policy alternatives. *Evaluation and Policy Analysis, 12*(2), 213–227.

Odden, A., & Marsh, D. (1987). *How state education reform can improve comprehensive secondary schools.* Berkeley, Calif.: Policy Analysis for California Education.

Rosenholtz, S. J. (1989). *Teachers' workplace: The social organization of schools.* New York: Longman.

Rossmiller, R. A. (1986). *Resource utilization in schools and classrooms: Final report.* Madison, Wis.: Wisconsin Center for Education Research.

Rossmiller, R. A. (1987). Achieving equity and effectiveness in schooling. *Journal of Education Finance, 12*(4), 561–577.

Rutter, M., Maughan, B., Mortimore, P., & Ouston, J. (1979). *Fifteen thousand hours: Secondary schools and their effects on children.* Cambridge, Mass.: Harvard University Press.

Sedlak, M. W., Wheeler, C. W., Pullin, D. C., & Cusick, P. (1986). *Selling students short: Classroom bargains and academic reform in the American high school.* New York: Teachers College Press.

Sizer, T. R. (1984). *Horace's compromise: The dilemma of the American high school.* Boston, Mass.: Houghton Mifflin.

Slavin, R. E. (1987). Ability grouping and student achievement in elementary schools: A best-evidence synthesis. *Review of Educational Research, 57*(3), 293–336.

Smylie, M. A. (1988). The enhancement function of staff development: Organizational and psychological antecedents to individual teacher change. *American Educational Research Journal, 25*(1), 1–30.

Stern, D. (1986). Compensation for teachers. In E. Z. Rothkopf (Ed.), *Review of research in education, 15,* 285–316.

Stevens, R. J., & Slavin, R. E. (1995). The cooperative elementary school: Effects on students' achievement, attitudes, and social relations. *American Educational Research Journal, 32*(2), 321–351.

Strike, K. A. (1985). Is there a conflict between equity and excellence? *Educational Evaluation and Policy Analysis, 7*(4), 409–416.

Strike, Kenneth A. (1988). The ethics of resource allocation in education: Questions of democracy and justice. In D. H. Monk & J. Underwood (Eds.), *Microlevel school finance: Issues and implications for policy.* The Ninth Annual Yearbook of the American Education Finance Association. Cambridge, Mass.: Ballinger.

Summers, A. L., & Wolfe, B. L. (1977). Do schools make a difference? *American Economic Review, 14*(3), 639–652.

Tannenbaum, A. S. (1962). Control in organizations: Individual adjustment and organizational performance. *Administrative Science Quarterly, 7*(2), 236–257.

Walberg, H. (1984). Improving the productivity of America's schools. *Educational Leadership, 41*(8), 19–30.

Walberg, H. T., & Fowler, W. J. (1987). Expenditure and size efficiencies of public school districts. *Educational Researcher, 16*(7), 5–15.

Walberg, H. T., & Shanahan, T. (1983). High school effects on individual students. *Educational Researcher, 12*(7), 4–9.

Wang, M. C., Haertel, G. D., & Walberg, H. J. (1993). Toward a knowledge base for school learning. *Review of Educational Research, 63*(3), 249–294.

Wilson, W. J. (1987). *The truly disadvantaged: The inner city, the underclass, and public policy.* Chicago, Ill.: University of Chicago.

6

Understanding Resource Allocation in High Schools

William T. Hartman

INTRODUCTION

The literature on effective schooling suggests that the most-effective schools operate in a rational, purposive manner (Murphy, Hallinger, & Mesa, 1985). They engage in a deliberate, schoolwide effort to improve student achievement, the most common measure of their success being student test scores. The leaders in the school are supposed to identify which pedagogical, organizational, and social arrangements are the most beneficial for student learning and to implement them. All school resources—teachers, administrators, other staff, facilities, supplies, equipment—are focused on improving student outcomes. "The effective schools research lays out an action plan for enhancing achievement in schools. The plan is rational in that it deliberately expects and designs outcomes," (Thompson, Wood, & Honeyman, 1994, p. 40). This is both a description of the best schools and a normative prescription for other, less-effective schools to follow.

In spite of the national prominence and most-favored status given to this view of how education should operate, there are competing, and possibly more accurate, interpretations of the objectives, decision-making processes, and actions of school personnel, even in schools that have been nationally recognized as having achieved "excellence in education." Alternative explanations emphasize bureaucratic routine, administrative convenience, self-interest of school personnel, and political motivations—rather than improvement of student outcomes—as the primary determinants of school personnel behavior.

The resource allocation process offers a largely unused window from which to observe and analyze important building-level educational choices. Through the distribution of resources among the various instructional, support, and administrative units in high schools, administrators and faculty have an opportunity to influence student outcomes, as well as their own working conditions and relationships. Drawing on an earlier report describing the resource allocation process in high schools (Hartman, 1985), this study analyzes the behaviors and decisions of the major participants in the resource allocation process, the manner in which the schools actually operated, and the underlying motivations of school personnel. Particular attention is paid to the objectives pursued through the distribution of resources in the schools and the results that the decision makers expected to achieve.

EXPLAINING RESOURCE ALLOCATION BEHAVIORS

Three contrasting perspectives are examined to help understand and explain the behaviors of those responsible for allocating resources within high schools. The first is a rational model approach, which assumes that administrators and others involved in the process act in a logical fashion to improve student outcomes. The second approach is a bureaucratic organization model, which assumes that resource allocation decisions are based on existing standard operating procedures and reflect the organization's primary concern with limiting and controlling changes to the present operation. The third approach is a political economy model, which assumes that persons involved in the resource allocation process operate in a bureaucracy in which "individuals try to maximize their own welfare (or benefits) within the context of the institutional or organizational reward structure they face" (Boyd, 1982, p. 113). These three approaches offer very different explanations of the objectives and motivations of school officials.

Rational Model Approaches

The common feature of rational approaches applied to the educational process is the presumption of rationality on the part of the decision makers. Cibulka's (1987) description of the rational approach provides an excellent example: "Organizational behavior is both purpositive and deliberate. . . . [Decision makers] should establish priority among their goals, weigh the costs and benefits of alternative methods, and evaluate program results in reformulating policy. Budget setting should involve systematic procedures guaranteeing that policy will not be reacting merely to short-term pressures, but rather will reflect reasoned consideration of optimal choices" (p. 12).

The fundamental assumption of the rational model as applied to education is that the goals of the organization are to improve student learning (usually measurable cognitive achievement). Consequently, high school personnel behave in a rational manner when they make decisions or take actions designed to enhance student outcomes. Decisions or actions based on other objectives or motivations are "irrational" in the sense that they are inefficient in producing student learning. Administrators and teachers operating in accordance with the rational model (a) pay explicit attention to student outcomes and (b) use the expected impact on student outcomes as a primary criterion in making both administrative and programmatic decisions.

A strict specification of the rational model would require that the linkages between inputs into the educational system and the student outcomes be known and that administrators be capable of specifying an educational production function for their operation (Hanushek, 1986). From a managerial perspective the rational model assumes that administrators have the authority to organize the production process in the most productive manner, the knowledge to select the appropriate types and mix of resources, and the ability to utilize information about the achievement of student outcomes in managing the educational process (Levin, 1971). Finally, administrators are assumed to be accountable through their reward structure for student learning.

A loosening of these conceptual constraints is necessary to reflect more accurately the actual abilities of administrators and their management of high schools and to avoid setting up the rational model as a "straw man" to be easily rejected when theoretical standards are not met. It is not necessary that administrators and other school personnel exhibit perfectly rational behavior (that is, make every decision and take every action based on an expected test score increase) in order to confirm the functioning of the rational model in high school resource allocation decisions. What is more significant for the rational model analysis is if they act and make resource allocation decisions as if they had such knowledge. Whether their decisions are based on past experience, personal belief, or on the research findings of effective educational practices (Edmonds, 1979; Purkey & Smith, 1982; MacKenzie, 1983; Rosenholtz, 1985), administrators acting in accordance with the rational model will utilize improved student achievement as a major criterion for resource allocation decisions.

The rational approach is represented in school budgeting, the formalized aspect of resource allocation, by approaches like the Planning-Programming-Budgeting-Evaluation System (PPBES) (Hack, Candoli, & Ray, 1995), Performance Budgeting (Mundt, Olsen, & Steinberg, 1982), and Zero-Based Budgeting (Phyrr, 1973). All of these budgeting approaches feature specification of objectives, estimation of results or outcomes to be achieved, linkage of resource allocation choices to maximization of outcomes, and use of analysis to justify budget decisions. As a description of PPBES states, "The PPBES cycle is directed to significant reallocation of the organization's resources in an effort to put those resources to more effective and efficient use" (van Geel, 1973, p. 2). Although implementation of these rational budgeting approaches has generally not succeeded in elementary and secondary school systems (Kirst, 1975; Lee & Johnson, 1977; Johnson, 1982; Wildavsky, 1986), the concept of alignment of organizational objectives with budget decisions remains a useful measure of rationality in evaluating the resource allocation process. At a minimum, educators acting rationally should consider student outcomes and allocate resources in a way that they believe will improve student learning.

Label/Libel Gambit

The predisposition toward the rational approach is fostered by the terminology involved. Calling these practices and procedures "rational" establishes a strong implication that other approaches are "irrational." This is a subtle version of the label/libel gambit: Something becomes perceived as what it is labeled, regardless of reality. The label eliminates the need to evaluate the item or process in question and serves as a shorthand for thinking about it. In this case the gambit cuts both ways: The rational approaches receive the positive connotation of logic, fairness, thoughtful consideration, and goal achievement, whereas other, "nonrational," approaches suffer a negative image that, even though perhaps superficial, is the major way in which they may be perceived.

Bureaucratic Organization Models

In bureaucratic models, schools are viewed as bureaucratic organizations in which high schools operate as part of a larger school system. Their choices in the resource allocation process are constrained not only by the policies and rules of the school district in which they are located but by state and federal statutes and regulations as well. Consequently, high school personnel develop a set of "standard operating procedures" to guide their actions. The behaviors of schools can be interpreted as "*outputs* of large organizations functioning according to a standard pattern of behavior" (Allison, 1970, p. 67).

The central feature of the bureaucratic approach is the dominance of the existing organizational process. "Existing organizational routines for employing present physical capabilities constitute the range of effective choice" (Allison, 1970, p. 79). This translates into a strong preference for the status quo. The best prediction of what an organization will do in the next time period is what it is doing in the current time period (Allison, 1970, p. 88). In this model, resource allocation decisions for the next budget year are heavily influenced by the current distribution of resources.

In a bureaucratic organization the formal objectives, which provide the public rationale or purpose for the existence of the organization, are frequently not the goals pursued by the organization's members.

> The operational goals of an organization are seldom revealed by formal mandates. Rather, each organization's operational goals emerge as a set of constraints defining acceptable performance. Central among these constraints is organizational health, defined usually in terms of bodies assigned and dollars appropriated. The set of constraints emerges from a mix of the expectations and demands of other organizations in the government, statutory authority, demands from citizens and special interest groups, and bargaining within the organization. (Allison, 1970, p. 82)

For schools this means that the maintenance or increase in budget allocations, personnel allotments, and building space supersede the formal educational goals of student learning.

Uncertainty avoidance is another important characteristic of bureaucratic organizations. Unpredictable occurrences can upset the existing and familiar procedures and relationships. Consequently, organizations attempt to minimize uncertainty in their operations. "The primary environment . . . is stabilized by such arrangements as agreed budgetary splits, accepted areas of responsibility, and established practices" (Allison, 1970, p. 84). It is the "better the devil you know" syndrome that is behind the "organization's interest in controlling, rather than presenting, choices" (Allison, 1970, p.90).

In spite of members' efforts, bureaucratic organizations are not static entities. Changes in practices and procedures occur through reaction to outside influences, experiences with success or failure of present routines, and learning over time. However, such changes are largely incremental from the present base of operations. Further, they are shaped by the procedures present in the existing organization.

Incremental budgeting (Wildavsky, 1986) is an example of the bureaucratic approach applied to the budget process. In incremental budgeting, the organization's decision makers concentrate primarily on additions to the existing budget. The base amounts, which are the bulk of the budget, receive continued funding without examination. Budget behavior consists of attempting to maximize the annual increment added to the base. There are no radical shifts among budget areas because of the stability of the base of each area, the relatively small incremental amounts, and some expectation that all areas will receive a similar incremental percentage increase. The focus of the budget effort and of resource allocation decisions is internal and bureaucratic—who gets how much. Little, if any, consideration is given to the performance of the organizational units or to the outcomes they are expected to produce.

Political Models

Explanations utilizing a political perspective of fiscal and organizational behavior in educational systems view the results of any resource allocation process as determined by bargaining among self-interested individuals and groups. These groups are assumed to have different objectives (although some may overlap) and to work to satisfy their personal needs. Some of the groups may be internal to the organization (school board, district administrators, building principals, high school department heads, and the district teachers' association), and others may be external (special interest or advocacy organizations, business organizations, voters). The distribution of resources in a school or district is based on objectives, power, and negotiating skills of the individuals and groups involved (Hoy & Tarter, 1995).

A prominent approach in this area is that of public choice theory. This analysis, focusing on the internal members of the organization, seeks to explain "how individual preferences are aggregated into collective decision-making in institutions in which markets fail or are not permitted, as in cases of government monopolies" (Cibulka, 1987, p. 9). In education, public choice theory has been utilized to interpret actions of public school personnel that do not appear to be aimed at the stated goals of schools but instead work to advance the individual administrator's or teacher's personal objectives.

Boyd (1982) has used a public choice approach to explain the behavior of educational bureaucrats. The analysis observes that schools operate a government monopoly rather than a competitive, market-oriented enterprise. In the non-market economy, revenues received by schools do not depend on satisfying consumer demand or client needs but instead are derived primarily from local taxes levied by the school district and from grants from the state. Thus, the funds to operate schools depend on the mere existence of the district, not on any performance measures. Without an unambiguous and measurable goal for education, such as profitability in the private sector, educational administrators generally have few incentives to increase efficiency or productivity. As described by Michaelsen (1977), "Since there are, in the bureau, no profits which can be privately appropriated, we may assume that the bureaucrats, including schoolmen, seek instead to survive, to enlarge the scope of their activities, to gain prestige, to avoid conflict, to control the organization and content of their daily round as much as possible. All these are, as it were, profit in kind" (p. 239).

The lack of agreed-upon goals, of criteria for measuring their achievement, and of an information system to provide performance results means that administrators and other school personnel are not evaluated on how well they accomplish their tasks. As characterized by Hanushek (1996), "Rewards are only vaguely associated with performance, if at all" (p. 31). The focus of organizational members is shifted away from student outcomes. The result is goal displacement in which the employees are free to substitute their own goals for the conflicting demands of the public and the official goals of the organization. Behaviors are based on individual interpretation of the official goals colored by self-interest. Thus, the public choice model argues that the pattern of operation is a bureaucratic bargain between the building administrator and building personnel in which accommodations are reached to satisfy their individual needs (Michaelsen, 1977). These include minimizing conflict (or potential for conflict) from inside and outside the organization, ease of administration, equal treatment of teachers and/or students, maintaining stability in the organization, improving staff morale, promoting favored programs, shifting or maintaining the direction of the curriculum, and modifying or retaining the pedagogical approaches utilized.

Budgeting under the public choice model tends to be internally oriented and less concerned with the results produced by expenditures. The budget amounts are decided on the basis of the bureaucratic bargain described earlier. This view does not mean that school administrators are deceitful or act illegally. "By accepting this theory of motivation, we do not rule out altruism. Administrators and teachers, like entrepreneurs, take pride in their work and strive for excellence. The issue is not whether bureaucrats are altruistic, but rather whether there are mechanisms available to harness their self-seeking to the public interest" (Michaelsen, 1977, p. 239).

Some of these objectives may indeed be self-serving and status enhancing for the administrators and teachers involved. Other objectives, particularly those concerning curriculum, pedagogy, or staffing, may represent beliefs that certain approaches will be better than others for student learning; however, these assessments and subsequent resource allocation decisions are largely subjective and intuitive rather than linked formally to measures of specified student outcomes.

METHODOLOGY

To examine both the resource allocation procedures and the basis for decisions made during the process, detailed case studies were made of four high schools located in three separate districts in Oregon. The schools were chosen specifically to represent a range of characteristics believed to have the capability of influencing resource allocation practices: budget processes ranging from participatory to dictatorial, a variety of instructional and administrative arrangements, some range in size (from approximately 1,000 to 1,740 students), student populations with different socioeconomic status, and principals who had been at the schools for at least four years. Schools from several districts were included so that the effects of varying district policies and of different communities could be observed. The schools have been given fictitious names in this study (Advance, Bridge, Central, and Delegate).

Resources were defined as personnel and other items, such as services, supplies, and equipment, that were purchased and used in the educational process. Resources that did not appear in the schools' budgets (for example, volunteer efforts, or resources provided by other agencies) were excluded.

During the 1984–85 school year, the author made approximately forty visits to the four high schools to observe the resource allocation processes. Almost half of these visits were concentrated during the two to three months of the budget development period, and the remainder were scheduled periodically throughout the year to examine the full range of school planning, budgeting, and financial management activities.

In each school, interviews were conducted with the principal, one or more assistant principals, two to four department heads representing both academic and nonacademic areas, and school-level business managers and budget secretaries. Structured interview guides for each type of school personnel were employed to ensure that similar questions were asked in each school. The questions asked were divided into two general types: those to obtain a description of the resource allocation process, and those to analyze which models best matched the behavior of school personnel in allocating resources under their control. Examples of each type of question are provided in Figure 6.1.

Some of the most interesting and fruitful time in the schools was spent attending staff meetings and budget meetings. From three to ten small and large group meetings were visited in each of the three schools that used these procedures as part of the budget process. As a nonparticipant observer, it was possible to witness the actual resource alloca-

Descriptive

Who is involved in the resource allocation process in your school? What role does each individual play in the process?

What are the primary steps in the process?

What information do you have when preparing your budget request?
  Where do you obtain this information?

What information do you use when making decisions among competing budget requests?
  Where do you obtain this information?

What rules and guidelines are there governing the budgeting process?
  Who imposes them (principal, district office, school board)?
  Are they closely followed? Why or why not?

Are there differences in the way different types of resources are allocated? Personnel, supplies, equipment?

Analytical

What is the basis for making a budget request?
What justification is required for various items?

Are there any new budget items this year?
  Why were these requested?
  How did you justify these items?

Do you have access to prior years' expenditures?
How, if at all, are they used in deciding current allocations?

How are teachers allocated to departments?
  Who does it? Is there much change in the number of teachers in a department from year to year?
  What causes changes?

How are departmental budget allocations for nonpersonnel items determined (for example, supplies, equipment)?
  What is the basis for these decisions?
  How and for what reasons are cuts made if the total requests are greater than the school's available dollars?

Do any outside groups participate in or influence the budget process? Who? How?

Figure 6.1. Interview Guide for School Personnel.

tion practices firsthand. This allowed independent verification of the reported processes, as well as the opportunity to record the behaviors and expressed motivations of the participants.

All documents relevant to the budget process were collected from the schools: guidelines and instructions for making budget requests; budget request forms; formal policies and administrative memoranda specifying priorities, procedures, or constraints for the budget process; prior year budget allocations by department; initial departmental budget requests and final allocations for the study year; individual teacher assignments by department and class; student enrollments by class; teacher handbooks; and student handbooks.

Interviews with superintendents, assistant superintendents, business managers, and personnel directors in each district were also conducted. These sessions were used to learn about district policies and procedures for allocation of personnel and other resources to schools, to collect instructions utilized in the budget development process, to determine the flexibility school principals had when distributing their allocations within their schools, and to obtain available budget and other data for examining resource allocation decisions.

The descriptive school documents and interview data were utilized to develop a picture for each school of its instructional and budgeting organization, the process used for deciding allocation of resources, and the principal's management approach. Particular emphasis was placed on the roles and responsibilities of personnel involved in resource allocation decisions. Budget, personnel, and student data were analyzed to compare actual resource allocation patterns and the relative distribution of each among the schools' departments.

The written interview responses and budget meeting observations were analyzed for evidence of each of the three explanatory models. Each instance of a verbal or written comment or participant behavior related to either a rational, bureaucratic, or political approach was noted. These results were aggregated by major area in the resource allocation process to identify the prevalence of activities associated with each model. Conclusions about the validity of each of the three explanatory models of the resource allocation processes found in the high schools were based on a comparison of the actual practices with the theoretical behaviors predicted by the models.

FINDINGS

District Allocation Policies

District policies for allocating resources to high schools were based on equality. In the districts that contained more than one high school, districtwide standards were utilized to distribute teachers and other certified personnel (student/teacher ratio), classified personnel (ratios or number of hours/week), administrators (fixed number), and supply and equipment monies (dollar-per-student or lump sum) to the schools.

All these factors were established by school board policy and indicated that board members favored an equal distribution of resources.

As a district business manager explained, "It is easier to treat everybody the same than it is to explain and defend different allocations to each of the high schools in the district." However, in some cases, this equal treatment was not considered fair treatment; complaints were voiced in several of the high schools. "Even though we have 1,800 students and [another high school] has just over 1,000 students, we both get the same number of administrators." "We are in an older building, and we should get more funds for maintenance and upkeep than [another high school in a newer building]."

Personnel Allocations within the High Schools

In all four high schools studied, personnel allocation decisions were the principal's province; they were not delegated to or shared with others in the school's organization. However, before making personnel changes, principals typically consulted with other administrators in their building and with department heads or other instructional supervisors to obtain more information, to seek advice, or to prepare them for the outcomes.

The bases for staffing allocation decisions among instructional departments were existing staffing, student enrollment patterns, and changes in course enrollments. These were combined with either explicit or implicit standards for class size to prevent overcrowded classrooms, overloaded teachers, or inefficient use of personnel. Annual changes in the number of teachers assigned to a department reflected changes in the number of course sections offered by the department, which in turn were determined by student enrollment. These changes tended to be marginal adjustments, not large shifts (for example, 0.4 FTE staff added to science department). The procedures provided principals with decision rules for making changes in staff allocations that left most teachers unaffected and could be readily understood and accepted by teachers.

The principal-controlled personnel allocations resulted in approximately equal loads in each department for the four high schools. As shown in Table 6.1 (next page), the average number of students per day for teachers in the academic departments was approximately the same as those in the nonacademic departments. In spite of the national and local concern about academic achievement, teacher workload was actually higher in academic departments in three of the schools, and no school provided workload reductions for teachers in the academic subjects. For example, in three of the high schools the number of class assignments was generally equal for all teachers. In the other school,

Table 6.1.
Average Number of Students per Teacher by Department

Department	Advance	Bridge	Central	Delegate	4-School Average
Social Studies	134	134	125	138	133
Mathematics	127	134	123	143	132
Science	133	117	123	130	126
Foreign Language	117	119	120	133	122
Language Arts	113	125	119	123	120
Academic Average	125	126	122	133	127
Physical Education	111	173	143	178	151
Arts & Crafts	128	132	119	158	134
Health	134	108	135	148	131
Business Education	135	122	125	128	128
Music & Drama	128	116	118	140	126
Homemaking	111	135	82	147	119
Industrial Arts	110	91	82	119	101
Nonacademic Average	122	125	115	145	127
School Average	123	127	119	136	126

Note: Delegate High School numbers tend to be higher because they had a seven-period school day rather than the six-period day utilized by the other three schools.

Advance High School, teachers in traditional academic departments (English, mathematics, science, foreign languages, social studies) were assigned five classes per day; teachers in nonacademic departments (business, fine arts, home economics, industrial arts, physical education/health) had six classes per day. However, in the academic departments the average class size was greater, which resulted in a general parity of the total number of students taught among all teachers in the school.

Within both the academic and nonacademic departments of each school a range of teacher loads existed, but in most cases the differences were not too large. The exceptions that existed were largely explained by individual school circumstances, space or equipment limitations that restricted class capacity, and the preferences and educational priorities of administrators. For example, in Advance High School, the most academically oriented of the four schools studied, the principal explained, "We offer a number of elective courses in language arts and foreign languages which by their nature have low enrollments. We think that these are important because they meet the needs of our student body." However, these administrators balanced the load somewhat by giving teachers one or two smaller elective classes combined with high-enrollment basic classes for the remainder of their assignment.

Some of the personnel changes represented principals' efforts to implement curriculum changes that they believed appropriate for their students. For example, administrators at Advance High School reduced the number of positions in the industrial arts department (to shift the emphasis of the curriculum); increased the instructional positions in the computer science, physical education, health, and music and drama departments (in response to increasing enrollments); and added a librarian and a substance abuse counselor (to respond to schoolwide priorities). Similarly, at Bridge High School the principal informed the faculty members involved that it was necessary to "refocus the vocational educational program into a principles of technology program to meet the future needs of students or to reduce the size of the program substantially."

Of the four schools, only Bridge High School had explicit criteria for terminating a program:

1. Class size below twelve for two consecutive years
2. Class offered at another high school in the district or at a local community college
3. Class not needed to meet district or state requirement

Using these criteria, their electricity program and a specialized mathematics section had been terminated in the past few years. Implicit criteria used in the other high schools were similar, but their vagueness allowed more administrative discretion.

Budgeting Procedures for Nonpersonnel Resources

Advance High School utilized a participatory approach in its internal distribution of nonpersonnel resources (Hartman, 1989). The department heads, with the assistance of teachers in their instructional department, prepared departmental budget requests for supplies and equipment. To assist in this task, the administration provided them with all available budget-related information: district instructions and timelines, historical allocation amounts by department, enrollments, the lump sum amount provided to the high school for supplies and equipment. The requests were aggregated by the school business manager and copies provided to each department head.

The key feature of this school's resource allocation process was a marathon meeting of the faculty council (principal, assistant principals, department heads, and support unit leaders) to reduce the total departmental budget requests ($314,000) to the school's allocation ($251,000). During the seven-hour meeting, each department head presented the department's budget request, answered any questions about it, offered reductions in their budget request, and made a case why certain reductions should not be made. Department heads also questioned other departmental requests and suggested cuts in other departmental budget requests. The administration's budget request was considered along with the others; no special treatment was given to it during the deliberations.

In **Bridge High School** a budget committee, composed of the principal, assistant principals for curriculum and for administration, four division leaders (responsible for curriculum articulation among several instructional departments), librarian (for media items), two budget assistants (teachers on special assignment), and one teacher volunteer, was responsible for reducing the total budget requests for supplies and equipment ($240,220) to the total amount allocated to the school ($168,488). Five short meetings after school, lasting approximately one hour each, were held by the committee. The committee was guided in its deliberations by a budgeting procedures memorandum prepared by the principal.

The principal served as the chair of the budget committee, and in this position he directed and controlled the process by setting the agenda, making comments and suggestions during the meetings, and by using his knowledge of where he wanted the resources channeled to implement his vision of the school's educational programs. Because Bridge High School operated without department heads, the committee was without strong advocates for specific departmental requests. Consequently, the committee members generally deferred to the principal's suggestions on difficult decisions.

At **Central High School** the allocation of supply and equipment funds was closely controlled by the assistant principal for curriculum and budgeting. The centralized pattern in the school mirrored the concentrated authority at the central-office level maintained by the district superintendent.

The assistant principal made a preliminary allocation of general instructional supply monies to each department, based on their past year's expenditures, his knowledge of the departments' operations, and an estimate of departmental enrollments for the upcoming year. He then met individually with each department head to discuss the department's plans and budgetary needs for the next year. With this input the assistant principal made any adjustments that he thought appropriate to the initial allocation amounts, informed the principal of his decisions, and forwarded this information to the district office and to each department head.

Allocations for equipment were treated separately. The assistant principal informed the department heads that "a little bit of money" was available from the district office for equipment and solicited their requests for three or four low-cost items. When the department head requests exceeded the available allocation, the assistant principal requested reductions from several department heads to reach the allocation amount ($12,000).

Although **Delegate High School** had a traditional department head organizational structure, the school also had three area coordinators, each of whom functioned as the budget administrator for one-third of the academic departments. (Two of the three area coordinators were also department heads.) Departmental supply budget requests (built from individual teacher requests) were submitted to an area coordinator who screened them for accuracy, proper coding, and reasonableness.

The three area coordinators made the nonpersonnel resource allocation decisions for the school. Their job, as assigned by the principal, was to meet as a group and jointly to allocate the available supply monies among the departments. Other than not exceeding the total amount allotted to the school, they were not given further direction or constraints from the principal. The area coordinators were also responsible for reviewing and prioritizing the equipment requests received from departments.

The principal deliberately stayed out of the allocation process himself. He felt that if he made or influenced departmental budget decisions, he would be unable to function as an arbitrator for any disputes that might arise. He defined his role as reviewing, approving, and transmitting to the district office the allocation decisions made by the school staff. The principal was prepared to lobby the district office for additional funds beyond the school's original allocation if he felt that the requests were justified.

Supply and Equipment Allocations

The per student amounts allocated to supplies and equipment varied substantially among departments. Table 6.2 (next page) presents the allocation amounts for each school. The academic departments received very small amounts on a per student basis, whereas the nonacademic departments, in some cases, were allocated very large amounts. Only science among the academic areas had an allocation averaging over $5.00 per student, but the average of nonacademic departments was almost $30.00 per student, and the industrial arts department in Advance High School had an allocation of $93.54 per student. The large differences among the dollar-per-student amounts for academic and nonacademic depart-

Table 6.2.
Supply and Equipment Allocation
per Student-Period by Department

Department	Advance	Bridge	Central	Delegate
Academic				
Social Studies	$3.45	$1.93	$1.99	$4.50
Mathematics	$3.19	$1.96	$0.86	$1.97
Science	$14.26	$15.51	$6.37	$19.06
Foreign Language	$3.98	$6.14	$1.19	$5.64
Language Arts	$3.72	$4.14	$2.42	$10.94
Academic Average	$5.70	$5.94	$2.55	$8.42
Nonacademic				
Physical Education	$18.93	$12.62	$4.07	$8.41
Arts & Crafts	$23.51	$36.86	$14.47	$31.65
Health	$3.42	$14.16	$2.61	$4.14
Business Education	$19.51	$28.19	$5.01	$24.24
Music & Drama	$23.64	$41.11	$25.49	$69.55
Homemaking	$49.64	$40.83	$37.95	$42.75
Industrial Arts	$93.54	$65.17	$28.19	$64.03
Nonacademic Average	$33.17	$34.13	$16.83	$34.97
Support Units				
Counseling	$4.31	$0.78	$0.53	$2.03
Testing	$1.09	$0.26	$0.00	$1.03
Library	$4.56	$0.94	$0.91	$4.34
Audiovisual	$7.20	$7.02	$2.67	$11.81
Office of Principal	$15.05	$6.01	$16.55	$23.21
Support Total	$32.21	$15.01	$20.66	$42.42
Schoolwide Items				
Textbooks	$23.94	$35.48	$29.21	$23.01
Library books	$8.27	$5.73	$4.87	$14.11
Reference books	$2.59	$2.45	$1.13	$0.00
Periodicals	$2.20	$1.99	$4.98	$2.16
Computer	$12.64	$20.77	$24.53	$23.07
Schoolwide Total	$49.64	$66.42	$64.72	$62.35
School Average	$144.16	$149.86	$122.00	$220.41

ments were commented upon during several of the high schools' budgeting processes, primarily by members of departments with low allocations.

There were logical reasons for these disparities. Allocations to departments were made for dollar amounts; the dollar-per-student amounts (which were calculated for this analysis) had relatively little, if any, impact on the allocation decisions. Academic departments relied heavily on textbooks as a teaching device, and these were included in a schoolwide textbook allocation, not in their departmental allocation. Nonacademic departments had a greater use of consumable materials and expensive equipment in their operation, which required higher allocations. Finally, academic departments tended to have high enrollments, which reduced the per student costs, whereas some of the nonacademic departments had relatively low enrollments, which increased their per student costs.

Equipment requests received the greatest scrutiny in the process. Each specific piece of equipment required justification to be included in the budget; this was the case whether it was a formal written justification (Delegate High School) or a verbal explanation (Advance and Bridge High Schools). Justifications tended to be of the "needed for teaching," "to replace a broken unit," or "to modernize our equipment" variety. The orientation was to the needs of teachers in the instructional process, not to the results that were anticipated to be achieved.

Historical Influences and Stability

The personnel allocation decisions represented a strong commitment to the maintenance of existing programs and staff. Administrators preferred "to handle long term attrition through retirements and resignations." If this was not possible, a variety of short-term strategies were described to minimize the impact on the teachers affected: shifting teachers to related classes (for example, from Woods to Metals in Industrial Arts); part-time supervision of work-study students; transfers between schools. In Delegate High School the principal's reluctance to disrupt teachers' lives and careers through involuntary changes led to imbalances between student enrollments and departmental staffing. Seventy-five students who had registered to take foreign language classes were turned away because of too few class sections. The principal commented that although "many colleges strongly recommended a foreign language in high school, students don't really have to have it to go on to college. It's not really necessary." He felt that these courses were really electives, and the benefits to students were not worth the personal cost to the teacher in the industrial arts department whose position would have been reduced to increase the staff allocation in the foreign language department.

Past allocations to individual high school departments played a large part in determining the new allocations for the budget year in all four schools. In Advance High School a printout of the prior two years' supply and equipment allocations by department was given to each department head and was used repeatedly during the budget allocation meeting as a reference point to judge current budget requests. "What did they get last year?" was a frequent comment during their budget meeting. With the centralized organizational structure, the assistant principal in Central High School worked from the current departmental allocation amounts listing in preparing the distribution of supply monies for the upcoming year. The general tendency in all four high schools was to adjust departmental supply allocations upward by the percentage increase in the school's allocation from the district. However, the most-recent actual expenditures were compared to that year's allocation amount in an attempt to correct discrepancies that may have crept into the system.

CONCLUSIONS

Student Outcomes

Student outcomes were not explicitly considered in the resource allocation process of any of the four high schools studied. Neither administrators nor faculty made decisions (or even comments) that were based on allocating or reallocating personnel, supplies, or equipment in order to improve student achievement (as indicated by higher test scores) or any other explicit student outcomes. There was no mention made in any of the interviews, budget meetings, or documents of a connection between resource allocation policies, decisions, or alternatives and student outcomes.

The inescapable conclusion is that administrators and teachers in the high schools studied did not operate in accordance with the fundamental assumption of the rational model. Their actions and decisions were not based on improving student outcomes. In fact, they knew only very generally what student outcomes were in their schools. Statewide testing of selected grades provided some standardized results for some of the students, but this information was not used to direct resources to areas of need during the budgeting process.

There are several possible explanations for this inattention to student outcomes and the apparent failure of a rational model approach to explain resource allocation decisions in high schools. The first, and most obvious, is that the objectives of the high school administrators and teachers were not student-outcome oriented. They did not pay direct attention to student achievement because other motivations and incentives were more important to them. What these might be are explored through the other behavior models discussed later in this section.

Another explanation could be the lack of necessary knowledge that would enable administrators and teachers to predict the relationship between inputs and outputs in education. If administrators could not "optimize" the educational outputs as required by the rational model, those operating in accord with its general tenets could be expected at least to "satisfice" by seeking to achieve adequate, not necessarily optimal, student results (Allison, 1970, p. 72). Even this lesser standard was not attempted.

Another reason for the inattention paid to student outcomes by administrators and teachers could be the corresponding lack of public interest in specific school results. Without a clear signal from their clients (parents and students) that outcomes are important, school personnel have little incentive to attempt improvement (and risk internal conflict or public failure) in this difficult area. In fact, it has been argued that "if there were clearer evaluative criteria for schools (brought about when like-minded consumers had an opportunity to choose their preferences), this would lead to more responsive employee behavior" (Cibulka, 1987, pp. 23–24).

However, even without public pressure for attention to student outcomes, it is possible that administrators and teachers as professionals could (or even should) be expected to make decisions in the best interests of their clients (students). In these high schools, there appeared to be no internalized professional norms that would highlight student outcomes in budgetary decision making.

Process Orientation

In spite of the lack of attention paid to specific student outcomes, participants did believe that resource allocation decisions and the items purchased as a result were important in the educational process. The budget decisions and resource allocation choices for supplies and equipment were made to meet teachers' instructional needs rather than to be student-outcome oriented.

"We need these new microscopes for our biology class. The old ones are worn out."

"In order to function, the teachers in the social studies department must have a working typewriter."

"This is the third year in a row that this teacher has requested a new [science instrument]. She'll be furious if it's turned down again."

Even though faculty and student handbooks in three of the four schools contained specific educational goals for students (academic, social, and personal) and school personnel from all schools verbally supported these goals, there were no measures utilized to link resource allocation alternatives with program results. Indeed, the idea of this type of assessment was not even considered. Although administrators and teachers subscribed to the general goals of the district and school, the connection between teaching assignments or supply and equipment allocations to each department and student achievement was more of a generalized feeling, an intuitive calculus about what was needed. As one vice principal said, "We hire good people and turn them loose to do their things."

Organizational Approaches

Both centralized and decentralized approaches to resource allocation were utilized by the high schools in the study. The choice of approach seemed to be determined by the organizational relationships between the district office and school, the principal's beliefs of the appropriateness (or inappropriateness) of sharing resource allocation decisions, and the abilities and expectations of the faculty.

The participatory approaches used in Advance and Bridge High Schools were implementations of explicit strategies by the principals to increase shared decision making between administrators and teachers. More points of view could be presented, and more individual and group interests were represented. They were deliberately open processes; all participants were party to the decisions that were made, and no special deals favoring a single department were cut. Further, they were processes that shared internal accountability for the resource allocation decisions made for the schools. Department heads (who were teachers) and administrators were jointly responsible for distributing the resources provided by the district. However, all of those participating were school personnel; no students, parents, or anyone outside the school faculty were involved.

The centralized decision-making process, represented in Central High School, provided school administrators with stronger control over the manner in which resources were distributed. The amount of time school staff spent on budget matters was greatly reduced, and the process was more efficient in that sense. However, even with input from department heads, the decisions were primarily those of a single administrator. The forum for reaching resource allocation decisions was much more limited, and the range of possibilities considered was probably narrower.

The intermediate approach, utilized in Delegate High School, was designed to remove the principal and assistant principals from resource allocation decisions. The decision-making process was viewed as a mechanical and educationally unimportant function with the potential for creating ill feelings among faculty members whose budget requests were reduced or denied.

Basis for Resource Allocation Decisions

Historical and Incremental. High school budget decisions were strongly influenced by historical expenditure patterns. Current-year personnel allocations and supply and equipment amounts were generally the starting point for the next year's allocations. All schools exhibited a substantial tendency to stability and continuation of existing programs and an avoidance of radical shifts.

As a result, personnel and supply allocations followed an incremental budgeting pattern; the base was by and large secure, and changes in allocations, even for cause, were at the margin. Changes in departmental allocations of personnel or supply dollars (beyond an adjustment for inflation) required justification to modify the status quo. Shifts in enrollment, addition of a new section or course, and modification in state graduation requirements were the types of events that caused modifications in previous allocations. With a few exceptions, the causes were external to the high school administrators and faculty and not internally generated.

Equality. The distribution of personnel resulted in similar teaching loads across departments within each of the four high schools. This was a result of the principals' choices; state regulations did not specify class sizes, nor were such provisions present in any of the districts' collective bargaining agreements. The basis for this allocation was more a consideration of equal treatment of teachers rather than of the educational needs of students or of appropriate pedagogy. Even in the one case when there was some differentiation of number of class assignments between teachers of academic and nonacademic subjects, this was balanced by an equal total number of students. Administrators, who made the personnel allocation decisions, practiced a standard of equality for their teachers based on workload and designed to treat all teachers in a similar fashion.

Supply and equipment allocations superficially violated the equality principle for resource distribution. However, the dollar amounts appeared to reflect differences in supply and equipment requirements among departments. Even this rationale, however, focused on inputs to the educational process; no linkage with student outcomes was considered.

Overall, the impression was that the allocation process functioned to provide something for everyone. The amount or type of item varied from department to department, but every teacher and administrator received more or less what the decision makers believed to be a fair share.

Efficiency. Personnel allocations were largely enrollment driven; principals used target class sizes, anticipated student enrollments, and graduation requirements to make their decisions. As noted before, the changes in personnel allocations were generally marginal and did not alter personnel allocations abruptly. However, low-enrollment classes, unless balanced with higher-enrollment classes, were very expensive and threatened the equality of teacher workload.

Educational Priorities. Overall, there appeared to be some match among the perceived needs of the students in each of the high schools, the direction of the curriculum, and the resources allocated to departments. Advance and Bridge High Schools had higher percentages of college-bound students and wider academic curriculum offerings, particularly in the foreign languages and mathematics areas. Both of these schools had instituted changes in the course offerings and personnel allocations away from industrial arts to academic areas.

Central and Delegate High Schools, which had fewer students who were planning to attend college, had higher enrollments in business and industrial arts programs with resource allocations to match. These principals were more concerned about maintaining a wide range of course offerings to serve all their students. "[Delegate] is a comprehensive high school, meant to serve the needs of all students, not just the upper 10 percent."

Internal Bargaining. Throughout the processes there were numerous examples of bargaining among personnel in the resource allocation decisions. In the high schools that used group processes for decision making (Advance, Bridge, and, to a lesser degree, Delegate), explicit trade-offs between departments occurred, negotiations were common, and a variety of accommodations were made. For example, at the general budget meeting in Advance High School the mathematics department successfully argued for several more microcomputers for student and faculty use, whereas the drama department's request for a new sound system was delayed for a year. On the other hand, the same group approved an expensive optical scanner for attendance reporting ahead of competing academic requests because of the administrative needs (absences reported two to four days late and inability to identify class cutting) and teacher benefits (reduced attendance reporting requirements). At Central High School the direct individual discussions between the assistant principal and each department head were negotiating sessions in which the department head had to bargain for an increase if a greater allocation was desired.

Which Model Is Appropriate?

Resource allocation in the high schools studied did not operate according to a rational model. School personnel were not attempting to maximize some measure of student outcomes, such as test scores. The possibility of linking distribution of resources to improving student achievement was never considered explicitly. No evidence was found that the use of any consistent achievement measures to provide information for decision making had been contemplated.

Much of the behavior of the participants in the resource allocation process can be explained by the bureaucratic organization model. Current allocations for both personnel and nonpersonnel were based on past allocations, and any changes were incremental. Standard operating procedures guided decisions in modifying personnel allocations; these were based on enrollments, minimum class sizes, and teacher workloads.

In and of itself this finding is not surprising. Many public organizations, such as schools, have been studied as bureaucratic organizations with similar conclusions (Herriot & Firestone, 1984). However, although the bureaucratic organization model explains *how* these high schools operated, it does not explain *why* they functioned as they did. What is it about the structure and organization of these high schools that permitted such disregard for their formal goals of student achievement when allocating resources essential to achieving these goals?

An answer is found in the public choice model. School personnel are so loosely connected with and unaccountable for the outcomes of schooling that other, more-personal objectives replaced student outcomes in the resource allocation process.

The primary objective of the allocation process in the four high schools examined was equality among teachers in workload and in the teachers' self-declared needs for instructional supplies and equipment. In each school the allocation process worked differently but functioned to distribute resources in such a way as to minimize conflicts among school personnel and to establish a perception of fairness among teachers. Similar to Mann (1981), this analysis found that "the current procedures for resource allocation at the building level have more to do with the equitability of adult working conditions than with the production of responsive learning environments for children" (p. 4).

Explicit attention to student outcomes as required by the rational model might have necessitated differential treatment of teachers and could have disrupted the internal harmony achieved by equal treatment. The combination of the bureaucratic organization model (to explain how) and the public choice model (to explain why) provides the most thorough explanation of the resource allocation process observed in these high schools.

REFERENCES

Allison, G. (1970). *Essence of decision: Explaining the Cuban missile crisis.* Boston: Little, Brown.

Boyd, W. (1982). The political economy of public schools. *Educational Administration Quarterly, 18,* 111-130.

Cibulka, J. (1987). Theories of educational budgeting: Lessons from management of decline. *Educational Administration Quarterly, 23,* 7-40.

Edmonds, R. (1979). Effective schools for the urban poor. *Educational Leadership, 37*(1), 15–24.

Hack, W., Candoli, I. C., & Ray, J. (1995). *School business administration: A planning approach,* 5th ed. Boston: Allyn and Bacon.

Hanushek, E. A. (1986). The economics of schooling: Production and efficiency in public schools. *Journal of Economic Literature, 24,* 1141-1177.

Hanushek, E. A. (1996). The quest for equalized mediocrity: School finance reform without consideration of school performance. In L. O. Picus & J. L. Wattenbarger (Eds.), *Where Does the Money Go? Resource Allocation in Elementary and Secondary Schools.* Thousand Oaks, Calif.: Corwin Press.

Hartman, W. T. (1985). *Resource allocation in high schools.* Eugene, Ore.: University of Oregon, Center for Educational Policy and Management.

Hartman, W. T. (1989). Participatory budgeting in high school. *Planning and Changing, 20*(1), 15–25.

Herriot, R. E., & Firestone, W. A. (1984). Two images of schools as organizations: A refinement and elaboration. *Educational Administration Quarterly, 20,* 41–57.

Hoy, W. K., & Tarter, C. J. (1995). *Administrators solving the problems of practice: Decision-making concepts, cases, and consequences.* Boston: Allyn and Bacon.

Johnson, H. (1982). *Planning and financial management for the school principal.* New York: Teachers College Press.

Kirst, M. (1975, April). The rise and fall of PPBS in California. *Phi Delta Kappan 56,* 535–538.

Lee, R. D., & Johnson, R. W. (1977). *Public budgeting systems.* Baltimore, Md.: University Park Press.

Levin, H. M. (1971). Effect of different levels of expenditure on educational output. In R. L. Johns et al. (Eds.), *Economic Factors Affecting the Financing of Education,* Vol. 2, 173-206. Gainesville, Fla.: National Educational Finance Project.

MacKenzie, D. (1983). Research for school improvement: An appraisal of some recent trends. *Educational Researcher*, no. 12, 5–17.

Mann, D. (1981). *Education policy analysis and the rent-a-troika business.* Paper presented at the American Educational Research Association Annual Meeting, April, Los Angeles.

Michaelsen, J. (1977). Revision, bureaucracy, and school reform: A critique of Katz. *School Review, 85,* 229-246.

Mundt, B., Olsen, R., & Steinberg, H. (1982). *Managing public resources.* Peat Marwick International.

Murphy, J., Hallinger, P., & Mesa, R. (1985). School effectiveness: Checking progress and assumptions and developing a role for state and federal government. *Teachers College Record, 86,* 615-641.

Phyrr, P. (1973). *Zero-base budgeting.* New York: John Wiley and Sons.

Purkey, S., & Smith, M. (1982). To soon to cheer? Synthesis of research on effective schools. *Educational Researcher*, no. 40, 64–69.

Rosenholtz, S. J. (1985). Effective schools: Interpreting the evidence. *American Journal of Education, 93,* 352–388.

Thompson, D. C., Wood, R. C., & Honeyman, D. S. (1994). *Fiscal leadership for schools: Concepts and practices.* White Plains, N.Y.: Longman.

van Geel, T. (1973). PPBES and district resource allocation. *Administrators Notebook, 22,* 1-4.

Wildavsky, A. (1986). *Budgeting: A comparative theory of budgeting processes,* Rev. ed. New Brunswick, N.J.: Transaction Books.

7

Allocation and Distribution of Resources in High Schools

M. Barbara Sartori

To achieve educational excellence in the 1990s and beyond, demands continue to be placed on educators to increase productivity and accountability (Boyd and Hartman, 1988). Effective schools literature suggests that improvement of student outcomes should be the focus for a more productive educational process. Educational administrators should be expected to be accountable for the results produced within their schools. Although constrained by many factors, resource allocation and distribution decisions offer administrators an important means by which productivity can be improved. With calls for restructuring and decentralization, an examination of resource strategies and practices utilized in education is essential.

The primary purpose of this study was to examine "how" and "why" resources are distributed, that is, both the process of distributing resources in high schools and the objectives of these distribution decisions. The high school budget was the vehicle in this study for determining resource distribution. Throughout the budget, available resources were distributed among instructional, support, and administrative units. Distribution among these various units forced choices among alternatives competing for limited resources. Budgetary decisions required educators to select which resources were going to be provided to which programs.

Three distinct decision-making models were utilized to interpret both the behaviors and attitudes of personnel involved in the budget process in high schools. The rational (objective problem solving) approach assumes the use of formal goals and objectives and production function analysis in the decisions that evolve in the budget process. The bureaucratic decision-making model focuses on the rules, regulations, and "top-down" structure of the organization, leading to the use of the incremental budget process. The political decision-making model (subjective problem solving) examines "power" and the dominant effect goal displacement can have in the budgetary process. These three models were the basis for analyzing and understanding the decision-making processes of central administration and building-level educators.

In this research three primary issues were examined:

1. Process of resource allocation from central administration into the high school building
2. Process of resource distribution within the high school building
3. Analysis of which decision-making model or models best explain these distribution behaviors

ALTERNATIVE MODELS FOR DECISION MAKING

The Rational Decision-Making Model

The rational decision-making model is an objective, logical, definitive method for making decisions. The criteria for making decisions in the educational realm involve the use of goals and objectives specifically oriented toward the improvement of student achievement. Cibulka (1987) discusses the rational model as emphasizing that the internal organizational processes and structures are determinative and that the "organizational behavior has both a purpose and a deliberate set of goals and objectives from which to function; ends are carefully identified by decision makers, means are selected and weighed according to their costs and benefits, and so on" (p. 9).

An additional assumption of the rational approach is that resource allocations are understood and distributed in the most efficient and effective way, which assumes that the primary persons responsible for resource allocations and distribution possess knowledge of the needed combinations of various inputs (cognitive and/or affective learning). The prioritization of goals, the decisions dealing with costs and benefits, and an evaluation of program results are all necessary within the framework of the rational decision-making model (Cibulka, 1987, p. 10–12).

In order to determine if resources are being allocated and distributed in a rational manner, production function analysis can be utilized to determine which inputs produce the most-efficient and most-effective results. The production function approach relies on the assumption that the production process being assessed operates with what is called technical efficiency. Technical efficiency assumes that all people with discretion over production strive to produce the maximum level of output possible from a set of given inputs (Monk, 1981). An additional assumption of the technical efficiency is that all persons striving for outcomes attempt the pursuit of the same specific goals. However, various professionals within the educational system have different ideas regarding the inputs and outcomes of education. This multiplicity of goals contributes to one of the major criticisms of public education: that there are no clearly defined goals and objectives. Brown and Saks (1981) described schooling "as a process in which student time and teacher time are combined with other resources to produce an output called learning" (p. 219). The generality and vagueness of this statement illustrates the problem of applying specific production-type criteria to education. Consequently technical efficiency is difficult to accomplish in the educational realm.

The budgeting process includes prioritization of goals, weighing costs and benefits of alternative methods, and the evaluation of program results. These assumptions are built into PPBS or Planning-Programming-Budgeting System (Anthony and Herzlinger, 1980), Performance Budgeting (Mundt, Olsen, & Steinberg, 1982), and ZBB or Zero-Based Budgeting (Mundt, Olsen, & Steinberg, 1982).

Building principals making use of the rational decision-making model would have as a major goal the improvement of student learning. They would understand and seek to manipulate educational expenditures (inputs) to produce the best and the most efficient student learning (outputs). As was previously stated, the relationship between input and output in public education is difficult to define, but principals acting in accordance with the rational model make resource distribution choices that they, at least, believe will enhance student outcomes.

The Bureaucratic/Incremental Decision-Making Model

Marton, as quoted in Herriott and Firestone (1984), describes a bureaucracy "as a formally organized social structure with clearly defined patterns of activities on which, ideally, every series of actions is functionally related to the goals of the organization." The basic guidelines for the bureaucratic model of decision-making suggests that the organization makes decisions based on rules and procedures (Gavin, 1984, p. 73). Because rules and regulations are the basis of the bureaucratic theory, decisions are based upon predetermined directives or simply "standard operating procedures." The predetermined set of rules does not allow for creativity or participative management.

> Bureaucratic decision-making may result in stability in the organization, with past decisions and activities determining future decisions and organizational actions. Bureaucratic decision-making may also result in the use of standard measures of performance as a means of evaluating efficiency and effectiveness. Either decision process tends to be highly structured and the consideration of alternative courses of action very limited. Investigating bureaucratic decision-making requires that decision outcomes be examined in relation to the previous operation (incrementalism) and in relation to the organization's use of standard measures of performance or activity. (Gavin, 1984, p. 74)

With incremental budgeting, the existing budget—the "base"— serves as the starting point.

> The base is the general expectation among the participants that programs will be carried on at close to the going level of expenditures, but it does not necessarily include all activities. It means establishing the expectation that the expenditure will continue, that it is accepted as part of what will be done, and, therefore, that it will not normally be subjected to intensive scrutiny. (Wildavsky, 1964, p. 17)

The base is then transformed into a new budget by making minimum changes in the existing levels of allocations.

In incremental budgeting, the major determining factor of the size and content of this year's budget is last year's budget. Most of the budget is a product of previous decisions. Generally, agreement on the budget can be obtained easier with the incremental approach than with any of the comprehensive approaches. "It is much easier to agree on the addition or retention of monies as opposed to deciding the value of maintaining or eliminating an entire program. Conflict is reduced by an incremental approach because the area open to dispute is reduced" (Wildavsky, 1964, p. 136).

Building principals using the incremental process would instruct department heads to take their budgets from the previous year and add a percentage to that budget. All department heads would receive the same percentage (for example, 5 percent or 10 percent) to add to the previous year's budget. There would be no favoritism, decisions would be equal, and conflict would be minimal.

THE POLITICAL DECISION-MAKING MODEL

The idea of politics playing an important part in budgetary decision making has received a great deal of attention. There are authors who contend that the terms "budget" and "politics" are almost synonymous. "Perhaps the 'study of budgeting' is just another expression for the 'study of politics' yet one cannot study everything at once, and the vantage point offered by concentration on budget decisions offers a useful and much neglected perspective from which to analyze the making of policy" (Wildavsky, 1961, p.190). Wildavsky's theory sees budgetary decisions as less than rational because they entail no clear delineation of ends, weighing of options, or selection of the best direction. Instead budgets reflect political realities (Wildavsky, 1964). This perspective argues that the political model describes the way budget decisions actually are made (Cibulka, 1987, p. 8).

The political elements involved in the decision-making process can be looked at from two different perspectives: the concept of "power" as the central element of the decision; or the public choice theory, which explains how "goal displacement" plays a large part in the determination of the budgetary process.

Dahl (1957) argues that power is the capability of one social actor to overcome resistance to achieve a desired result or objective (p. 210). Among the most significant forms of power are: authority; expertise; control of rewards; coercive power; and personal power (Bolman & Deal, 1985, p. 116). Bolman and Deal emphasize how the authority one possesses, if relied upon solely, often undermines their use of power: "They generate resistance and are outflanked, outmaneuvered . . . by individuals or groups who are more versatile in the exercise of multiple forms of power" (p. 117).

Conflict is seen as normal or customary in political organizations. Choices result from bargaining and compromise, and the resulting decision seldom reflects the complete preferences of any one person or group of persons. Political models of choice further presume that when preferences conflict, "the power of the various actors determines the outcomes of the decision process. Power is used to overcome the resistance of others and obtain one's way in the organization" (Pfeffer, 1981, p. 28).

Another concept considered in the political realm is the public choice theory. According to Boyd (1982), "the public choice theory assumes that rational, self-interested individuals try to maximize their own welfare (or benefits) within the context of the institutional or organizational reward structure they face" (p.113). The public choice approach is also concerned with "the action of individuals when they choose to accomplish purposes collectively rather than individually (Buchanan & Tullock, 1962, p. 13).

In a competitive environment, such as a profit-seeking corporation, there is an incentive structure that will encourage self-interested employees to engage in behaviors that will lead to the maximization of profits. Boyd explains how "this structure" necessitates satisfying customers, thereby presumably achieving (or at any rate approaching) the organization's announced goals. A public school system, on the other hand, is non-profit seeking, and the announced goal is the production of student learning (Boyd, 1982, p. 114). The school's budget does not come from satisfying customers or producing more sales, but from the public arena. The budget must satisfy politicians, not satisfy customers (Michaelsen, 1977).

Niskanen (1971), Michaelsen (1977), and Boyd (1982) discuss how there is really no mechanism to "harness their self-seeking to the public interest." With multiple and often conflicting goals, administrators and teachers must select and interpret for themselves organizational goals and the connection these goals have to the public good. As a result, the official goals of the organization can be displaced by the unofficial or personal goals of employees. In the political decision-making model, decisions are seen as arrived at either by political power (persuasion or influence) of some individuals or groups over that of others or by employee collective choice based on self-interest, which in the non-profit organization is likely to lead to goal-displacement (that is, the official goals of the organization are displaced by the unofficial or personal goals of employees).

Both political power and collective choice in nonprofit organizations, such as schools, lead to goal displacement, but the latter dynamic is especially likely to produce systematic goal displacement in which adult (employee) welfare concerns take precedence over student learning.

METHODOLOGY

In order to determine which decision-making models and objectives were used by high school personnel as resource allocations were distributed throughout the high school budget, the exploratory case study gathered data through interviews with actual participants of the process, by attendance at various budgetary meetings from the building level to the school board level, and by collecting pertinent documentation (school district budgets, high school building budgets, memos, instruction sheets, and so on). Three school districts in southeastern Pennsylvania agreed to participate in this case study. One school district has two high schools, and the other two districts each have one high school. The participating high schools exemplified a range of characteristics appropriate for this study: budget processes ranging from centralized to participative; high schools having the same grade composition (10–12); and building principals who have held such a position for at least three years. Even though the size of the student body was not a criterion for consideration, the high school student body ranged from 1,150 to 2,269 per building. The high schools chosen for the study were found in suburban public school districts that were located in predominantly white and middle- to upper-middle-class communities. For purposes of this study the high schools were given fictitious names. Anderson and Stanley are from the same school district; Palmer and Meyers are the only high schools within their districts.

The study began with the initial stages of budget preparation at the district level (in late fall) and carried through the final stages of school board adoption. According to the laws of the Commonwealth of Pennsylvania, school district budgets were to be adopted every year by June 30.

Interviews began with central office administrators (superintendents, assistant superintendents, business managers, personnel directors, and subject area supervisors), followed by building-level personnel (principals, assistant principals, and four to five department heads, of which at least two were within the major subject areas, and two were from the minor subject areas). Decision-making processes used by central administrators provided the context for understanding the decision-making models within the high school buildings. Forty interviews were conducted, with each interview lasting forty-five minutes to an hour.

Once all interviews and budget meetings and hearings were completed and the budget approved for the 1988–89 school year, the researcher organized and analyzed the data. A data categorization scheme was developed from which all information was divided into descriptive and analytical, and then into allocation and distribution of nonpersonnel and personnel resources. The researcher went through every transcribed interview and identified responses by data category. Any responses that indicated the existence of one or more of the decision-making models were separately noted. Answers in each section were summarized and written down for each interview and then aggregated for all respondents.

Because interviews were not the only method of data collection, the information gathered from meetings, memos, and observation was reviewed in similar fashion and added to the data from the interview questions. After all the information was collected and combined in similar groupings, then the researcher determined appropriate data necessary for reporting in the study. Conclusions were drawn from all these data as to whether decision-making models used by high school personnel were classified as either rational, bureaucratic, political, or a combination of these models. The results that were primarily qualitative were provided in a narrative form. Descriptive information was used to compare characteristics of different school districts.

FINDINGS

For purposes of this study the term "allocations" referred to the total resource amounts that were issued to each building. The term "distribution" referred to the actual disbursement of these resources throughout the various budget categories.

District Allocations for Nonpersonnel Resources

Resource allocations for nonpersonnel items (consumables, textbooks, new equipment, conferences, principal office supplies, and library books/supplies) were allocated to all four high school buildings on a per pupil allocation. This allocation was what the principal received to create the building budget for the following academic year. Among the high schools, differences in allocation basically dealt with nonpersonnel items the building principal was to include in the building budget, the amount of dollars included in the per pupil allocation, when the dollar amounts were determined, and lump sum allocations as opposed to specific categorical allocations.

In each of the high schools, this allocation was based on an incremental increase over the previous year's budget. Anderson, Stanley, and Palmer received a 5 percent increase, and Meyers received a 10 percent increase. Because the enrollment at the high school level at all four of the high schools was declining, and the percentage increase was based upon the present number of students, the actual dollar increase ranged from 0.3 percent at Anderson to 7.5 percent at Meyers.

Principals in each of the four schools had minimal input into the allocation process. Categories included in the per pupil allocation ranged from five to seven items, with new equipment included in the per pupil allocation at Anderson and Stanley. Replacement equipment and new textbooks for all four high schools were separate line items in the budget and purchased through district funds. At Anderson and Stanley, conference money was to be budgeted in the per pupil allocation, whereas at Palmer conference money came from district funds and at Meyers conference money was budgeted with the assistant superintendent.

How Nonpersonnel Resources Were Distributed within High School Buildings

Anderson High School's distribution of resources within the high school budget was completed by the principal himself. There was little, if any, input from any of the interviewed staff as to the actual distribution of resources. In the middle of November the building principal distributed a memo to all department heads with all information needed for the completion of their budgets. The per pupil allocation for Anderson ($133,800) was not shared with department heads. Completed budgets were to be returned to the building principal the day Christmas vacation began, with the principal reviewing the budget over the holidays.

When the department heads returned from Christmas vacation, one of two things occurred: Either they received their budgets back from the principal with a note attached to cut a specified dollar amount from a certain category within their budget, or they received no note (which led them to believe that their budgets had been approved and there was no need for any cuts).

Because replacement equipment was not included in the per pupil allocation, the principal took all requests from every department and submitted them along with the per pupil portion of his budget. Initial requests for replacement equipment was $119,479. Central administration told the principal that cuts needed to be made; he went back to the department heads and asked them to prioritize and cut equipment. When he resubmitted requests for replacement equipment, his total was $39,259. This amount (about 38 percent of the original requests) was approved.

Stanley High School utilized a participative approach throughout the building budget. Toward the middle of November the building principal discussed the budget at a meeting with department heads and assistant principals. Information regarding the budget process, timelines, last year's budget, and total per pupil allocation ($139,000) was reviewed. As the principal indicated, "They [department heads] were asked to use as a guideline the figure their department had last year, plus 5%, and that is the allotment of money per department." Budgets were to be prepared by December 20 and turned into the principal or one of the assistant principals.

When the budgets were returned, the total amount requested exceeded the allocated amount. The principal constructed a chart of each department and all categories within the budget and indicated the dollar requests by department by category. On December 22 the principal, assistant principals, and the department heads met to discuss the budget; through a cooperative effort and two meetings, the requests were cut, and the budget was balanced at $139,000.

Replacement equipment was also not included in the per pupil allocation. Department heads were requested to list all replacement equipment needed for their departments (along with justification and rationale). The requests (which totaled $66,400) were sent to central administration. About the middle of April the principal received word to cut requests for replacement equipment. The principal then met with assistant principals and department heads, and together they cut back on replacement equipment. A list was resubmitted to central administration with totals now at $44,795. The resubmitted list was approved. The principal received about 70 percent of the original requests.

At Palmer High School the majority of the budget for nonpersonnel resources was coordinated and developed by one of the assistant principals. The process itself was found to be partially participative, with final decisions for the budget being made by the principal and the assistant principal. The assistant principal began the process in late October when an initial meeting was held with department heads, where all information necessary for budget completion was distributed. Budgets were to be compiled by the end of November, at which time they were to be turned into the assistant principal. There was no dollar figure given, and the per pupil allocation ($145,103) was not shared with the department heads. The principal wanted people to build their budgets based upon what they felt they needed.

Along with their budgets, department heads were asked to submit a prioritized list of new and replacement equipment. The principal and the assistant principal at Palmer made many decisions (especially about new and replacement equipment) in terms of five-year plans. Each department head was expected to produce a five-year plan for new and replacement equipment. Department heads were also reminded about the Five Year Cycle, which identified any curricular area in the first year of the cycle (Goal 1) that was to review the curriculum and order new textbooks. If department heads failed to do this, they would have to wait another five years (until they were back at Goal 1) to order new textbooks.

During December the principal and the assistant principal met with each department head for fifteen to twenty minutes. Each department head was expected to be able to justify any requests in that budget. After the meetings were completed, the principal and the assistant principal sat together and made decisions as to where the actual per pupil allocation would be distributed. After the per pupil portion of the budget was balanced and equipment identified, the principal presented his budget to the Director of Secondary Education. Requests for new equipment ($68,667) and replacement equipment ($84,665), totaled $153,332. The principal was proud of the fact that he received his total requests and that there were no cuts to be made.

At Meyers High School the building budget was divided into various stages with different rules for different areas under consideration. A participative approach to the budgetary process was evident. In November the principal began the capital outlay portion of the budget. Department heads, assistant principals, and the principal met, and each was to indicate all new and replacement equipment necessary, plus items were to be prioritized. When all the information was returned to the principal in January, he placed all the requested items on a list and forwarded the information to the business manager and the superintendent. Identifying new and replacement equipment was not an easy task because it included furnishing a seventeen-room addition then under construction.

Initially the total amount for new equipment ($284,917) and replacement equipment ($81,020) was approved. Unfortunately, the school board altered their initial decision, and the new equipment amount needed to be cut back to $212,348. Together the principal and the department heads looked at the prioritized equipment list and made decisions together as to what to cut. The principal eventually received about 74 percent of his original requests for new equipment. Replacement equipment was cut by the school board to $59,020, allowing for purchase of 73 percent of the original requests.

The per pupil allocation portion of the budget was allocated in the following manner. These amounts were based upon final board approval (which did not come until June):

	Per Pupil Allocation	Total Allocation
Consumable Supplies	$57.70	$66,125
Replacement Textbooks	$18.00	$20,700
Audiovisual	$10.00	$11,500
Library	$20.00	$23,000
Principal's Office	$11.50	$13,225
Total	$117.20	$134,550

The principal was to distribute resources according to the listed amounts. The resources were allocated in April, and the principal did not have to return any portion of this budget to central administration.

Audiovisual the library, and the principal's office merely prepared their budgets based upon these figures. The principal did not have any decisions in terms of these categories. When it came time for the consumable portion of the budget, the principal used a totally participative approach to the process. All the department heads, the assistant principals, and the principal met and were instructed to build their budgets according to their needs. There was also a curriculum cycle similar to Palmer's. As a result of the curriculum cycle, certain departments would have priority for resources. After the budgets were built, everyone met again, and it was determined that the requests exceeded the allocation. Together everyone decided where cuts would occur.

The following month the same process was used for replacement textbooks. In this instance the requests did not exceed the total allocation, so there was no need for cuts. As it turned out, there was $5,000 left to be encumbered for use in the second semester.

District Allocations for Personnel Resources

Instructional staff (FTEs) at all four high schools was based upon the number of courses selected by students for the following academic year. School boards established policies or guidelines for minimum and maximum class size, with some variations by district. Palmer's policy was a result of efforts by school board, administration, and teachers, and did allow more flexibility than others.

Staffing for guidance/counseling and nurses at all four high schools was generally based upon state recommended guidelines with all of the schools staffing toward the lower end of the recommendation. Administration at Anderson, Stanley, and Meyers was a result of "tradition" with no one being able to define exactly why the number of administrators assigned per building existed as it did. Palmer did not have a definite guideline for high school administrators, but the high school principal identified a need for an additional administrator and the school board authorized hiring an additional administrator.

Clerical staff at all four high schools was not a result of any identified rule, ratio, or rationale. The administrator who could convince the superintendent that there was a need for additional clerical help might receive the person. The only area where there were strict guidelines for assignment of educational aides was with special education.

How Personnel Resources Were Distributed within the High School Buildings

In all four high schools it was the principal's decision as to "who would go where and who would do what" after staff were assigned to the building. Distribution of instructional staff (FTEs) was accomplished almost the same within each high school. Principals asked department heads to provide them with recommended teaching assignments for each staff member and also an actual class schedule. The principals did not have to follow the recommendations of the department heads, but if possible the principals did try to accommodate these recommendations.

One of the most important aspects considered in the distribution of teaching assignments was the issue of equity. Teacher contracts indicated how many classes teachers were allowed to teach; maximum number of students per class was set by recommended board policies. Additional factors affecting distribution of staff were the master schedule, nonteaching assignments, coaching responsibilities, seniority among staff, certification, assignment of part-time staff, and personal requests.

Because assignments of teaching staff were based upon student requests, the largest concentration of FTEs was in the academic area and the smallest in the nonacademic areas. Noninstructional staff (nurses, guidance/counseling, and the librarian) were allocated by central administration for placement within the buildings. Clerical staff was allocated by central administration, and the principal distributed them among administration, guidance, the library, audiovisual, and special education.

DECISION MAKING USED IN THE DISTRIBUTION OF RESOURCES

Nonpersonnel Resources

After information was collected as to how the budget process operated, the next step was to examine why decisions were made as they were. The decision-making models used to evaluate the study were rational (objective problem solving), bureaucratic (rules, regulations, and incrementalism), and political (power or collective choice).

The primary motivating factor that functioned at Anderson was the political decision-making model. The principal had total control of the process and made all decisions as to distribution of resources. He expressed a concern for fairness and equity among the curricular departments, but the interviewed department heads did not share his view. For the most part, when taken collectively, there was equality among the major areas and the minor areas, but if taken by individual areas this was not the case. The building principal wanted to build a budget that would distribute the per pupil portion of the budget without creating dissension among the teachers or have central administration question his distribution of funds.

It appeared that the principal wanted to make all the decisions and felt, as building principal, that he had the right to make these decisions. In addition he had many tasks that needed to be completed, and the completion of the budget was another task. There were no incremental changes across the board, and there did not appear to be any specific objective criteria for decisions. He did what he wanted to do with the allocation. There were no expectations for results of the spending, and because the principal felt that there was "only 10 percent of the budget which could be used in a creative manner," he would be the one to make the decisions, based on his assessment of "whose turn it might be" to receive more of the allocated resources.

At Stanley the decision-making model demonstrating the most evidence was the bureaucratic/incremental. The principal at Stanley instructed department heads to add 5 percent to last year's budget.

Department heads took the indicated 5 percent and created their budgets. There was no conflict, and the interviewed department heads felt that they were treated fairly and equally. The combination of the participative and the incremental approaches enabled the participants to be satisfied with the results. Even though the process was satisfactory for all concerned, there was no discussion as to the results of resource spending or improvement of student outcomes/learning.

Budgets were to be built on a 5 percent increase over last year, but in actuality there was only a 0.3 percent increase in actual dollars. As a result there was a need for cuts to be made because the totals were well over the allotment. Together everyone helped make decisions to balance the budget. If a department head was asked to justify a certain request and could do so to the satisfaction of everyone, the item would remain in the budget. If the reason for the request was "not good enough," cuts would have to be made. The principal did indicate that "together we will make decisions as to where the cuts will occur, but if need be I have the final say."

When looking at the decision making used at Palmer, one of the obvious differences from Anderson and Stanley was that goals and objectives were recognized and played a major part in the budget process. The goals were divided into six areas (staff development, curriculum development, student development, employee relations, community relations, and facilities management), with curriculum development having the greatest budgetary implications. However, even though goals and objectives were evident, the improvement of student learning was not one of the stated goals.

The building principal offered all the department heads equal opportunity to the budget allotment. The principal expected department heads to be able to justify requests in a logical, well-planned manner. After all department heads had the opportunity to present their budgets, the principal and the assistant principal made decisions as to who would receive what based upon all the presentations. Consequently, the end result would favor the department who could "talk a better game."

After the budget decisions were made and the budget was presented to one of the central office staff, the process continued. "If the principal is a good salesman he can get what he wants. The principal must convince the Director of Secondary Education and he in turn must convince the cabinet." Politics was evident in the central office as well as the high school building.

Bureaucratic/incrementalism was seen to a lesser degree. Goal 1 of the curriculum cycle indicated that there were certain rules and regulations that the principal needed to consider as the budget was being prepared. Curricular areas in Goal 1 were to be given budgetary priority for curriculum review and purchase of new textbooks, whether there was a need or not. Every five years the curriculum was reviewed, yet student outcomes was not a part of the review. The principal did indicate that audiovisual was not to exceed more than 5 percent over the previous year's budget, indicating there was one category within the budget where incrementalism was utilized.

For the most part the principal wanted to build a budget that was representative of the needs and the wants of department heads. The principal's attitudes and answers indicated his interest in doing what was best for the students. He also believed his department heads should obtain what was best for their students by planning, preparing, and justifying needs. The department heads who prepared the best would obtain results.

Meyers High School's budget was mostly controlled and directed by the central administration. Rules and regulations were established by central administration for the actual dollar figures awarded in each of the five categories within the budget. This process did not allow much decision making by the principal. Most of the decisions he had to make relative to the budget were confined to capital outlay, consumables, and replacement textbooks. Anderson, Stanley, and Palmer principals needed to make decisions as to equalization of the resources among the noninstructional and the instructional areas of the budget, whereas the Meyers principal did not. The bureaucratic model was very evident throughout the budgetary process in this school.

When there was need to make cuts in the capital outlay and consumable portions of the budget, the principal sought input from all the department heads to decide how and why items would be cut or not cut. Capital outlay reductions involved searching priorities and together deciding what to cut to arrive at a lower figure. When it came to the consumable budget, even though everyone met to decide how to make cuts, the principal had an idea as to where the cuts would occur. Although the principal indicated that there was a totally cooperative approach to the process, he also indicated, "I have one more vote if need be." He anticipated that department heads would add a percentage from last year's budget to this year's budget. He could almost determine where requests were excessive, while at the same time accepting input and information from all department heads to decide how to cut the budget.

One of the goals and objecti/es of the district, a five-year curriculum cycle, played a part in budget decisions. Departments identified as "being up for review" would have priority in the budget. As with Palmer, the curriculum cycle was not based upon student outcomes.

Bureaucratic/incrementalism was evident from the central office down through the high school itself. Decision-making for capital outlay and consumables enabled a cooperative effort to arrive at the final figures, but the principal maintained the right to make final decisions. The principal wanted to prepare a budget that would best meet the needs of the school and still work under the rules and regulations set forth by the central administration.

Personnel Resources

Equality among instructional staff was the primary motivating factor for distribution of instructional personnel. The total number of classes taught, the total number of students taught by each teacher, and how many noninstructional duties each teacher assumed were the primary factors that each of the four high school principals tried to balance. When the principals made decisions as to who would teach what, they would try and follow recommendations of the department heads in order not to create conflict.

When actual instructional assignments were made, the principals considered many factors as the process unfolded. The building of the master schedule was one of the most important objectives the principal needed to accomplish. To build the master schedule, the principal needed to consider who requested what period for planning, who and where staff were needed for noninstructional duties, how many classes the department heads taught, what time of the day part-time instructors began or finished, and what requests the coaches had. All these requests were (in most cases) considered before the needs of the students. Principals tried to accommodate all requests and still schedule between 70 percent and 75 percent of all student requests. The football coach, who coached one of the best football teams in the country and requested to teach four classes first semester and have them in the morning, was always accommodated, regardless of what might best serve the academic needs of the students.

CONCLUSIONS

There were a variety of methods used for the distribution of nonpersonnel resources within the high school buildings. A centralized approach, partially participative, and a totally participative dominated the processes used by the principals in this study. At Anderson High School there was little communication, which resulted in confusion and resentment as to the distribution of resources, whereas at the other three high schools the interviewed participants were usually satisfied with the process—which found all the participants satisfied with not only the process but also the results.

The decision-making choices for the distribution of nonpersonnel resources, most evident at all four high schools, were either bureaucratic and/or political. Anderson was evident of a pervasive political approach, whereas Meyers represented a strong bureaucratic model. At Anderson the principal made all decisions without assistance from anyone else in the building. No one had any idea as to who did what or who received what. The principal felt there was really only 10 percent of the allocated resources allowing for creativity, and the distribution of this 10 percent was to be his choice. At Meyers there were very strict rules and regulations for every budget category. There was little flexibility and few decisions for the principal to make. Stanley and Palmer combined both the bureaucratic and political models.

Teaching positions were allocated to buildings based upon student course requests and school board policies for minimum and maximum students allowed per section or course. For the most part there was a very bureaucratic and in one district "a very mathematical approach to the assignment of staff." The student requests and the teacher contract represented the rules to be followed.

After the staff were assigned to the buildings, it was the province of the building principal to make actual teaching assignments. Many noneducational factors (noninstructional duties, coaching responsibilities, lunch duty coverage, and so on.) were considered as teaching assignments were decided. Even though there were many factors to be considered, the needs and the wants of the students did not receive primary consideration. Equality of teaching responsibilities, equality in number of student contacts per teacher, and equality of noninstructional assignments were of prime importance.

Whether distribution of nonpersonnel or personnel resources were evaluated, the end results indicated that decision making was either bureaucratic or political. The rational decision-making model was not evident in any of the decisions that had to be made. Improvement of student outcomes or student learning was not considered in any budgetary decisions. Principals in this study shared a desire to create a budget that would (to the best of their knowledge) most adequately meet the needs of the staff and their buildings. Process as opposed to product was the primary educational pursuit seen in these schools.

REFERENCES

Anthony, R. N., & Herzlinger, R. E. (1980). *Management control in non-profit organizations.* Homewood, Ill.: Richard D. Irwin.

Bolman, L. G., & Deal, T. E. (1985). *Modern approaches to understanding and managing organizations.* San Francisco, Calif.: Jossey-Bass Publishers.

Boyd, W. L. (1982). The political economy of public schools. *Educational Administration Quarterly, 18*(3), 111–130.

Boyd, W. L., & Hartman, W. T. (1988). The politics of educational productivity. In D. H. Monk & J. Underwood (Eds.), *Microlevel school finance: Issues and implications for policy.* Cambridge, Mass.: Ballinger.

Brown, B. W., & Saks, D. H. (1981). The microeconomics of schooling. *Review of Research in Education,* 217–252.

Buchanan, J. M., & Tullock, G. (1962). *The calculus of consent.* Ann Arbor: The University of Michigan Press.

Cibulka, J. G. (1987). Theories of education budgeting: Lessons from the management of decline. *Educational Administration Quarterly, 23*(1), 7–40.

Dahl, R. A. (1957). The concept of power. *Behavioral Science,* 201–215.

Gavin, T. J. (1984). *Departmental budget allocations and power in a community college.* Unpublished doctoral dissertation, University of Oregon, Eugene, Ore.

Herriott, R. E., & Firestone, W. A. (1984). Two images of schools as organizations: A refinement and elaboration. *Educational Administration Quarterly, 20*(4), 37–52.

Michaelsen, J. B. (1977). Revision, bureaucracy, and school reform: A critique of Katz. *School Review, 85,* 229–246.

Monk, D. H. (1981). Toward a multilevel perspective on the allocation of educational research. *Review of Educational Research, 51*(2), 215–226.

Mundt, B. M., Olsen, R. T., & Steinberg, H. I. (1982). *Managing public resources.* Peat Marwick International.

Niskanen, W. A., Jr. (1971). *Bureaucracy and representative government.* Chicago: Aldine-Atherton Publishing Company.

Pfeffer, J. (1981). *Power in organizations.* Marshfield, Mass.: Pitman Publishing, Inc.

Wildavsky, A. (1961). Political implications of budgetary reform. *Public Administration Quarterly, 21*(4), 183–190.

Wildavsky, A. (1964). *The politics of the budgetary process.* Boston, Mass.: Little, Brown and Company.

8

Transcending the Effects of School Size on the High School Curriculum

David H. Monk

INTRODUCTION

It is well known that enrollment levels of high schools are positively related to the discrete number of courses offered by high schools (Barker 1985; Fowler 1992; Haller et al. 1990; McKenzie 1989; Monk 1987; Monk and Haller 1993). It is less well known that this relationship is characterized by numerous exceptions such that some relatively small schools offer numbers of courses that rival the number offered by considerably larger schools. This "overlap" is troubling from a policy-making perspective because a commonly pursued means of expanding educational opportunities in communities served by small high schools are efforts to increase enrollments, usually by means of consolidating separately organized schools. The overlap suggests that there are means by which some small schools are able to offer a complement of courses similar to what is offered by larger schools without increasing their enrollment. The overlap also suggests that some larger schools are failing to take full advantage of whatever capability their size permits regarding the provision of a broader array of educational opportunities.

The analyses reported here are designed to show how high schools deploy resources for the purpose of offering courses. The focus of the inquiry is on the variation in curricular offerings that remains after the effects of high school size (as measured by enrollment) have been removed. The goal is to see how much of the remaining variation in numbers of discrete courses offered can be explained by largely exogenous community as well as by more endogenous school characteristics.

The assertion that decisions made by administrators and teachers within schools can transcend the constraining effects of school size and community characteristics on course offerings is important to this ongoing program of research into the microeconomics of curriculum development. The longer-term goal of the research is to assess the role administrative leadership plays in the formation of the high school curriculum. For now, the focus will be on individual administrative practices as well as on more-global measures of teacher dedication to their duties. As the research moves forward, more-explicit attention will be paid to the linkages across administrative and teacher decision making.

The balance of the chapter is divided into three sections. Attention turns first to a series of conceptual issues that influenced the selection of variables for the analysis. This is followed by a description of the data that were used and the results that were found. The chapter concludes with some tentative conclusions and some speculation over the implications for policy.

CONSTRAINTS ON THE OFFERING OF COURSES

High school curricular offerings vary for reasons stemming from two conceptually distinct sources. On the one hand there may be differences in the demands communities make on their schools for courses. One community may be very attentive to the academic portion of the curriculum and insist on seeing a broad range of courses, including advanced placement courses suited for college bound students. A second community may be much less interested in these courses and place a higher priority on courses that have more-immediate vocational implications. A third community may seek to offer as few different courses as possible on the grounds that the taxpayers' responsibility is to provide a common basic program for all students. In such a school, multiple sections of a relatively small number of courses would be the result.

On the other hand there are influences on curricular offerings that stem from supply conditions. These influences arise from constraints school officials encounter as they seek to provide course offerings. A good example of a supply-based constraint arises from the size of the school. As indicated earlier, high school size is related to curricular offerings, and the relationship is readily explained in economic terms.

In smaller high schools, diseconomies of scale are likely to be present. The resulting higher operating costs can generate downward pressure on the number of different courses that are offered. Even if two communities exerted the identical demands on their schools for additional courses, the expectation is that the smaller of the two schools would provide fewer discrete courses than would the larger.

Although this distinction is reasonably clear conceptually, in practice it is difficult to disentangle the effects of demand and supply on the decision to offer or not to offer courses. The impact of school size illustrates the difficulty, because school size may also be related to the demands and expectations a community has for its schools.

The strategy pursued here is to control statistically for the effects of both school size and selected community characteristics on curricular offerings. With these controls in place, the focus can be on the supply-related constraints administrators and teachers encounter as they seek to broaden or otherwise modify their curricular offerings. These supply-related influences warrant special scrutiny if for no other reason than the fact that constraints are more readily manipulable via public policy than are what may be deep-seated tastes and preferences for one or another type of education.

Characteristics of the Community

It is less than obvious that the average socioeconomic status of a community will have straightforward effects on the breadth of curricula found in the local high school. This is particularly true for general measures of curricular breadth that do not distinguish among types of courses offered. A relatively uneducated community that assigns a low priority to preparing students for postsecondary education may provide a wide array of vocationally oriented courses and as a result offer a relatively large number of discrete courses. In contrast a highly educated community that seeks to place its youth in colleges and universities may concentrate on a relatively small number of high-quality courses and appear to offer a curriculum of limited breadth. The vocationally oriented community may place a similarly high emphasis on the quality of its offerings rather than their breadth.

Measures of the diversity of a community's social and economic characteristics are more directly relevant to the breadth of course offerings. High schools in communities with a more varied mix of parents and taxpayers can be expected to feel more pressure for diversified course offerings. The degree to which this diversity translates into curricular breadth can be assessed empirically.

In addition, external labor market conditions can play an important role in curriculum building. To the extent that administrators have discretion over who they hire, they will be more able to meet demands for additional courses when labor markets are relatively large and populated by individuals with varied combinations of talent. The availability of a part-time teacher can make it possible to offer courses that would otherwise be impossible for a school. When labor markets are more limited, administrators will face an additional constraint in their efforts to staff additional courses that may be sought by the community.

Characteristics of the High School

Spending in the context of external labor market conditions. One means of overcoming the effects of low enrollment levels on curricular offerings is to spend at higher levels. There is nothing to prevent a very small high school from offering a full complement of even highly specialized courses if there is willingness to spend at a sufficiently high level. Hedonic wage theory holds that even the most-specialized and difficult-to-hire teaching resources can be attracted to the least-attractive school settings if the package of benefits is sufficiently generous (Antos and Rosen 1975).

However, increased curricular breadth is not the only outcome of high education spending levels. A school district may spend at high levels to raise the quality of existing offerings rather than to increase the range of courses in the curriculum.

Thus, although increased spending is one means of overcoming the constraining effects of size, it does not follow that spending more necessarily translates into an increased diversity of curricular offerings.

Internal resource allocation practices. Schools can enhance their course offerings to the degree that administrators have flexibility in making teacher assignments. One of the difficulties administrators face in small settings involves the sometimes awkward combinations of teaching talent needed to staff courses. In settings where part-time teachers are difficult to hire, administrators can be expected to desire flexibility in making teaching assignments. The idea is to avoid having to find teachers capable of teaching substantially different subject matters, and the presumption is that flexibility makes it easier for administrators to achieve this result. When flexibility is limited and when all else is equal, there will be less ability to offer a broad array of courses than when flexibility is greater.

There is an additional dimension of internal resource allocation that comes into play as soon as the focus shifts to more narrowly defined areas of the curriculum.[1] One means of enriching the offerings in one content area is to make do with a less rich offering in one or more other areas of the curriculum. In other words, trades can be made such that courses in one area are "financed" at the expense of courses in other areas. To the extent that trades along these lines are an important means of financing curricular offerings in the face of size-related constraints, there are potentially serious equity issues embedded in the impact of school size on educational opportunities. Some types of students may be bearing more of the cost of small school size than are others.

Commitments of professional staff. An additional means by which expanded curricular offerings may be financed involves the degree to which teachers and other educational professionals are willing to make an extra commitment to broadening the educational opportunities available within their respective schools. When teachers and others make this commitment, a possible result is a broadened, more diversified curriculum. In the absence of such a commitment, particular courses could be missing from the curriculum.

In such a setting, the teachers themselves can be viewed as the source of financing for the additional courses. The courses are available thanks to the additional commitment made by the teachers.[2] Their willingness to teach a course above and beyond what might otherwise be expected comes at some cost, and even though this cost may never appear within financial records, it is nevertheless real and has bearing on schooling processes.

DATA AND METHODOLOGY

The data for this study come from various files of the *High School and Beyond* surveys conducted by the U.S. Department of Education. These data, collected between 1980 and 1982, include the responses of administrators, teachers, and parents to questions about their schools and communities. Properly weighted, the 1,015 schools in the primary sample are representative of all public and private high schools in the United States in 1980.

The sample was narrowed to be more relevant to the policy issues examined here. In particular, all private schools, all specialized schools (those coded as vocational or intended specifically for the handicapped), and all schools that failed to provide curriculum data were eliminated. This left a total of 652 "standard" public United States high schools. From this sample, all four-year high schools (grades 9–12) were selected as a means of eliminating the effects of alternative grade structures on course offerings.[3] This yielded a sample of 352 schools.

However, not all of the high schools participated in all phases of the survey. In particular, the teacher and parent files involved a subset of the larger sample. As a consequence when variables coming from these files are used, the sample size drops considerably.

The dependent variables used throughout the analyses are the residuals that arise after various predictors are entered into ordinary least squares regression models. The analysis begins by regressing the number of unduplicated credits on high school size as measured by the size of the graduating class. Credit counts were selected because they capture full- as well as part-year course offerings. The credits are "unduplicated" in the sense that they measure unique courses. Multiple sections of the same course do not add to the number of unduplicated credits offered by a school.

The resulting residuals serve as the dependent variable in the following analyses where the effects of community characteristics are examined. The residuals of the community characteristics analyses are then used as the dependent variable in the analysis of school characteristics. The residuals produced by the school characteristics analyses are, in turn, used as the basis of the final analyses focused on the commitments of teachers.

The analyses deal with counts of credits regardless of their location within the high school's curriculum. In addition, the residuals for academic credits only are examined,[4] as are the residuals for mathematics and science course offerings. Mathematics and science courses were chosen for special attention because of the attention they are receiving within the ongoing school reform movement.

The independent variables are assigned to the categories explored in the previous section. The community characteristics include the average socioeconomic status of the high school (as reported by sampled students from within the high school), the standard deviation of the socioeconomic status variable for the high school, and dummy variables indicating whether or not the high school is located in an urban or rural labor market.

The spending variable is the beginning B.A. teacher salary divided by the county's per capita income. It also would have been desirable to examine overall spending levels, but the district spending level variable was plagued by questionable entries and was dropped from the analysis. The teacher salary variable is expressed as a fraction of the county's per capita income as a means of controlling for the effects of regional differences in the cost of living. The goal is to identify those districts spending at high levels relative to a second indicator of income levels.

Insight into the impact of spending variables was also obtained by considering principals' perceptions of the offered salaries' ability to attract candidates for teaching positions. Two principal perceptions in particular were examined: the principal's assessment of the degree to which salaries are insufficient to attract teacher candidates, and the principal's assessment of the degree to which there is a shortage of qualified applicants.

The internal resource allocation variables include the percentage of classroom teachers who are new, the percentage of classroom teachers with more than ten years of experience in the school, the percentage of classroom teachers with fewer than three years of experience in the school, and the percentage of teachers with tenure. These variables were chosen to capture various aspects of administrative flexibility within the school. They were also chosen on the grounds that they reflect phenomena over which administrators exercise some discretion.

In addition, the residuals associated with various areas of the curriculum (vocational and non-mathematics/science to be specific) were also included as predictor variables. These residuals measure the degree to which a school is offering an unusually large or small number of courses in the indicated curricular area, given its size.

Finally, there are variables intended to capture the level of commitment made by the professional staff. Teachers' responses to the following questions were used to build a scale of teachers' willingness to make extra efforts on behalf of their students:

1. You can count on most staff members to help out anywhere, anytime—even though it may not be part of their official assignment.
2. In this school I am encouraged to experiment with my teaching.
3. Routine duties and paperwork interfere with my job of teaching (reverse scale).
4. Teachers in this school are continually learning and seeking new ideas.
5. There is a great deal of cooperative effort among staff members.
6. I sometimes feel it is a waste of time to try to do my best as a teacher (reverse scale).

The reliability coefficient for this six-item scale was .70.

A second scale attempted to measure the degree to which teachers actually make additional efforts on behalf of their students. This scale is based on teacher reported amounts of time devoted outside of class to the following activities: background reading in the subject area taught, contacting employers on students' behalf, conducting makeup work for students, counseling students, and tutoring students. Activities were chosen that are not likely to be explicitly linked to extra compensation for the teacher. The reliability coefficient for this five-item scale was .59.

Relationships among the variables were estimated using multiple regression techniques. The variables were looked at collectively using the categories introduced here. They were also examined individually. Sample weights were adjusted to avoid artificially inflating tests of statistical significance.

RESULTS

High School Size

The size of a high school's graduating class alone explains 50 percent of the variance in the total number of unduplicated courses found within the high school's curriculum. In the case of academic credits, the percentage of the variation explained is 58; in the case of science and mathematics credits, the percentage explained is 40. Thus, in all three measures of curricular offerings, the size of the high school alone explains roughly one-half of the variance. Clearly, size is an important predictor of course offerings within high schools. However, it should be equally clear that in two of the three areas of the curriculum considered, more than one-half of the total variance remains unexplained by size.

Further analysis of the residual variation indicates that its magnitude increases with the size of the high school. The rank order correlations between the absolute values of the residuals and school size ranged between .279 for total credits and .386 for academic credits. These are moderately large coefficients that suggest that there is some tendency for enrollment to be more of a constraining influence on curricular offerings in small compared to larger schools. However, they are not so large in magnitude as to call into question the prudence of inquiring into the additional sources of variation even among the smaller schools in the sample. Indeed, visual inspection of the residuals indicates that substantial variation does exist among like-sized small schools in terms of curricular offerings.

Characteristics of the Community

Table 8.1 reports the results of regressing the residuals for all courses, academic courses, and mathematics and science courses on a series of community characteristics. Although the explanatory power of these models is not large (the R^2 statistic never exceeds .087), consistent positive relationships are revealed between communities' average socioeconomic status and course offerings in the selected areas of the curriculum. In other words, communities with higher average socioeconomic status tended to fall above the regression line estimated in the first stage of this analysis, and communities with lower average socioeconomic status tended to fall below the line.[5]

Variation in socioeconomic status, as measured by the standard deviation of the distribution of SES scores reported by students within each high school, is also positively related to curricular offerings, but not within the academic portion of the curriculum. More-varied communities offer a larger number of discrete courses than do others. The lack of a statistically significant positive relationship between

Table 8.1.
Community Characteristics and Unduplicated Counts of Course Credits with the Effects of School Size Removed
Regression Coefficients with Standard Errors in ( )

	Residuals for All Credits	Residuals for Academic Credits	Residuals for Science & Math Credits
Average Socioeconomic Status	14.49** (6.60)	15.57** (3.07)	3.29** (.97)
Standard Deviation of Socioeconomic Status	35.44* (20.39)	15.22 (9.48)	4.58 (3.00)
Location in a Rural Region	4.77 (4.46)	2.14 (2.07)	.08 (.66)
Location in an Urban Region	15.01** (6.99)	7.46** (3.25)	.33 (1.03)
Constant	-24.02* (12.98)	-9.24 (6.03)	-2.46 (1.91)
R^2	.035	.087	.043
F	3.11*	8.29***	3.92***

n = 352
* = p<.10
** = p<.05
*** = p<.01

SES diversity and academic course offerings suggests that most of the effects of diversity are felt within the vocational area of the curriculum. However, it is worth noting that of the 35.44 additional courses associated with a unit increase in the standard deviation of SES, 15.22 or roughly half arise in the academic curriculum. The relatively large standard error estimated for the academic coefficient accounts for the lack of statistical significance and suggests that substantial variation in the impact exists within the sample. Whatever tendency there is for state curricular regulations to be more focused on academic rather than vocational offerings can explain a tendency for community diversity to have greater impact on vocational rather than academic offerings.

Location within an urban area is also associated with being above the regression line constructed in the first stage of the analysis. In other words, urban communities are more likely to offer larger numbers of courses than would be expected given their size alone. Location in a rural area made little difference in terms of course offerings, and these results are consistent with earlier findings (see Monk and Haller 1993).

Table 8.2.
School Characteristics and Unduplicated Counts of Course Credits with the Effects of School Size and Community Characteristics Removed

Regression Coefficients with Standard Errors in ( )

	Residuals for All Credits	Residuals for Academic Credits	Residuals for Science & Math Credits
Beginning B.A. Teacher Salary Divided by the County Per Capita Personal Income for 1981	14.24 (18.06)	1.82 (7.29)	.15 (1.99)
Principal Perceives Salaries of Teachers to Be Insufficient	-5.30** (2.37)	-2.65*** (.96)	-.21 (.27)
Principal Perceives a Shortage of Qualified Teacher Applicants	4.56* (2.26)	.84 (1.07)	.06 (.29)
Percentage of Teachers with Tenure	-.03 (.26)	-.03 (.10)	.00 (.03)
Percentage of Teachers with >10 Years' Experience	.83 (1.61)	-.13 (.65)	-.28 (.18)
Percentage of Teachers with <3 Years' Experience	.27 (2.15)	-.41 (.86)	-.10 (.24)
Percentage of New Teachers	-.05 (.16)	-.06 (.00)	-.00 (.02)
Residual for Vocational Credits		.26*** (.05)	
Residual for Non-Science & Math Credits			.25*** (.03)
Constant	-11.63 (39.07)	11.93 (15.75)	2.07 (4.31)
R^2	.061	.249	.412
F	1.04	4.62***	9.73***

n = 120
* = p<.10
** = p<.05
*** = p<.01

Characteristics of the High School

Spending in the context of external labor market conditions. In Table 8.2, attention turns to the impact of school level characteristics on the residuals constructed as a by-product of the analyses reported in Table

8.1. In the absence of significant correlation among the predictor variables, these residuals can be interpreted as the variation in course offerings remaining after the effects of both school size and community characteristics have been removed.

The absence of a relationship between the measure of real spending on teacher salaries and curricular offerings is interesting. Recall that this variable measures the degree to which spending on beginning B.A. teacher salaries is high relative to per capita county incomes. It is not a general measure of real spending on education but instead reflects decisions already made about the degree to which education spending is devoted to teacher salaries.

It is not possible *a priori* to predict the effect that spending more in real terms on teacher salaries will have on the breadth of curricular offerings. On the one hand, higher salaries will make it possible to hire teachers who are trained to a given level of excellence in a wider range of areas, and this could increase the number of courses offered. On the other hand, the higher salary may permit districts to hire teachers trained to a higher level of excellence in a narrower range of areas, and this could reduce the number of courses offered. Moreover, as teacher salaries reach higher levels, the school limits its ability to hire larger numbers of teachers, and this too can reduce the school's ability to offer a broad array of courses.

The results in Table 8.2 indicate that higher beginning salaries for teachers are unrelated to the number of courses offered in all three areas of the curriculum. It is more likely that a general spending variable with a control in place for teacher salary levels would be positively related to these residuals than the salary variable alone. This is the case because the addition of a general spending variable would capture a willingness on the part of school boards to hire a relatively large number of teachers at a wage equal to the regional average and to thereby broaden the curriculum. Salary variables alone are not capable of discerning this possible effect of spending.

Despite the absence of a relationship between real salaries and course offerings, principals' perceptions of labor market conditions are related to course offerings. In cases where the principal perceived the offered salaries to be barriers to hiring the people the principal sought, course offerings were below what would be expected given the school's size and community characteristics. This negative relationship was found in all three areas of the curriculum examined.

The second principal perception variable captures the principal's assessment of teacher shortages in his or her labor market. The positive coefficient suggests that when shortages are perceived, more courses are offered than would otherwise be expected. Though the positive direction of the relationship is surprising, it needs to be interpreted in light of the other variables being simultaneously entered. In this formulation, the perception of shortage is being assessed among schools with comparable real spending levels on teacher salaries as well as comparable perceptions of the degree to which salaries are barriers. The perception of a shortage under these conditions may be reflecting higher standards and expectations for the school on the part of the principal. The relationship between a principal's dissatisfaction with the available labor market for teachers and the supply of more courses than would otherwise be expected to be found within the school may be an indication of the impact an administrator can have on increasing educational opportunities for students.

Internal resource allocation practices. Table 8.2 also makes it clear that neither the indicators of increased flexibility (the percentage of new teachers, and the percentage of teachers with less than three years of experience) nor the indicators of reduced flexibility (the percentage of teachers with more than ten years of experience and the percentage of teachers with tenure) are related to the residual variables. These insignificant relationships are not surprising, given how crudely flexibility is being measured. But there is an alternative explanation for these results that is more damaging. Specifically, it is hardly obvious that flexibility will necessarily translate into additional courses. Flexibility could also stimulate efforts to improve the quality of a given array of educational opportunities. The presumption that there is always an underlying desire to expand course offerings may be quite faulty. Nevertheless, a broader range of course offerings is a relevant indicator of educational opportunity, and it is important to know how it is related to various community and school characteristics.

An additional internal allocation variable that warrants attention is average class size. Unfortunately, this has been a difficult variable to construct cleanly using these data. Average class size is important because it reflects a number of prior internal resource allocation decisions. In this sense it is quite analogous to the teacher salary variable discussed earlier. A willingness to tolerate relatively small classes suggests an interest in offering a broader array of curricular offerings, all else being equal. Two key allocation decisions can be discerned that permit insight into the link between spending on education and the range of curricular offerings: (a) the salaries (as well as other benefits) paid to teachers; and (b) the practices regarding class sizes and their distribution. It appears clear that more needs to be done with class size variables.

The relationships found between the residuals pertaining to vocational as well as science and mathematics courses are quite interesting. Recall that one means of financing a relatively rich offering in one area of a curriculum involves providing a more modest offering elsewhere.

The reasoning was that being above the regression line for academic courses would logically be associated with being below the regression line for vocational courses. With this in mind the residual for vocational credits was entered into the regression model for the academic credit residuals. As Table 8.2 indicates, the result was a striking *positive* relationship. What this means is that schools offering unusually large numbers of academic credits also offer unusually large numbers of vocational credits. In other words, larger numbers of academic courses do not appear to be financed via a reduced number of vocational courses. A similarly strong positive relationship emerged when the focus was on the linkage between the residuals for mathematics and science courses with the residuals for all other academic courses.

These results suggest that the sort of triage envisioned earlier is not an important part of how some high schools overcome the constraints size imparts on their ability to offer courses.

Commitments of professional staff. Next, the residuals produced by the regressions reported in Table 8.2 were regressed on the two scales measuring the level of teacher willingness to commit additional time and effort on behalf of students as well as the actual expenditure of additional (uncompensated) time on noninstructional but instructionally relevant activities. The results are reported in Table 8.3.

Table 8.3 makes it clear that these measures of teacher commitment are not strongly correlated with the incidence of additional courses. In only one equation is even one of the variables statistically significant. Expressed teacher willingness to make extra efforts on behalf of students is associated with a larger number of courses than would otherwise be expected given the numerous other school and community characteristics that have been considered. The fact that no relationship exists between actual allocations of teacher time to uncompensated instructionally relevant activities and course offerings is perhaps not surprising given the likely possibility that the effort required by these activities can limit the inclination of teachers to accept additional course preparations.

Further conceptual as well as empirical work needs to be done at this level of the analysis. More-refined scales of teacher as well as administrator (especially principal) commitments to students need to be developed. More work also needs to be done linking administrator, teacher, and student activities. There is a widespread presumption that administrative leadership plays an important role in creating educational opportunities for students.[6] The means by which this is accomplished need to be better understood, and assessments of the role administrators play in broadening curricular offerings could be very insightful.

Table 8.3.
Professional Staff Characteristics and Unduplicated Counts
of Course Credits with the Effects of School Size,
Community Characteristics, and School Characteristics Removed

Regression Coefficients with Standard Errors in ( )

	Residuals for All Credits	Residuals for Academic Credits	Residuals for Science & Math Credits
Teacher Willingness to Make Extra Effort on Behalf of Students	3.48* (1.82)	.12 .73	-.17 .20
Extra Time Actually Devoted to Instructionally Relevant Activities by Teachers	1.00 (2.33)	-1.18 .94	.14 .26
Constant	-39.92 (34.95)	13.39 14.10	-.36 3.87
R^2	.030	.015	.011
F	1.83	.90	.63

n = 120
* = p<.10

CONCLUSIONS AND IMPLICATIONS

The results presented here are disturbing for at least two reasons. First, the magnitude of the inequalities in curricular offerings among the sampled high schools is substantial. The reality is that high school size is important but certainly not determinative of how broad the range of courses will be in a given school and that schools continue to vary dramatically in the courses they offer when the effects of school size have been removed.

Second, the results show clearly how little is known about what explains variation in curricular offerings. We need to face up to the fact that none of the school level variables measuring spending levels, perceptions of labor market conditions, flexibility in the internal allocation of resources, and the commitment levels of teachers made much of a substantive difference in explaining the residual variation.

The one school-level attribute that did make a noteworthy difference was the ability of the school to offer courses in other areas of the curriculum. And although the strong positive direction of this relationship came as a surprise, it is understandable but not very enlightening. It really amounts to just a different way of admitting to the ignorance that persists. We are in effect saying that there are some schools that somehow seem able to overcome the effects of size. When this happens, it seems to happen throughout the entire curriculum.

The results are also relevant to an important and ongoing policy debate. School and school district reorganization have been widely pursued for many years as a means of broadening the curricular opportunities of students, particularly at the secondary school level. The results demonstrate the upper bounds on how successful such policies are likely to be. The findings suggest that focusing solely on the school-size-related sources of curricular inequalities will not be adequate if the goal is to eliminate inequalities in curricular opportunities among high schools.

These are early results in an ongoing effort to explore the microeconomics of curriculum building. It is worth noting several other recent efforts that focus on gaining greater understanding of the allocation of resources to points deeply embedded within schools and their effect on curricular offerings (see Monk, Roellke, and Brent 1996; Picus, Tetreault, and Hertert 1996; and Nakib 1996).[7] Although progress continues to be made, the phenomenon is quite complex and advancement toward a deeper understanding is limited and slow moving. Nevertheless, the enterprise is important and warrants further attention. Indeed, the ignorance of from whence the residual inequality in curricular offerings comes is an embarrassment and ought to serve as inspiration for more-thorough and successful analysis.

ACKNOWLEDGMENTS

I wish to thank Professors Emil J. Haller and William Sparkman for their helpful comments on an earlier draft of this chapter. Professor Haller was particularly helpful with the analyses focused on school-level phenomena, and I am very grateful to him for his counsel. Of course, I remain responsible for any remaining deficiencies.

NOTES

1. The same logic suggests that offerings of certain types of courses (for example, advanced placement courses) can come at the expense of different kinds of courses within the same subject area (for example, remedial courses).

2. This phenomenon goes beyond instances where teachers teach an additional course beyond what their contract requires. It includes situations where a teacher substitutes a new course for an additional section of a course already being taught.

3. For more on the effects of grade configurations, see McKenzie (1989) and Monk and Haller (1993).

4. The following subject areas were considered academic: Area and Ethnic Studies, Computer and Information Science, Foreign Language, English, Liberal Studies, Biology, Mathematics, Multidisciplinary Studies, Physical Education, Philosophy and Religions, Science, Science Technologies, Psychology, Public Affairs, Social Sciences, and Visual and Performing Arts.

5. These results are consistent with earlier findings using a reduced form model that was constructed using a less restricted sample. See Monk and Haller (1993) for more details.

6. This is a common theme within the effective schools literature. See, for example, Purkey and Smith (1983); Rosenholtz (1987); and Rutter et al. (1979).

7. For insights into the impact of education reform efforts on teacher staffing patterns see Roellke (1996).

REFERENCES

Antos, Joseph R., and Sherwin Rosen. (1975). "Discrimination in the Market for Public School Teachers." *Journal of Econometrics* 3(3): 123–150.

Barker, Bruce. (1985). "Curricular Offerings in Small and Large High Schools: How Broad Is the Disparity?" *Research in Rural Education* 3(1): 35–38.

Fowler, William, (1992). *What do we know about school size? What should we know?* ERIC Reproduction Service Document ED 347675.

Haller, Emil J., David H. Monk, Alyce Spotted Bear, Julie Griffith, and Pamela Moss. (1990). "School Size and Program Comprehensiveness." *Educational Evaluation and Policy Analysis* 12(2): 109–120.

McKenzie, Phillip A. (1989). "Secondary School Size, Curriculum Structure, and Resource Use: A Study in the Economics of Education." Doctoral dissertation, Faculty of Education, Monash University.

Monk, David H. (1987). "Secondary School Size and Curriculum Comprehensiveness," *Economics of Education Review* 6(2): 137–150.

Monk, David, and Emil J. Haller. (1993). "Predictors of High School Academic Course Offerings: The Role of School Size," *American Educational Research Journal* 30(1): 3–21.

Monk, David H. , Christopher F. Roellke, and Brian O. Brent. (1996). *What Education Dollars Buy: An Examination of Resource Allocation Patterns in New York Public School Systems.* ERIC Reproduction Service Document 399 664.

Nakib, Yasser A. (1996). *Beyond District Level Expenditures: Resource Allocation and Use in Florida's Public Schools.* Paper presented at the Annual Meeting of the American Education Finance Association, Savannah, Ga.

Picus, Lawrence O., Donald Tetreault, and Linda Hertert (1996). *The Allocation and Use of Education Dollars at the District and School Level in California.* Paper presented at the Annual Meeting of the American Education Finance Association, Savannah, Ga.

Purkey, S. C., and M. S. Smith. (1983). "Effective Schools: A Review." *The Elementary School Journal 83:* 427–453.

Roellke, Christopher F. (1996). The Local Response to State Initiated Education Reform: Changes in the Allocation of Human Resources in New York State Schooling Systems, 1983–1995. Unpublished Ph.D. dissertation, Department of Education, Cornell University.

Rosenholtz, Susan J. (1985). "Effective Schools: Interpreting the Evidence." *American Journal of Education* 93(3): 352–388.

Rutter, Michael, Barbara Maughan, Peter Mortimore, and Janet Ouston. (1979). *Fifteen Thousand Hours.* Cambridge, Mass.: Harvard University Press.

9

Resource Use and Student Achievement in Elementary Schools

Richard A. Rossmiller

This research was undertaken with the recognition that student learning results from the interaction of many variables. They include variables associated with the students themselves and their home environments as well as variables associated with their schools. Classroom teachers are important school resource inputs, and they play an important role in managing school resources. Although some teacher union leaders are reluctant to admit that classroom teachers are managers, even an unskilled observer in an elementary school classroom soon realizes that the teacher is responsible for managing a large set of human and material resources—instructional materials and equipment, space, time, and students with varying aptitudes and interests, to name a few. Teachers try to help their students master a body of knowledge, acquire specific skills, or understand a process. Observation of teachers at work also reveals that they are not all equally skilled in managing classroom resources. Some teachers are able to actively engage their students in the task at hand nearly all of the time, and others struggle to maintain a semblance of order in their classroom. There has been much discussion of the important role that principals play in managing school resources, but the crucial role that teachers play in managing these resources has not received as much attention.

This chapter summarizes the results of a three-year longitudinal study of individual students in four Wisconsin elementary schools.[1] An education production function model was employed, and the design of the research drew upon the results of previous research in which several types of resources have been shown to influence students' academic achievement. The design of this longitudinal study called for data on individual students to be gathered over a three-year period. Data were gathered on the use of time in classrooms, particularly time on-task; per pupil expenditures for core subject areas—reading, mathematics, language arts, social studies, and science; the students' home environment and involvement in out-of-school activities; the preparation, experience, background, attitudes, and beliefs of teachers in the classrooms we observed; and student academic achievement and gain each year in reading and mathematics.

Students in four Wisconsin elementary schools who were enrolled in grade 3 during the 1979–80 school year were followed through their third-, fourth- and fifth-grade years. Two of the schools were located in urban areas with populations over fifty thousand, and the other two schools were located in smaller communities with populations of less than ten thousand. The four communities were relatively homogeneous with respect to median family income and poverty levels.

The four schools were similar in size of enrollment but dissimilar in their physical plant and organizational patterns. Schools A and B were housed in traditional buildings with separate self-contained classrooms joined by common hallways except for a new wing in School A containing a large open space for students in grades 5 and 6. Although the teachers in School A were nominally assigned to multigraded teams, planning and instruction took place on a graded basis and the two schools were organized in a relatively traditional manner. In Schools C and D students were housed in multigraded instructional units in large open areas with movable walls, chalkboards, and bookshelves. Cross-grade planning and grouping practices occurred in both schools during all three years of the study.

The demographic characteristics of the student sample were quite similar in the four schools. The number of students in the sample ranged from fifty-one in School C to eighty-eight in School A. About 54 percent of the students were male, 3 percent were nonwhite, 28 percent had attended a preschool program, and their average age at entry to third grade was 102 months. Most of the students were from middle- or lower-middle-class families. The families tended to be small to medium in size; very few had less than two or more than five children. All but nine of the students lived at home with their natural mothers, all but twenty-nine lived with their natural fathers, and only nine students lived in homes in which there was no adult male present. All the students spoke English as their primary language. About 12 percent of the students in the sample were involved in special programs, with the percentage ranging from 6 percent in School D to 18 percent in Schools A and B.

Most of the third-grade teachers were women, but by fifth grade the number of males had increased so that half the teachers were men. The teachers averaged more than ten years of teaching experience, were between thirty-five and forty years of age, and approximately half of them held a master's degree.

The major dependent variables in our model were student achievement in reading and mathematics as measured by the Stanford Achievement Test, which was administered near the end of each school year by members of the project staff. Basic information on each student's personal characteristics (age, sex, race, handicaps, attendance, involvement in special programs, and so on) was obtained from school records. About one-third of the parents were interviewed by telephone during each year of the study to obtain information about students' daily activities outside of school and about a wide range of home background variables.

Each student was observed in the classroom by a member of the project staff for a full school day in the fall, winter, and spring of each school year. Highest priority was given to observing each student during the time he or she was involved in reading, mathematics, language arts, science, and social studies classes. The observer recorded at two-minute intervals whether the student was on- or off-task and the instructional mode being used at the time—large group, small group, independent study, and so on.

Information about the personal, educational, and professional background and activities of teachers was obtained from school personnel records and from an instrument completed by each teacher that provided information about their background, personal preferences, and professional opinions. The preferences and opinions section was adapted from an instrument used by Murnane and Phillips (1979) and included questions about the instructional practices the teachers used, as well as elicited their opinions and beliefs about various aspects of schooling.

THE USE OF TIME AND STUDENT ACADEMIC ACHIEVEMENT

It is tempting to view the amount of time a student spends on-task as a primary determinant of their learning because it offers such a simple explanation of student performance. If it is true that the more time students devote to studying a subject, the more likely they are to master it, it follows that the prescription for improving student performance is simple and straightforward—maximize the time students spend on-task and minimize interruptions and distractions that might divert their attention from the subject.

Interest in the way time is used in schools can be traced to Carroll (1963), who recognized that students' time is an important resource in the learning process. He defined on-task time as the time during which the student is "paying attention" and "trying to learn." Carroll acknowledged that the amount of time needed to achieve mastery is influenced by a student's aptitude and ability to understand and follow directions, and by the quality of instruction. Carroll's model of learning suggested that, other things being equal, learning is a function of the amount of time a student is on-task.

From an economic perspective, time is one of many resources that, in combination, determine school productivity. A student's time in school is a particularly important variable because it is one over which educators can exercise considerable control—in contrast with variables such as a family's household income or the parents' level of schooling that are beyond the reach of school authorities. As Thomas (1971) observed, the opportunity cost associated with alternative uses of student time is "foregone learning."

This aspect of the study examined the relationship between the allocation and use of time in elementary school classrooms and the student's achievement test scores in reading and mathematics and the gain the student made each year in those subjects. As noted earlier, each student was observed in the classroom throughout each of three days per year (fall, winter, spring). The observer recorded at two-minute intervals the subject, the mode of instruction, and whether the student was on- or off-task or engaged in process behavior at the time of the observation.

Time on-task, the time in which a student is actively engaged in learning, was categorized in one of five modes of instruction:

1. *Independent study*, in which the student was working alone—either reading, studying, writing, or working with other instructional materials
2. *One-to-one*, in which the student was working with an adult—a teacher, an aide, or a volunteer
3. *Small group*, in which the student was working with an adult in a group smaller in size than the entire class
4. *Large group*, in which the student was working with a teacher and other students in a class-size or larger group
5. *With other students*, in which the student was working with one or more other students but not with an adult

Process behavior was defined as time when the student was in transition from one activity to another, waiting for instructions, obtaining directions, and so on. Off-task time was defined as time when the student was not attending to the task at hand, or any other assignment, but was "wasting" time that could have been used for learning.

The amount of class time spent on the basic academic subjects—reading, mathematics, language arts, science, and social studies—dropped from an average of 209 minutes per day for third graders to 179 minutes per day for fourth graders and to 154 minutes per day for fifth graders (see Table 9.1). The decline in minutes per day devoted to these five academic subjects was not a result of shorter school days; in fact, the total length of the school day increased from third grade to fifth grade. Rather, the decline in the amount of time devoted to the academic core subjects was a result of the growing amount of time devoted to other activities during the school day.

Two instructional modes predominated in these classrooms—independent study and large group instruction. Small group instruction was used only a small amount of the time—an average of eighteen, seven, and six minutes per day in third, fourth and fifth grade, respectively. Very little time was devoted to either one-to-one instruction or to working with other students.

Individual students varied greatly in their use of time. In some instructional modes at least one student was observed to spend no time at all on-task, whereas other students were on-task nearly all of the time in each of the academic subjects. Overall, students were on-task approx-

Table 9.1.

Average Minutes of Daily Instruction Time Spent by Students in Five Subject Areas (Reading, Mathematics, Language Arts, Science, and Social Studies)*

	Third Grade (n=196)	Fourth Grade (n=227)	Fifth Grade (n=192)
Independent study	69.7	52.7	44.5
One-to-one	1.9	1.7	1.0
Small group	18.5	7.2	5.8
Large group	57.2	69.6	60.9
W/other students	4.1	2.5	3.5
Total on-task	151.4	133.7	115.7
Process time	34.1	20.7	17.7
Off-task time	20.5	19.8	16.5
Not observed	3.4	3.0	3.9
Total instructional time	209.4	179.2	153.8

*Includes only students for whom observations were available for each of the five academic subjects.

imately three-fourths of the time. (It would, of course, be unrealistic to expect all students to be on-task all of the time.) The amount of classroom time devoted to process behavior was a bit disconcerting. It accounted for over 16 percent of instructional time in grade 3 and over 11 percent in grades 4 and 5, although it varied widely from one classroom to another. Process behavior, as we defined the term, is one indicator of a teacher's skill in classroom management. Time lost when the student is waiting for the teacher to correct a paper or answer a question, or when the teacher repeats instructions over and over and over again, or when the teacher fails to start the class on time are examples of what we considered process behavior.

Information concerning student time on-task in reading and mathematics for each mode of instruction is presented in Table 9.2. Two modes of reading instruction predominated in the third grade. Independent study and instruction in a small group setting accounted for 87 percent of the instructional time in reading, with relatively little time spent in other instructional modes. In mathematics, independent study and large group instruction were the modes most commonly employed with very little time spent in the other three instructional modes. An average of about ten minutes per day was taken up by process time in both reading and mathematics instruction.

Table 9.2.
Minutes per Day of On-Task Time by Mode of Instruction in Reading and Mathematics

	Grade 3			Grade 4			Grade 5		
	Mean	S.D.	Range	Mean	S.D.	Range	Mean	S.D.	Range
Reading									
Independent Study	25.7	10.5	5-55	17.5	10.3	2-68	16.0	8.0	0-37
One-to-One	0.5	1.1	0-11	0.6	1.3	0-13	0.2	0.5	0-4
Small Group	13.6	8.1	0-36	5.4	9.5	0-49	4.0	6.8	0-39
Large Group	4.0	5.1	0-23	14.8	8.7	0-38	10.2	8.3	0-39
W/Other Students	1.5	2.3	0-14	1.3	2.7	0-11	0.4	1.7	0-13
Process Time	9.3	4.1	2-26	5.6	2.9	0-16	4.4	2.1	0-12
Mathematics									
Independent Study	20.5	6.2	4-39	18.5	6.4	3-36	15.4	7.8	0-34
One-to-One	0.9	1.2	0-7	0.7	1.1	0-8	0.4	0.8	0-4
Small Group	1.7	4.2	0-20	1.2	3.1	0-20	1.1	2.7	0-19
Large Group	8.7	8.2	0-35	10.7	7.8	0-33	10.2	6.5	0-28
W/Other Students	1.4	2.6	0-17	0.7	1.4	0-7	0.4	1.4	0-9
Process Time	10.0	5.0	2-27	5.9	2.9	1-15	4.5	2.3	0-11

At the fourth-grade level independent study was still the most prevalent mode of reading instruction, although greater use was made of large group instruction in fourth grade. Time spent in small group instruction averaged about five minutes per day. In mathematics, independent study and large group instruction again were the most common instructional modes with very little time spent in the other three modes. Process time declined to an average of less than six minutes per day in grade 4.

Independent study remained the most prevalent instructional mode for reading at the fifth-grade level and was followed by large group instruction. In mathematics, independent study and large group instruction still were the dominant modes. Process time in both reading and mathematics had declined to about 4.5 minutes per day.

ON-TASK TIME AND STUDENT ACADEMIC ACHIEVEMENT

Multiple regression analysis was used to examine the relationships between achievement test scores in reading and mathematics and the amount of time students spent on-task and in process activities in these subjects. Table 9.3 shows the coefficients of determination (R^2) for reading and mathematics achievement scores and the six variables measuring time on-task and process time in these two subjects. Time on-task accounted for a relatively small amount of the variation in student achievement in these four schools—from as little as 17 percent of the variance in reading scores in grade 3 to as much as 27 percent of the variance in reading scores at grade 5. In most cases, a two-variable model accounted for nearly as much of the variance in reading and mathematics achievement scores as did all six variables. Time on-task in independent study was the first variable to enter two of the three equations for reading achievement, whereas time on-task in small group instruction entered first in two of the three years for mathematics achievement. Although all of the individual variables from which the R^2 values reported in Table 9.3 were derived were statistically significant at the .05 level, it appears that many factors other than time on-task were involved in the achievement of this sample of students.

Perhaps the percentage of time an individual student spends on-task is a better descriptor of the student than it is a predictor of the student's academic achievement. For example, we observed that the most able students were likely to be on-task less of the time simply because they were able to complete their assignments more rapidly than other students. Failure to identify a consistent relationship between time on-task and student achievement also may reflect the repertoire of instructional practices and classroom management skills of individual teachers. Al-

Table 9.3.

Relationship of On-Task Time and Process Time in Reading and Mathematics to Achievement in Reading and Mathematics*

Reading			Mathematics		
Grade 3 (n=231)			**Grade 3 (n=231)**		
Regression Model	*Variable*	R^2	*Regression Model*	*Variable*	R^2
One variable	Independent	.16	One variable	Small group	.12
Two variables	Independent w/Students	.16	Two Variables	Small group Process	.18
All six variables		.17	All six variables		.23
Grade 4 (n=241)			**Grade 4 (n=241)**		
One variable	Large group	.07	One variable	Small group	.11
Two variables	Independent Large group	.15	Two variables	Small group Large group	.18
All six variables		.20	All six variables		.21
Grade 5 (n=205)			**Grade 5 (n=210)**		
One variable	Independent	.13	One variables	Large group	.10
Two variables	Independent w/Students	.19	Two variables	Large group Process	.13
All six variables		.27	All six variables		.18

* All correlations statistically significant at .05 level of confidence.

though the relationships revealed in these analyses were based on the behavior of individual students, they also reflected the patterns of instructional practice selected by individual teachers. Only two or three teachers were involved in reading instruction with these students in any one school each year, and they generally chose among alternative modes of instruction on the basis of their personal preferences as well as their judgments concerning the most-effective mode of instruction for particular students. The number of students in a given class, the availability of teacher aides, and the use of instructional teams are also factors that may influence the choice of an instructional mode.

To assess whether the importance of time on-task differed for various types of students, the sample was divided into quartiles based on students' reading and mathematics achievement scores. When students in the bottom quartile, the middle half, and the top quartile in reading and mathematics achievement scores were analyzed separately, time on-task proved to be a better predictor of achievement scores for students in the lowest quartile than for those in the middle half or the highest quartile, particularly in reading (see Table 9.4). For students in the bottom quartile, the six variables accounted for 45, 31, and 31 percent of the variance in reading achievement in third, fourth, and fifth grades, respectively. For students in the top quartile, these variables

Table 9.4.
Relationship of On-Task Time in Reading and Mathematics
to Achievement in Reading and Mathematics in
High and Low Quartiles*

| | Reading Achievement | | | | Mathematics Achievement | | | |
| | Low Quartile | | High Quartile | | Low Quartile | | High Quartile | |
	Var.	R^2	Var.	R^2	Var.	R^2	Var.	R^2
Grade 3	(N = 53)		(N = 55)		(N = 56)		(N = 57)	
One variable	F	.33	D	.04	F	.14	E	.04
Two variables	D, F	.41	A, D	.10	E, F	.17	E, F	.07
All variables		.45		.15		.19		.09
Grade 4	(N = 61)		(N = 61)		(N = 63)		(N = 60)	
One variable	C	.13	B	.06	A	.04	C	.04
Two variables	C, F	.24	B, C	.09	A, B	.07	C, F	.06
All variables		.31		.12		.12		.08
Grade 5	(N = 49)		(N = 50)		(N = 50)		(N = 52)	
One variable	C	.15	F	.04	B	.05	D	.07
Two variables	C, F	.22	A, F	.05	B, D	.08	D, E	.09
All variables		.31		.10		.15		.13

Variables: A = Independent Study

B = One-to-One

C = Small Group

D = Large Group

E = With Other Students

F = Process

* All correlations statistically significant at .05 level of confidence.

accounted for 15, 12, and 10 percent of the variance in reading achievement for students in third, fourth, and fifth grades, respectively. The results for mathematics achievement were less striking, with time on-task and process time accounting for 19, 12, and 15 percent of the variance in mathematics achievement for students in the bottom quartile in grade 3, grade 4, and grade 5, respectively. For students in the top quartile, these variables accounted for 9, 8, and 13 percent of the variance in mathematics achievement at the third, fourth, and fifth grade levels.

Caution must be exercised in generalizing from these results. Although the correlations were statistically significant, they may be of limited practical significance to teachers and principals because much of the variance in student achievement was not accounted for by differences in time on-task. Furthermore, no consistent pattern of relationships between time on-task in various modes of instruction and student achievement in reading or in mathematics was evident. Although time on-task is important and should not be ignored as a source of variance in student achievement, it is quite clear that merely increasing time on-task is not a panacea. Time on-task may be a covariate of other variables (such as academic aptitude) known to be related to student achievement, or it may exert a mediating influence on student achievement.

EXPENDITURES FOR INSTRUCTION AND STUDENT ACADEMIC ACHIEVEMENT

The relationship between expenditures for education and student performance has been a subject of enduring interest. Although the "cost quality studies" of Mort and his associates (Mort, Ruesser, & Polley, 1960) were begun in the 1920s, the *Equality of Educational Opportunity* study (Coleman et al., 1966) was the first large-scale study to use disaggregated variables in the specification of an educational production function. Over the past seventeen years Hanushek (1981; 1986; 1989; 1994; 1996) has published extensively based on his syntheses of the education production function literature and still holds to a conclusion he reached in 1986 that "there appears to be no strong or systematic relationship between school expenditures and student performance" (1162). More recently, Hedges, Laine, and Greenwald (1994; 1995; 1996) have challenged Hanushek's findings. Using different methodology, their meta-analysis of the studies Hanushek reviewed, and of a larger set of education production function studies they assembled, led them to conclude that school resources are "systematically related to student achievement and that these relations are large enough to be educationally important" (Greenwald, Hedges, & Laine, 1996, 384). Although they differ as to the appropriate methods to be used in synthesizing the results of a set of education production function studies, Hanushek and his critics seem to agree that merely spending more money will not guarantee higher student achievement. Rather, the question for which we do not yet have a good answer, is "*How* does money make a difference?" That is, which of the many resources that money can buy will have the greatest impact on student achievement and, even more complicated, what particular combination of resources will be the most efficient and effective?

Most of the earlier education production function studies used data aggregated at the school or the school district level rather than at the individual student or classroom level. The data collected in this study enabled us to conduct analyses of the relationship between expenditures for instruction in reading and mathematics using individual students as the unit of analysis rather than data aggregated to the school or the district. The data on the use of instructional time described in the preceding section and disaggregated data on expenditures for individual teacher salaries and for supplies and materials for various instructional purposes enabled us to approximate very closely the actual expenditure per student for instruction in reading, mathematics, and other subjects. The following cost variables were calculated:

- *Total cost per student (total instruction)*—the total instructional cost directly attributed to each student, plus the administrative cost and instruction-related costs that were prorated across all students in a school
- *Instructional cost per student (direct instruction)*—the direct instructional cost per student for all subjects including art, music, physical education, and any direct nonacademic special services such as guidance
- *Instructional cost per student for reading (reading instruction)*—the direct instructional cost per student for reading only
- *Instructional cost per student for reading plus language arts plus social studies (word-related instruction)*—the total direct instructional cost per student for instruction in these three subjects
- *Instructional cost per student for mathematics (math instruction)*—the direct instructional cost per student for mathematics only
- *Instructional cost per student for mathematics plus science (math-related instruction)*—the total direct instructional cost per student for instruction in both mathematics and science

One set of analyses was conducted with special needs students included in the sample, and a second set of analyses was performed with special needs students excluded. The results of these analyses are summarized in Table 9.5.

The most noteworthy characteristic shared by the correlations in Table 9.5 is the fact that all of them were negative when the analysis included special needs students. That is, there was a consistent inverse relationship between each expenditure measure and both student achievement and student gain in reading and mathematics. All the correlations between the various measures of expenditure and reading achievement were statistically significant and negative for all three years. For mathematics, ten of the twelve negative correlations between achievement and the various expenditure measures were statistically significant. Correlations between the various expenditure measures and student gain in reading and mathematics achievement from one year to the next also were consistently negative, although generally not statistically significant. When students with special needs (who typi-

Table 9.5.
Correlations Between Various Measures of Expenditures for Instruction and Reading and Mathematics Achievement Scores and Gain in Achievement in Grades 3–5

	EXPENDITURE MEASURE					
	Total Instruction	Direct Instruction	Reading Instruction	Word-Related Instruction	Math Instruction	Math-Related Instruction
Reading Achievement						
Grade 3	-.40 (-.03)	-.39 (.01)	-.40 (-.08)	-.43 (-.11)		
Grade 4	-.28 (.04)	-.29 (.03)	-.24 (-.04)	-.23 (.10)		
Grade 5	-.37 (-.13)	-.38 (-.15)	-.30 (-.12)	-.36 (-.07)		
Math Achievement						
Grade 3	-.40 (-.06)	-.39 (-.04)			-.06 (.06)	-.12 (.02)
Grade 4	-.22 (.11)	-.23 (.11)			-.24 (.11)	-.26 (-.02)
Grade 5	-.28 (-.04)	-.29 (-.06)			-.24 (-.08)	-.27 (-.18)
Gain in Reading						
Grade 3	-.09 (.11)	-.10 (.10)	-.06 (.13)	-.06 (.17)		
Grade 4	-.16 (-.01)	-.16 (-.01)	-.09 (.04)	-.13 (-.02)		
Grade 5	-.20 (-.21)	-.19 (-.22)	-.17 (-.21)	-.17 (-.20)		
Gain in Math						
Grade 3	-.11 (-.10)	-.10 (-.08			-.07 (.03)	-.08 (-.02)
Grade 4	-.12 (-.02)	-.13 (-.03)			-.04 (.03)	-.07 (-.07)
Grade 5	-.13 (-.05)	-.13 (-.07)			-.05 (-.07)	-.09 (-.19)

Note: Figures in parentheses are correlations with special needs students excluded. Correlations greater than .22 are statistically significant at the .001 level.

cally were involved in "pull-out" programs in which they received more-intensive instruction) were removed from the sample, the correlations between spending and achievement or gain were virtually nil, that is, there were no statistically significant relationships between the various expenditure measures and student achievement or student gain in reading or mathematics.

The range of expenditures for students in regular programs was relatively narrow, particularly when contrasted with the range of expenditures for students in special programs. Recall from our earlier discussion that relatively little time was devoted to one-to-one instruction or to small group instruction. Thus, the appropriate share of the teacher's salary typically was prorated evenly across students because we had to assume that in large group instruction each student was receiving an equal share of the teacher's time. Similarly, in independent study each student was assumed to be receiving the same share of the teacher's time except at those times when the teacher was working individually with a particular student.

The lack of variation in the way instructional time was used with regular students served to constrain the variation in cost per individual pupil that could occur. By including the students who were in special programs in the analysis, the variation in both the cost variables and the dependent variables was increased, but the chance that a few outliers on either the cost or achievement variables would markedly affect the correlations also was increased. If one excludes special students, it appeared that teachers in these schools were allocating classroom resources among their students in a manner unrelated to their performance on achievement tests.

When one considers the nature of the programs for students with special needs that these schools were providing, it is not surprising to find statistically significant negative relationships between the level of expenditure and student achievement. The programs generally were characterized by a low pupil/teacher ratio and were staffed by experienced teachers who held an advanced degree and had special training. Because the teachers were paid primarily on the basis of their training and experience, their salaries were relatively high and consequently the per pupil cost of special needs programs was relatively high. Most students with special needs were in special programs precisely because they were low achievers. Thus, when the expenditure per student in programs for students with special needs is correlated with their achievement test scores, one could expect the correlations to be strongly negative and statistically significant.

HOME ENVIRONMENT AND STUDENT ACADEMIC ACHIEVEMENT

Our data permitted us to look at the association between the home environment of 198 elementary school students and their achievement in reading and mathematics. The telephone interview protocol included 113 questions assessing eight aspects of the home environment: (a) the family constellation, (b) the child's and (c) the parents' use of time, (d) the parents' education and occupations and other socioeconomic characteristics, (e) the quantity and variety of reading materials in the home, (f) the parents' priorities for the child's involvement in out-of-school activities, (g) the quality and quantity of interactions between the parents and the child's school, and (h) the parents' opinion about the school and its success in meeting their child's needs. Factor analysis and cluster analysis procedures were used to identify variables that appeared to be most useful in understanding the relationship between home environment and students' academic achievement.

Though it is generally accepted that a student's school performance is affected by their home environment, the nature of these relationships is not well understood. In their review of the literature pertaining to family characteristics and student performance in school, Iverson and Walberg (1982) identified four schools of research: the "socioeconomic school," the "family constellation school" (emphasizing family size and birth order, and so on), the "British school" (emphasizing parental attitudes and expectations), and the "Chicago school" (emphasizing family behavior and parent-child interactions). These are not competing schools of thought; researchers of one school seldom discredit the work done by others. The complex mixture of socioeconomic, attitudinal, and behavioral characteristics of families, together with the ability and motivation of individual students, must be sorted out before one can hope to understand why some students make rapid progress in school and others progress slowly or not at all.

After application of factor and cluster analysis procedures, the twenty-five variables shown in Table 9.6 were selected for use in multiple regression analyses. A cognitive aptitude index also was included to control for variations in the academic ability in students. (About 40 percent of the variance in students' third- through fifth-grade reading and mathematics achievement scores was accounted for by the cognitive aptitude index.)

Two home environment variables made substantial and consistent contributions to the variance in reading achievement when both boys and girls were included. The number of hours the mother worked outside the home was negatively associated with reading achievement and explained 3–4 percent of the variance in third-, fourth-, and fifth-grade reading achievement scores and nearly 7 percent of the variance in reading achievement gain from second through fifth grade. The family socioeconomic status index, which was constructed using both parents' education level and job status, was positively associated with student achievement and explained 1–5 percent of the variance. The association of these two variables with achievement appeared to increase somewhat as students progressed from third to fifth grade.

The number of hours the mother worked outside the home was negatively associated with achievement and was the most powerful predictor (other than cognitive aptitude) of student achievement in mathematics, explaining 2–4 percent of the variance in mathematics achievement scores. The mother's level of schooling was positively associated with student achievement in mathematics, accounting for 2–3 percent of the variance.

Table 9.6.
Home Environment Variables Selected
for Multiple Regression Analysis*

Variable Name	Variable Name
SOCIOECONOMIC VARIABLES	READING RESOURCES VARIABLES
Father's years schooling	Reading material variety
Mother's years schooling	FST professional magazine
Annual income	
Home	PARENT/SCHOOL INTERACTION
Family SES index	Father to P. T. conf.
Father's job status	
	PARENT'S TIME-USE
CHILD'S TIME-USE	TSD homework help
TSD on homework	TSD mother at work
TSD read to self	
Total TSD activities	HOME EDUCATIONAL CLIMATE INDICES
# sports activities	# of siblings
# church activities	# of organized activities
# art/music activities	Strong academics
	"School is good"
PROBLEMS IN SCHOOL	Child doing well
Child-child problems	
"Hates academics"	
Total # of problems	

TSD = Time spent daily; FST = family subscribes to.

* Variables were selected for examination in the regressions if they:

   (1) proxied for clusters that were correlated (R>.10) with a cluster of achievement variables;

   (2) demonstrated durable and statistically significant (p<.05) partial correlations to
      reading or math achievement or growth;

   (3) were identified in other research as being associated with measures of
      academic attainment.

The family socioeconomic status index was the only variable to make a consistent (though small) contribution to the prediction of growth in reading, accounting for 3–6 percent of the variance. Two variables—the perception of parents that the school offered a strong academic program and the variety of reading materials in the home—made small contributions to the prediction of growth in mathematics, accounting for 3–4 percent of the variance. The number of sports activities in which students were engaged was consistently and negatively associated with both reading and mathematics achievement, and the number of art/music activities was positively associated with reading achievement. These two variables each made small but consistent contributions, accounting for about 3 percent of the variance.

When boys and girls were analyzed separately, the cognitive aptitude index was found to be a useful predictor of achievement and growth for both groups, but otherwise there was relatively little commonality in the results. A negative association between maternal employment and achievement in reading and mathematics was evident for boys but not for girls. Two variables—the number of organizations and activities in which girls were involved and the parents' perception that the school had a strong academic program—both correlated positively and significantly with girls' reading achievement.

Family socioeconomic status was positively linked with the achievement of both boys and girls in reading, and the strength of the association appeared to grow from grade 3 to grade 5. It did not, however, contribute significantly to the variation in mathematics achievement scores.

The amount of time the student spent each day doing homework was weakly and negatively associated with achievement in reading and mathematics. This does not imply that doing homework is detrimental to academic performance; rather, it appeared that most of the students in our sample finished most of their work at school and only the low achievers found it necessary to do school work at home. Examination of the achievement profiles of students who received help from their parents with their homework revealed that the association between achievement in both reading and mathematics and the amount of time parents spent helping their child with homework assumed a curvilinear shape. There was a fairly steep positive slope up to 8–10 minutes of help per day followed by a gradual negative slope out to 120 minutes of help per day. This pattern was quite consistent across all three grade levels. The results suggest that parents who spend a small amount of time per day assisting their child with homework probably *supplement* the instruction the child receives in school, and that large amounts of parental help are probably *remedial* and are intended to help the child who has fallen behind or who is not doing well in school.

A student's involvement in cultural activities (music lessons, dance lessons, and so on) was significantly and positively associated with reading achievement, and the total number of activities in which girls participated was significantly and positively associated with reading achievement. For boys, participation in sports activities was significantly and negatively associated with their achievement in reading and in mathematics.

Nearly all the fathers and male heads of household in this study held full-time jobs requiring at least forty hours of work per week. Thus it was not surprising to find that the amount of time the father spent at work was not significantly correlated with any measure of student achievement or growth. Maternal employment, on the other hand, was found to be related to both the achievement scores and the year-to-year achievement gains of students. The data analysis yielded the following findings:

1. Children whose mothers were employed outside the home did not do as well on tests of reading and mathematics achievement as the children whose mothers were not employed.
2. The negative association between maternal employment and student achievement increased as the number of hours per day of maternal employment increased.
3. The significant negative association between hours of maternal employment and both reading and mathematics achievement was pronounced for boys but only slight or nonexistent for girls.

TEACHERS AND STUDENT ACADEMIC ACHIEVEMENT

Most people believe intuitively that teachers do make a difference! For example, one of the concerns raised most frequently by administrators when merit pay for teachers is discussed is how to respond to the parents whose child is assigned to a teacher who has not been identified as deserving of merit pay. Research also supports the view that teachers can make a difference in student learning (Summers & Wolfe, 1977; Murnane, 1975). Research on effective schools lends support to the important role the classroom teacher plays in student achievement. These studies support the view that student achievement is higher in schools and classrooms where there is a clear focus on academic goals, appropriately structured learning activities, a teaching method appropriate to the learning task to be accomplished, and an expectation of high achievement by students (Brookover et al., 1979; Purkey & Smith, 1983).

Monk (1996) has examined the teacher's role in student learning using the concept of instructional alignment, that is, the "fit" between (a) the capabilities the teacher brings to a classroom and the backgrounds, beliefs, and knowledge that shape the needs the student brings to the classroom and (b) the extent to which the teacher's capabilities are actually used. Monk's assumption is that the closer the alignment, the more likely that a student will enjoy academic success.

The data collected in this study enabled us to study relationships between the achievement of students in reading and mathematics and the personal characteristics, instructional behaviors, attitudes, and beliefs of their teachers. The first step in our analysis was to identify those students who received the preponderance of their instruction in reading and/or mathematics from a single teacher. Some students were observed with two or three different regular classroom teachers for reading or mathematics during the year; other students were observed with a regular teacher most of the time but occasionally spent time with a special teacher; still other students were observed with a special teacher most of the time. Only students who were observed with the same classroom teacher throughout the year were included in this portion of the study. In addition, only teachers for whom there were six or more student observations in the subject under study were included in the sample. Applying these decision rules, thirteen reading teachers were included in the third- and fourth-grade years and fourteen were included in the fifth-grade year. Ten mathematics teachers were included in third- and fourth-grade years, and seventeen were available in the fifth-grade year.

The unit of analysis for this portion of the study was the individual classroom teacher. The large pool of teacher-related variables was reduced by using factor analysis, cluster analysis, and regression analysis to identify the variables that appeared to be most closely related to student achievement in reading and mathematics. In selecting the variables to be retained, we considered the nature and quality of the data, results obtained by other investigators, and intuitively logical relationships between and among variables. Six variables describing teacher personal characteristics were retained:

1. Satisfaction with teaching
2. Gender
3. Graduate degree status
4. Number of graduate credits earned in the past twenty-four months
5. Number of professional journals and magazines read regularly
6. Years of experience in teaching

Six variables relating to teacher attitudes, beliefs, and behaviors also were retained:

1. Amount of daily homework the teacher assigned
2. A belief that the primary purpose of education should be to teach people what to think
3. A belief that making a lesson dramatic often results in students missing the point of the lesson
4. A belief that a teacher should talk to students just as they would to an adult
5. A belief that a teacher generally ought to engage in a fair amount of sheer repetition, even at the risk of boring some students
6. A belief that a teacher should take pains to explain things thoroughly

The results of the final stepwise regressions are shown in Table 9.7. Only the first four variables entering the equation are shown because

Table 9.7.
First Four Steps, Stepwise Regression of Mathematics and Reading Achievement on Teacher Personal Characteristics, Attitudes, Behaviors, and Beliefs

Step No.	Variable	R	R^2	Stand. Regress. Coeff.	Sig. Level
		Mathematics—3rd Grade			
1	Yrs. tchg. exper.	.25	.063	.346	.000
2	Import. of repetition	.32	.099	-1.642	.005
3	Tch. s.'s what to think	.42	.181	1.846	.000
4	# journals read	.61	.372	1.262	.000
		Mathematics—4th Grade			
1	Tch. s.'s what to think	.51	.256	.250	.000
2	# grad. credits	.59	.352	-.576	.000
3	Talk to s.'s as adults	.64	.411	-.359	.000
4	Tchr. gender	.67	.450	.202	.001
		Mathematics—5th Grade			
1	Yrs. tchg. exper.	.34	.119	-.467	.000
2	# journals read	.50	.248	.344	.000
3	Talk to s.'s as adults	.53	.279	.190	.011
4	Explain thoroughly	.56	.311	.179	.010
		Reading—3rd Grade			
1	# grad. credits	.35	.123	-.561	.000
2	Tchr. gender	.46	.216	-.288	.000
3	Amt. of homework	.52	.268	.250	.000
4	Make lesson dramatic	.54	.296	.169	.006
		Reading—4th Grade			
1	Explain thoroughly	.27	.074	.124	.000
2	Tchr. gender	.37	.139	-.405	.000
3	# journals read	.44	.190	.492	.001
4	Make lesson dramatic	.50	.255	.381	.000
		Reading—5th Grade			
1	Make lesson dramatic	.26	.066	.148	.000
2	Grad. degree	.45	.200	-.672	.000
3	Yrs. Tchg. exper.	.49	.244	.494	.002
4	Explain thoroughly	.51	.264	.187	.028

any variables that entered after the first four accounted for very little variance in achievement scores. The first four variables produced multiple correlations (R) of .61, .67, and .56 with mathematics achievement scores for grades 3, 4, and 5, respectively. For reading, the corresponding multiple correlations were .54, .50, and .51 for third, fourth, and fifth grade, respectively. The first four variables that entered the equation in no instance accounted for as much as 50 percent of the variance, ranging from 25 percent of the variance in reading achievement for fourth graders to 45 percent of the variance in mathematics achievement for fourth graders.

No consistent pattern in the order in which variables entered the equations was evident for either mathematics or reading. For example, years of teaching experience was the first variable to enter in mathematics at third and fifth grade but did not enter at fourth grade. Number of graduate credits entered first in reading for third grade but did not enter for fourth and fifth grade. One variable (making a lesson dramatic often results in students missing the point of the lesson) appeared in all three reading equations but did not appear in a mathematics equation. No variable entered each of the mathematics equations during each of the three years.

To control for the student's previous achievement, the student's achievement at the close of the previous school year was inserted as an additional variable in the data set. The results are shown in Table 9.8. The student's achievement at the close of the previous school year was the first variable that entered the regression equations in both mathematics and reading and by itself accounted for a great deal of the variance in student achievement. The student's previous achievement accounted for 61 percent and 73 percent of the variance in mathematics achievement and 48 percent and 62 percent of the variance in reading achievement in fourth and fifth grade, respectively. There was no clear pattern evident in the next three variables to enter the equations. The number of graduate credits earned by the teacher in the past twenty-four months entered twice in mathematics but did not enter in reading; whether the teacher held a graduate degree entered twice in reading but did not enter in mathematics. Only two variables—the main purpose of education should be to teach people what to think and years of teaching experience—entered at least one equation in both mathematics and reading.

Although our sample of teachers was quite small and was not randomly selected, it was nevertheless surprising to find that no single set of teacher-related variables showed consistent and stable relationships with student achievement across grade levels and subjects. Rather, one subset of variables was about as good as another, at least in terms of the multiple correlation coefficients they produced. It is possible, of course, that the way in which teacher personal characteristics, attitudes, and beliefs bear upon the academic achievement of their students does vary from grade to grade and from subject to subject. It is also possible that the variables we used did not capture the crucial attributes of teachers that affect student learning, either because we selected the wrong variables or because our instruments were not sufficiently sensitive.

Table 9.8.
First Four Steps, Stepwise Regression of Mathematics and Reading Scaled Scores on Teacher Personal Characteristics, Attitudes, Behaviors, and Beliefs, Controlling for Student's Achievement at Close of Previous School Year

Step No.	Variable	R	R^2	Stand. Regress. Coeff.	Sig. Level
	Mathematics—4th Grade				
1	S.'s prev. ach.	.78	.607	.613	.000
2	Tchr. gender	.81	.660	.227	.000
3	# grad. credits	.83	.689	-.160	.000
4	Tch. s.'s what to think	.83	.695	.191	.087
	Mathematics—5th Grade				
1	S.'s prev. ach.	.86	.730	.816	.000
2	Yrs. tchg. exp.	.86	.748	-.138	.002
3	# grad. credits	.87	.754	.063	.053
4	Talk to s.'s as adults	.87	.758	.088	.140
	Reading—4th Grade				
1	S.'s prev. ach.	.69	.481	.649	.000
2	Explain thoroughly	.71	.498	.144	.016
3	Teach s.'s what to think	.72	.513	-.144	.026
4	Grad. degree	.72	.520	-.090	.116
	Reading—5th Grade				
1	S.'s prev. ach.	.78	.617	.718	.000
2	# journals read	.80	.634	-.080	.003
3	Yrs. tchg. exper.	.80	.641	.236	.066
4	Grad. degree	.81	.662	-.246	.001

Another possibility is that each teacher-student dyad is so unique that aggregated data are not useful, or perhaps that certain teacher attributes are especially important in dealing with certain types of students and that such relationships are masked when aggregated data are used.

Certain variables did appear in the final stepwise regression equations quite consistently. Years of teaching experience was often one of the first variables to enter and usually produced standardized regression coefficients with positive values. The number of professional magazines and journals teachers read regularly also appeared in the final regressions quite frequently, usually entered relatively early, and produced relatively stable standardized regression coefficients. On the other hand several variables seldom entered the final regression equations, or they entered late and contributed little to the multiple correlation coefficient. Satisfaction with teaching, for example, was not very useful in explaining variation in student achievement.

SCHOOL RESOURCES, HOME ENVIRONMENT, AND GAIN IN STUDENT ACADEMIC ACHIEVEMENT

Twenty-four variables that had displayed the strongest relationships with student achievement were selected from the data sets discussed earlier for inclusion in stepwise regression analyses of students' gains in reading and mathematics achievement. Four variables related directly to students, eight variables reflected aspects of the student's home environment, and twelve variables reflected teacher characteristics. No expenditure variables were included because the analysis of expenditures had yielded no significant relationships with student achievement.

Although a total of 281 students were observed during the course of the study, the sample available for these analyses was much smaller because only students for whom complete data were available for all three years of the study were included. For reading, a sample of 100 students was available for analysis of gains from grade 3 to grade 4, and 95 students were available for analysis of gains from grade 4 to grade 5 and from grade 3 to grade 5. For mathematics, 100 students were available for the analysis of gain from grade 3 to grade 4, and 71 students were available for the analysis of gains from grade 4 to grade 5 and from grade 3 to grade 5.

The analyses of gains in reading and in mathematics scores did not yield consistent results. Five variables entered the final regression for gain in reading during fourth grade and together accounted for about 24 percent of the variance in reading gain. They included one teacher-related variable (the purpose of education is to make students think), two home-related variables (number of music/art activities and mother's years of schooling), and two student-related variables (academic aptitude and percent of time on-task in reading). In the analysis of gain in mathematics from grade 3 to grade 4, six variables entered the final equation and accounted for about 20 percent of the variance in mathematics gain. One variable (gender) related to students; three variables were home-related (involvement in sports, perceived strength of school's academic program, and amount of reading material in home), and two variables related to teachers (amount of homework assigned and teacher held a graduate degree).

For gain in reading from grade 4 to grade 5, five variables entered the final equation, but only one of them (academic aptitude) also appeared in the equation for gain from grade 3 to grade 4. The five variables accounted for approximately 21 percent of the variance in gain in reading. In addition to students' academic aptitude, three variables related to teachers (teacher held a graduate degree, years of teaching experience, and a teacher should engage in considerable repetition) and one related to the home environment (perceived strength of school's academic program) entered the equation. Only one variable (teacher held a graduate degree) entered the equation for gain in mathematics from grade 4 to grade 5 and accounted for about 7 percent of the variance in gain in mathematics. It was the only variable that appeared in the equations for both grade 3 to 4 and grade 4 to 5 gains in mathematics.

Student gain scores in any single year varied more widely than they did over a two-year time span so that using the gain occurring over a two-year period tended to smooth the data. The results of the analyses of gains in reading and mathematics from grade 3 to grade 5 are shown in Table 9.9. Six variables entered the final regression equation for gain in reading and accounted for approximately 23 percent of the variance in gain over the two-year period. One variable was student related (academic aptitude); two were home-related (parents' rating of the strength of the school program and time spent on homework); and three were teacher-related (one should talk to students as if they are adults, students may miss the point if lessons are too dramatic, and the purpose of education is to make students think), all having to do with teachers' attitudes, behaviors, and beliefs.

The teacher's graduate degree status was the only variable to enter the equation for mathematics gain from grade 3 to grade 5 and accounted for approximately 10 percent of the variance in student gain. The coding of the variable was such that holding a graduate degree affected students' gain negatively.

Table 9.9.
Summary of Stepwise Regression of Gain in Reading and Mathematics Scores, Grade 3 to Grade 5, on Home, School, and Teacher Variables

Step No.	Variable	R	R^2	Stand. Regress. Coeff.	Sig. Level
		Reading (n=95)			
1	S.'s academic aptitude	.24	.058	.170	.018
2	Parent rating of school programs	.32	.104	-.146	.033
3	Talk to s.'s as adults	.36	.133	.328	.086
4	Teach s.'s what to think	.40	.159	.268	.096
5	Make lesson dramatic	.46	.211	-.272	.018
6	Amount of homework	.48	.226	-.128	.199
		Mathematics (n=71)			
1	T. has grad. degree	.33	.110	-.332	.004

None of the regression equations specified in these analyses produced large multiple correlation coefficients; in no instance was more than 25 percent of the variation in student gain accounted for by the variables entering the equation. Although they were purposefully selected from a much larger universe of variables in each area (home, school, and teacher), they explained only a small portion of the variance in student gains. Although the student's academic aptitude entered each equation for gain in reading scores, it did not account for more than 8 percent of the variance in any of the three equations and it did not enter any of the three equations for gain in mathematics.

The dichotomous variable indicating the teacher's graduate degree status entered negatively for two of the reading equations (from grade 4 to grade 5 and from grade 3 to grade 5). It also entered each of the mathematics gain equations, entering with a positive sign for gain from grade 3 to grade 4 and with a negative sign for gain from grade 4 to grade 5 and from grade 3 to grade 5. One may not conclude, however, that teachers who hold a graduate degree are less effective in teaching reading or mathematics, because many of these teachers were working with students who had special needs and thus were not likely to score well on the achievement tests. Also, our data did not include information concerning the teacher's course of study for the advanced degree, and teachers might have pursued their graduate work in a field unrelated to the teaching of either reading or mathematics. The results of the analyses do raise a question about the cost-effectiveness of paying teachers for earning graduate credits, because the number of graduate credits the teacher had completed in the previous twenty-four months did not enter any of the regressions.

It also is noteworthy that time on-task entered only one equation (reading, from grade 3 to grade 4), and that the percentage of time off-task did not enter any of the equations. Although it was noted earlier that time on-task was a useful predictor of a student's achievement test score, it was not a significant predictor of student gain in either reading or mathematics. Although this finding does not prove that time on-task is unimportant, it does suggest that increasing the amount of time on-task will not guarantee a marked improvement in student gains in reading or mathematics.

OBSERVATIONS AND REFLECTIONS

Any generalizations from the results of this study must recognize that the students who comprised the sample differed in several ways from the samples used by many of the other researchers who have worked to specify educational production functions. The students in this study attended elementary schools in districts serving either small or medium-sized cities in Wisconsin. Most of the students were white, were from middle- or lower-middle-class families, spoke English as their primary language, and lived with their natural parents. The students were similar in most respects to those typically found in rural, small town, or small city school districts located in the upper Midwest, or in other regions of the United States.

Concerning Equity and Efficiency

With regard to equity, the four schools had taken seriously the legal requirement that they develop appropriate individualized programs to meet the special needs of students with disabilities. Whether the needs of such students were being served at the expense of meeting the needs of regular students adequately could not be determined from our data. However, when special students were excluded from the analysis, the range of expenditure per pupil narrowed markedly, and within the population of regular students we found no evidence of inequity in their access to classroom resources.

With regard to efficiency, the results provided no firm basis for conclusions concerning whether resources were being used efficiently in these schools. We observed very little variation in instructional practice, at least in terms of the modes of instruction used, and we did not find that the percentage of time spent in a particular instructional mode was consistently associated with student achievement in reading or mathematics. We did note, however, that some teachers were much more successful than others in keeping their students on-task. Although the four schools each professed a commitment to individualized instruction, teachers in the third-, fourth-, and fifth-grade classes we observed did not make extensive use of either small group instruction or of a teacher or aide working with individual students. Large-group instruction and independent work (typically "seat work") were the predominant modes of instruction. With the exception of one school, little overt attention was directed toward individualizing instruction for regular students, particularly when their programs of study were compared with those of students with special needs.

Time on-task was a much more potent predictor of achievement for low-ability students than for high-ability students. The percentage of time on-task accounted for a substantial amount of the variance in achievement for students in the lowest quartile, but for students in the highest quartile the percentage of time on-task made little difference. Students in the highest quartile typically finished their lessons rapidly and thus had less need to be on-task than students in the lowest quartile. An intriguing question, which cannot be answered from our data, is whether more-challenging and creative instruction for the high-quartile students would have increased both their time on-task and their achievement test scores. Perhaps the lack of a strong association between percentage of time on-task and achievement scores for high-quartile students simply reflected the fact that too frequently they were not challenged to make full use of their talents.

Concerning Resources

The socioeconomic status of the student's family was linked positively with both student achievement and student gain, and the strength of the linkage appeared to increase as the students progressed from third through fifth grade. We do not believe, however, that it was income per se that was the critical element in the home environment. Rather, it was the attitude toward learning in these homes that appeared to be important—the parents' attitude toward education, the expectations they held for the child, and the provision of supplemental educational activities. In short, our data show that the external environment does affect the achievement of elementary school students and their rate of growth in academic subjects. Even though these variables are not susceptible to control by school personnel, the relationships identified underline the importance of cooperative, supportive working relationships between the home and the school.

With regard to resource inputs, when special students were removed from the sample, the variation in resources provided to individual students was remarkably small, and no significant relationship was found between the cost of the resources flowing to individual students and their achievement. However, the differences in teacher time and physical resources flowing to regular students in these schools were quite small, which may be why they did not contribute significantly to the variance in student achievement.

The importance of viewing students as very significant resource inputs to the educational process, as well as the focus of the process, is highlighted by our findings. The student's cognitive aptitude index consistently accounted for more variance in student achievement test scores than did any other variable. It also made a significant (although smaller) contribution to explaining variance in student gains in reading and mathematics. The results of this study appear to lend strong support to the value of early childhood and preschool programs that will strengthen a child's cognitive ability and skills.

Our findings also suggest that the attitudes and beliefs of teachers were more important predictors of student achievement than more-easily-quantified teacher variables such as age, years of experience, graduate degree status, and so on. The results indicate that, with the exception of the student, the teacher is the most important input to the educational process at the elementary school level. Teacher-related variables accounted for a substantial amount of the variation in student achievement scores, even when the effects of the student's cognitive aptitude were partialled out. Our commitments to the teachers who agreed to participate in the study precluded gathering data concerning the quality of instruction in the classes we observed. We noted, however, that the quality of instruction varied rather widely from teacher to teacher, and we suspect the quality of instruction was at least as important as the amount of time on-task in its effect on student achievement.

Although the length of the school day actually increased between third and fifth grade, the amount of class time devoted to the study of the five core academic subjects (reading, mathematics, science, language arts, and social studies) declined an average of nearly one hour per day between third and fifth grade. Other activities increasingly cut into the amount of time available for academic subjects. Although these other activities may be important, the reduction in the amount of class time devoted to basic academic subjects is cause for concern.

The results of this study underline the complexity of the educational process and the difficulty of attempting to understand student achievement and growth based only on the events that occur within the school. Although our unit of analysis was the individual student, thus avoiding some of the problems encountered in research based on school- or districtwide data, we were not able to account for a large percentage of the variance in either student achievement or student gains. Our results suggest that the search for a single education production function is futile. Rather, we believe that there are many valid education production functions, that is, that the most-efficient and most-effective combination of resources will be a function of the specific student as well as many situational variables. Perhaps that is why the teacher is such an important element in the educational process. It is classroom teachers who must make hour-to-hour and minute-to-minute decisions about how to use most effectively the resources available to optimize learning for the students in their classrooms. Thus, teachers are in a very real sense the primary managers of the resources society allocates for the education of children.

NOTE

1. The research reported in this paper was funded by the Wisconsin Center for Education Research and was supported in part by a grant from the National Institute of Education (Grant No. NIE-G-84-0008). Appreciation is expressed to Lloyd Frohreich, who directed the analysis of expenditures, and to Jacque Evenson, who served as statistical consultant. The opinions, findings, or conclusions expressed are those of the author do not necessarily reflect the position, policy, or endorsement of

the National Institute of Education or the Wisconsin Center for Education Research. A complete report of the research summarized in this chapter will be found in Rossmiller, R. A., (1986). *Resource Utilization in Schools and Classrooms: Final Report.* Program Report 86–7. Wisconsin Center for Education Research, University of Wisconsin-Madison. (ERIC No. ED 272 490)

REFERENCES

Brookover, W. B., Beady, C. H., Flood, P. K., Schweitzer, J., & Wisenbaker, J. (1979). *School systems and student achievement: Schools can make a difference.* New York: Praeger.

Carroll, J. (1963). A model for school learning. *Teachers College Record, 64,* 723–733.

Coleman, J. S., Campbell, E. Q., Hobson, C. J., McPartland, J., Mood, A. M., Weinfeld, F. E., & York, R. L. (1966). *Equality of educational opportunity.* Washington, D.C.: Government Printing Office.

Greenwald, R., Hedges, L. V., & Laine, R. D. (1996). The effect of school resources on student achievement. *Review of Educational Research, 66*(3), 361–396.

Hanushek, E. A. (1981). Throwing money at schools. *Journal of Policy Analysis and Management, 1,* 19–41.

Hanushek, E. A. (1986). The economics of schooling: Production and efficiency in public schools. *Journal of Economic Literature, 24*(3), 1141–1177.

Hanushek, E.A. (1989). The impact of differential expenditures on school performance. *Educational Researcher, 18*(4), 45–65.

Hanushek, E.A. (With others). (1994). *Making schools work: Improving performance and controlling costs.* Washington, D.C.: Brookings Institution.

Hanushek, E.A. (1996). A more complete picture of school resource policies. *Review of Educational Research, 66*(3), 397–409.

Hedges, L. V., Laine, R. D., & Greenwald, R. (1994). Does money matter? A meta-analysis of studies of the effects of differential school inputs on student outcomes. *Educational Researcher, 23*(3), 5–14.

Iverson, B. A., & Walberg, H. J. (1982). Home environment and school learning: A quantitative synthesis. *Journal of Experimental Education, 50*(3), 144–151.

Laine, R. D., Greenwald, R., & Hedges, L. V. (1995). Money does matter: A research synthesis of a new universe of education production function studies. In L. O. Picus (Ed.), *Where does the money go? Resource allocation in elementary and secondary schools* (pp. 149–191). Newbury Park, Calif.: Corwin Press.

Monk, D. H. (1996). Resource allocation for education: An evolving and promising base for policy-oriented research. *Journal of School Leadership, 6*(3).

Mort, P. R., Ruesser, W. C., & Polley, J. W. (1960). *Public school finance.* New York: McGraw-Hill.

Murnane, R. J. (1975). *The impact of school resources on the learning of inner city children.* Cambridge, Mass.: Ballinger.

Murnane, R. J., & Phillips, B. R. (1979). *Effective teachers of inner city children: Who they are and what they do.* Institution for Social Policy Studies, Yale University. Mimeo.

Purkey, S. C., & Smith, M. S. (1983). Effective schools—A review. *Elementary School Journal, 83*(4), 427–452.

Summers, A. A., & Wolf, B. L. Do schools make a difference? *American Economic Review,* September 1977, 639–652.

Thomas, J. A. (1971). *The productive school.* New York: John Wiley and Sons.

10

A Policy Framework for School Resource Allocation

Douglas E. Mitchell

INTRODUCTION

One inescapable conclusion of the research reported in this volume is that resource allocation in public schools is rarely controlled by even rudimentary attempts at rationally linking educational goals with pedagogical means. Despite a half century of sophisticated research and evaluation work documenting more- and less-effective strategies for pursuing educational program goals and overcoming student learning problems, school- and district-level resource allocation continues to be dominated by political power and bureaucratic routines.

It has become common place for researchers, policymakers, and even educators themselves to lament this apparent irrationality and to attribute it to a collapse in the moral integrity or intellectual capacity of school leaders. Indeed, accusing today's educators of some combination of venal self-interest, gross insensitivity, limited intellectual capacity, or hopelessly inadequate training has become so common that many community and business leaders are persuaded that terms like educational "crisis" and system "collapse" are fully justified. Such beliefs support the view that radical restructuring is absolutely essential before the basic educational needs of the nation can be served.

Before we all jump on the bandwagon of despair and radical reform now rolling down the corridors of political power, however, it might be well to consider the possibility that local educators are responding with intelligence and sensitivity to problems that are poorly understood and inadequately appreciated by their most vocal critics. Of course, local educators do not always make good budget decisions, and the apparent disconnection between budget allocations and educational program planning is surely contributing to reduced school effectiveness. But we should take a little time to explore the possibility that local educators confront problems that are obscured rather than illuminated by the current emphasis on rationally linking resource allocation to school productivity.[1]

Two key ideas help to put the school and district resource allocation dilemmas described throughout this volume into proper perspective. One challenges the use of the concept of "productivity" in analyzing the economics of resource utilization in education, the other develops an integrated framework for analyzing the dynamics of allocation by taking into consideration the ways in which allocation decisions are controlled by local circumstances.

The discussion of productivity begins by recognizing that, despite the recent popularity of the term, it is a rather limited concept for analyzing how well schools are succeeding in meeting basic goals. Productivity analysis draws its basic analytic framework from the manufacturing sector of the economy, and it makes important assumptions about what kind of economic good education is. To analyze school productivity, it is necessary to assume that education is a product, generated by applying pedagogical techniques to students seen as "raw materials." As developed in greater detail later, at least three other conceptions of the economic nature of education highlight the limitations of productivity analysis. To anticipate the argument: The economic value of schooling, and the means for enhancing that value, take on very different meanings if education is viewed as a social service, an investment in human capital formation, or a means of generating cultural identity. These broader and more-complex conceptions of the economic value of schooling may ultimately prove more fruitful in explaining school resource allocation problems and outcomes than the current emphasis on production function analysis.

After examining the implications of competing assumptions about the economic character of schooling, a second key idea is developed to provide a common frame of reference for interpreting the dynamics of resource allocation across all four conceptions of the economic value of education. Development of this idea begins with the recognition that the dynamics of allocation decision making are shaped by political and professional conflicts over the applicability of competing economic conceptions of the legitimate goals of education and over the means of attaining those goals. Research reported in the earlier chapters of this book demonstrates that rational systems of resource allocation can only be pursued where local educators and the communities they serve share common goals and have agreed-upon programmatic strategies for pursuing those goals. Though the breakdown of rationality is easily documented, its alternatives are not as fully understood as we might hope. Indeed, as the analysis presented here reveals, each economic theory of the value of education implies a different conception of what a "rational" decision is and provides no adequate accommodation for the meanings of rational held by competing theories. Moreover, even when disagreements about economic value are overcome, there are endless opportunities for moral or political disagreements about how to pursue a particular value to destroy an otherwise rational decision-making process.

PROBLEMS WITH THE CONCEPT OF PRODUCTIVITY

High productivity, especially in the wake of recently reported declines in Scholastic Aptitude Test scores, is such a naturally appealing idea that it is hard to imagine how anyone could oppose it. Like mom and apple pie, this symbol of civic virtue seems an unquestionable standard for judging the actions of professional educators and school policymakers alike. The mere thought of raising questions about the propriety of judging resource allocation on the basis of productivity considerations appears doomed at the outset. Could anyone advocate *low* productivity for the schools? Of course not. Then how could an analysis of resource allocation in terms of the consequences for school productivity possibly be inappropriate or misleading? The answer to this question is as important as it is subtle. As discussed more fully later, critical problems confronting local educators are generally neglected when policy critics and educational researchers concentrate on identification and analysis of educational production functions. Close scrutiny of some of these problems can shed important light on why local educators do not approach school productivity improvement in a particularly rational way.

Table 10.1 presents an overview of how various definitions of the economic value of education would be modified if education were conceptualized as a matter of social service delivery, personal investment opportunity, or cultural identity formation rather than rely on the student achievement production concept that dominates most resource allocation discussions. In the first (unheaded) column of the table are four analytic dimensions for comparison among these competing conceptions. How each of these analytic elements is expressed in productivity and production function analyses is shown in column A of the table, and the three competing conceptions of education are shown in columns B through D. A policy framework for analyzing school- and district-level resource allocation emerges from a sequential comparison of the productivity concepts in column A with each of the other three economic conceptions.

PRODUCING GOODS VERSUS DELIVERING SERVICES

Critical differences between product and service industries can be seen by comparing columns A and B in Table 10.1. Though some analysts transcend its origins, production function analysis is conceptually grounded in product manufacturing and is best suited to interpreting economic parameters for industries whose goods can be stockpiled. These industries are able to separate marketing considerations from production issues. In service industries, by contrast, market delivery is inextricably bound up with service provision—services cannot be stored for later distribution, they are consumed just as they are being produced.

This distinction is, of course, an abstraction. Most industries produce a mix of product and service goods. Financial service institutions, for example, move money around and make various business decisions on behalf of their clients, but they also produce statements and reports that are stored and distributed. And aircraft manufacturers service their customers with special designs and delivery schedules developed to service special needs.

In the case of schooling, the question of whether education is to be defined as a product or a service is broadly contested. Which definition

Table 10.1.
Competing Conceptions of Education as an Economic Good

	Education is Defined as			
	A. Product	**B.** Service	**C.** Investment	**D.** Identity
1. Process Conceptions	Production	Delivery	Opportunity	Creation
2. Essence of the Good	Can be Stockpiled	Immediately Consumed	Value Delayed	Morally Sanctioned
3. Outcome of Interest	Residual Knowledge	Learning Experiences	Improved Life Chances	Quality of Life
4. Measures	Grades & Test Scores	Engagement/ Participation	Access to Jobs/College	Culture/ Values

of the economic character of education prevails depends on which features of the schooling process are seen as fundamental. For those who see education as a product, residual knowledge in students is what schools produce. The production of knowledgeable students is measured through grades and test scores, and knowledge is presumably stockpiled for later use when students become adult workers and citizens. By contrast, those who see education as a service industry focus their attention on the immediate interactions between teachers and learners. From this perspective, education quality is assessed in terms of student learning opportunities and is measured in terms of their levels of engagement and participation in the schooling process.

In product-producing industries, productivity analysis helps to focus attention on the cost, reliability, and efficiency with which raw materials are turned into finished goods. By documenting the ways in which changes in manufacturing materials and techniques affect the rate and quality of production, analysts are able to identify bottlenecks and improvement opportunities as well as cut costs and reduce waste.

It is, of course, quite possible to extend the manufacturing sector idea of production function analysis to a service industry. More-productive services are those that reach their goals more rapidly and more completely, or do so at a lower cost. An important but subtle change in understanding takes place when this translation is made, however. Think of the agricultural extension agents of an earlier era, for example. Their "productivity" depended heavily on the social norms and beliefs of their clientele, not just on the technical quality of their services. When farmers resisted crop rotation, hybrid seeds, or inorganic fertilizers, they were not lowering the productivity of the Department of Agriculture—they were redefining the service-delivery problem faced by its agents.

A similar shift occurs when education is conceptualized as a service industry while being subjected to productivity analysis. When we discover that some students are harder to serve than others, production function analysis draws attention to programs and techniques rather than to opportunities and relationships. Subtle social processes are easily neglected in favor of statistical studies connecting test scores with instructional materials or techniques.

RESOURCE ALLOCATION IN PRODUCT
AND SERVICE INDUSTRIES

Table 10.2 (next page) outlines some of the parameters that can be expected to control resource allocations in different economic sectors. Here again, columns A and B contrast product manufacturing with social service delivery. Rows 1 and 2 in this table contrast rational and

Table 10.2.
Parameters of Resource Allocation in Various Economic Spheres

| | Education is Defined as | | | |
	A. Product	B. Service	C. Investment	D. Identity
1. Rational Allocation	Efficiency & Quality	Interest & Flexibility	Riskiness; Return rate	Justice & Fairness
2. Power Allocation	Accountability	Co-optation	Collusion	Elitism
3. Rational Failure	Incompetence	Insensitivity	Unreliability	Alienation
4. Political Failure	Dysfunctional Bureaucracy	Unfair Favoritism	Insider Trading	Minority Domination
5. Human Capital Resources	Standard Practices	Reputation of Staff	Reputation of Alumni	Public Confidence
6. Critical Overhead Costs	Technique Research	Customer Relations	Opportunity Analysis	Public Relations

political power-based approaches to resource allocation. "Rational" allocations are those where alternative uses of available resources are the focus of analysis and decision making. "Power-based" allocations are those where interest and debate focus on *who* has the right to make the decisions.

As suggested by the research designs reported in the earlier chapters of this book, rational allocation of resources within a production system involves linking resource decisions to production efficiency and quality. Though efficiency and quality are valued in a service industry, these concepts do not constitute the primary criteria for rational allocation of organizational resources. Client satisfaction and support are the touchstones of service excellence. Hence, it is rational for a service industry to allocate resources in ways that maximize these factors, even if the technical quality of the service suffers. The importance of this shift from technical quality to client satisfaction is easily recognized in the entertainment industry. So long as audience attraction keeps patrons paying more for tickets than is spent on production, the entertainment expense is rational. Giving primary attention to efficiency, or to quality defined in technical terms, would put the integrity and attractiveness of the work at risk and threaten its economic success.

In education, this often means spending money where people expect you to spend it, even if there is no evidence that these expenditures actually improve knowledge acquisition among students. Thus, when communities resist abandoning band uniforms or football teams, service-oriented administrators will understandably think twice about cutting these expenses in favor of textbooks or program supports.

The principles of power-based resource control also differ sharply as we move from a product to a service conception of schooling. From a product perspective, control over resources is appropriately used to hold people accountable for the technical quality of their job performance. Accountability, with its emphasis on objectivity and measurement of results, is often not the best approach to resource management in a service industry, however. Because service quality is a subjective matter and its success depends on actively engaged participation by clients, power-based resource management in these industries is best described by co-optation. That is, resources are manipulated to improve a service when they are used to maximize feelings of engagement rather than attention to outcome criteria. It can be expected, then, that school managers who hold a service-delivery conception of education will use their control over resources to reward loyalty and attention to client feelings at least as frequently as they attend to pedagogical outcomes. This shift is a reasonable use of political power over resource allocation insofar as support for school programs is threatened more by client disaffection than by low measured achievement.

The third and fourth rows of Table 10.2 present the negative side of the rational and power-based allocation processes highlighted in the first two rows. When rationality fails in a product manufacturing firm, the failure is appropriately attributed to staff incompetency. The reason is simple enough—because rationality in this sphere means using means-ends analysis to put resources into activities that improve quality and efficiency, a failure to do so is logically explained as a failure to develop or apply appropriate analyses to the production process and its problems. It is not accidental that widespread concern about staff competence in the schools has arisen at the same time that production function analysis is being applied to educational resource allocation decisions.

In a service industry, by contrast, resource utilization is viewed as irrational whenever the staff making allocation decisions are regarded as insensitive to client needs and interests. Insensitivity is the obverse of the emphasis on client satisfaction and engagement that drives service industry planning. It is this conception of education that led to the politicalization of school budgets, the development of categorical funding for special needs populations, and the period of widespread belief that school resource managers were pursuing self-interested policies yielding high rewards for managers and neglect for the needs of teachers and students.

Failure of political power-based resource allocation decisions is also seen differently in product and service industries. Because political allocation processes are driven by the determination of who can or should control decisions, failure of these systems involves assigning blame for poor resource utilization. Productivity analysis tends to assign blame to organizational units, service to various social groups. Thus in a product-manufacturing firm, where political accountability is recognized as a legitimate (though often uncomfortable) control system, failure is signaled by a growing belief that the organization has become a rigid, inflexible, and dysfunctional bureaucracy unable to align resources with the productive process. By contrast, in a service industry failure of the political allocation process is seen as cronyism or favoritism—the use of an "old boys network" instead of client needs and interests to guide allocation decisions. This difference in viewpoint probably explains much of the shift from program and personnel improvement to school restructuring that has accompanied the shift of political concern from equal educational opportunity to how well schools are producing trained workers and competent citizens.

The last two rows of Table 10.2 describe key differences in the resource allocation contexts facing various economic sectors. Row 5 describes what might be called "human capital resources" that accumulate through the successful continued operation of a school. These are resources that enhance organizational capacity, and can be lost or damaged if resource managers give too much attention to new technologies or to short-term program effectiveness without adequately considering staff development and long-term operational needs. Where attention is focused on the products of schooling, critical human resources are built up through the development of performance standards for individual staff members and standardized operating procedures for the implementation of programs. Potential conflicts between short-term productivity and long-term accumulation of human capital can create dilemmas for even the most highly rational production-planning managers. Long-term effectiveness depends on having a loyal and cooperative staff, but loyal workers are not always the most capable. Similarly, continued effectiveness rests on using well-understood and effectively implemented programs, but they are not necessarily the most powerful ones. Hence, managers committed to improving educational productivity must often decide between maintaining efficient, well-run activities that have limited effectiveness or shifting to new programs that reduce short-term productivity by requiring organizational and staff development investments before they can become effective.

Service-oriented school managers will face a different set of capitalized resource questions. For the service industry, standard practices are less important than maintaining a strong staff reputation. Indeed, in service industries it is important to help staff recognize when to suspend standard practices and "bend the rules" to accommodate client problems. In public schools, individual teachers acquire reputations for sensitivity to various types of learning problems, and various programs acquire reputations for effectiveness that may not be fully justified by any measures of student learning. These reputations are extremely valuable. They not only enhance support for the school, they allow the school to respond in nonstandardized ways to unique needs and interests without having to always justify the actions taken. The economic value of a strong reputation was illustrated by a musician who remarked that Sir Georg Solti was able to present highly innovative performances of the Chicago Symphony Orchestra that would have raised questions of competence in conductors of lesser reputation.

The last row of terms in Table 10.2 highlights critical overhead costs that vary from one type of economic sector to another. Product manufacturing firms remain competitive only if they give continued support to research and development of improved techniques. This, of course, is one reason why schools are being urged to adopt a product definition for education. It is also widely recognized that manufacturing firms that gain monopolistic control over their markets tend to neglect this critical overhead function and to deliver products that are less efficiently produced than those where competition keeps the firm from becoming complacent. This concern with monopolistic dampening of investment in research and development encourages support for educational choice programs and voucher systems that promise to introduce competition into the educational system.

Service-delivery firms often find that customer relations is a more critical overhead cost issue than technique research and development. As Meyer and Rowan (1978) put the issue, public schools depend more on the "logic of confidence" governing support for their programs than on any technical excellence in their actual delivery. That is not to say that customer relations programs can make up for shoddy and incompetent services, but it helps to put the dilemmas of management into perspective if we recognize that client confidence is essential and that new technologies will often be evaluated on the basis of how well they will be received by clients rather than by how much better they will deliver the goods.

INVESTMENT VERSUS CONSUMPTION

Up to this point, the limitations of productivity analysis have been discussed entirely in terms of the difference between the product-manufacture and service-delivery conceptions of the economic value of education. We turn now to the conception of education as an investment good. In economic terms, investment is aimed at the generation of lasting value and is directly contrasted with consumption. The investment value of education is often described as "human capital formation." Analysis of human capital formation typically emphasizes analyzing the market value of schooling outcomes—comparing salary incomes for various levels of education and evaluating access to higher education in terms of the differential income streams for college graduates and nongraduates.

As suggested by the terms listed in column C of Tables 10.1 and 10.2, the product or service conceptions of schooling can be contrasted with the investment perspective along a number of dimensions. Perhaps the best place to begin a description of these differences is with the recognition that investors concentrate on delayed rather than immediate values. That is, investors enter the market seeking opportunities to put resources to work, not expecting an immediate difference between costs and outcomes. Investors not only expect that resources will be put to work, but that they will probably need to concern themselves with the performance of their investments on an ongoing basis. This contrasts sharply with product and service agencies that make proprietary decisions to generate goods and services, leaving clients to make postproduction marketplace decisions regarding purchase and consumption. Investments are expected to grow in value and are purchased in order to reap later benefits. In essence, then, an investment good is one whose value is time-delayed and dependent on investor resources for its realization.

As contrasted with the production emphasis on residual knowledge and the service-delivery emphasis on providing students with intrinsically interesting learning experiences, the investment value of education is reflected in the improved life chances of the students. In the case of K–12 public schools, investment payoff involves more than just the dollar value of the incomes commanded by graduates as opposed to dropouts. The investment value of schooling also includes such benefits as reduced welfare and crime statistics and higher levels of satisfaction with adult life. Where jobs and income streams are being assessed, the social status of available jobs may be valued separately from their cash income. Certainly, student access to, and success in, higher education is a major investment payoff at the K–12 level.

Taking an investment perspective draws attention to important differences between public investment in the school system and the private investments of students and their families. Public investment in schooling is motivated by the desire to maintain a healthy economy and secure a cooperative citizenry. From the public investment perspective, the universal or the average outcomes of schooling are generally given highest priority. The private investments made by students and families are evaluated rather differently. Here, the question is whether the payoff for a particular student will be substantial—and the value used to assess that payoff may be quite different from those used by public-policy makers.

Terms shown under the investment heading in Table 10.2 (column C), set out the parameters of rational and politically-based resource allocation that operate when education is conceptualized as an investment good. Perhaps the most distinctive feature of investment allocation is that attention shifts away from the productive process itself and onto the predictability and marginal value of schooling outcomes. As a result, rational decision making is guided by efforts aimed at containing the risks of loss and maintaining suitable rates of return for investors—regardless of whether those advantages come from better schooling or simply better control of the after-school market for graduates. Investment risk and rate of return can take on some rather complex meanings. Consider, for example, how investment-oriented school resource managers might rationally respond to the prospect of developing a tuition- or voucher-based school. Middle- and upper-class families with normal to high-achieving students would assess the marginal value of such a school on the basis of whether attendance by their children assures admission (or better yet a scholarship) to a prestigious university. The risk that this outcome would not materialize is reduced if the voucher school screens potential students by some combination of testing and advertising its academic goals. Unfortunately, the market for this type of school is rather limited. As the field becomes more crowded, the ability of any given school to select students and prepare them for competitive entry to prestigious universities diminishes. As a result, even though the quality of education offered may continue to improve, the risk that the investment will not payoff goes up. Eventually, families will begin to perceive that the investments associated with intense academic discipline, transportation, or other direct costs are too risky. As this sense of risk goes up, investment-oriented parents will consider lower-cost alternatives—cheaper schools, test preparation courses to improve admission possibilities, lowered aspiration for admission to the targeted universities, and the like.

The family investment logic governing support for various schooling options can be expected to influence investment-oriented resource allocation by school executives and public funding agencies. In offering school programs, public officials will need to balance risk containment and payoff-control strategies. A school serving a low-achieving population, for example, could rationally invest substantial resources in programs and activities that make very modest contributions to school attainment, if whatever contributions are made are highly reliable. General education courses might be supported more fully than special purpose programs because they minimize chances of student failure, and provide easy access to high school diplomas for students who will not be called upon to demonstrate high levels of school learning upon entry to an unskilled job market. Similarly, where minority enrollment is high and both students and staff have low expectations for the future, investment decisions might well shift resources to staff comfort or public relations campaigns at the expense of instructional program support.

Political power-based resource allocation in an investment environment is driven by the development of self-interested collusion among those who have the most to gain from alternative allocation strategies. Professional educators often combine forces to control public oriented investments in education. The evolution of recent policies suggests that differentiated school programs designed to address distinctive student needs will maximize the value of public investments. Such programs promise to provide each student group with the level and type of investment needed to assure their entry into the economy or participation in civic life. Such a strategy does not always respond to the private interests of families and students, however. Differentiated programs create risks for school clients—individuals cannot confidently pick the program that combines a low risk of failure with a suitably high rate of return. Moreover, when programs are differentiated, students attending lower-status programs are stigmatized and the investment value of their participation is reduced, even if they gain a technically superior education. Local educators are caught in the middle. They are professionally attracted to program differentiation to raise the rate of return on investment, but they are pressed by local constituents to assure that no programs risk failure or reduce long-term returns.

Public-policy makers have a similar difficulty. They must balance student and family interests against those of professional educators when deciding how to invest in schooling. For the professionals, public investment should lead to a combination of job security and wage rates that make career commitment attractive. Because school wage rates tend to be below those for similarly trained workers in other fields, job security and working conditions need to be more attractive. Families, however, want resources allocated to assure improved life chances for the students. Even though this requires attracting qualified staff, the staff need to be motivated toward high performance rather than job security. One of the reasons Japanese industrial management appears attractive to school-policy makers is that it seems to combine high performance with job security rather than define these as conflicting goals.

From the investment perspective, rational and political resource allocation failures damage schools in different ways. Investment decisions lose their rational basis when it is impossible to either calculate the rate of return to a particular use of scarce educational resources or to ascertain the reliability with which that return will be produced. When, for example, school programs have haphazard and unpredictable effects on student learning, or student learning does not have a reliable impact on job opportunities and college admissions, everyone loses the ability to determine whether additional investment is warranted. Thus, where policymakers, parents, or students lose confidence in the efficacy of schooling, they are likely to settle for lowered staff effort and more-comfortable school programs rather than offer to make higher commitments to activities that do not guarantee success.

Where rational investment failures are generally the result of uncertainty about outcomes, political investment failures are reflected in what might be called "insider trading." If the alliances formed to control investment succeed in directing the benefits of schooling toward some groups or individuals and away from others, the political system proves itself unfair and undemocratic. Urban schools; language, racial, and ethnic minorities; and non-Protestant religious groups have all suffered from this sort of political failure. Where insider trading is controlling school investment decisions, we can expect vitriolic conflict—even a willingness to damage the entire school system in order to politically punish the insiders.

Finally, an investment perspective directs attention to unique aspects of human capital accumulation and necessary operational costs of schooling. Accumulated value in a successful school is, from the investment perspective, found largely in the reputation of the alumni. The success of previous students plays a major role in determining the perceived investment value for subsequent student groups. Because alumni are an important human capital resource for good school programs (and a liability for weak ones), allocating resources to their care and nurture is a rational investment strategy expenditure. Operationally, investment-oriented schools need evidence of the payoff to students that comes from graduation. Thus, schools can attract the support of public and private investors if they undertake convincing opportunity analyses, tracking the linkage between public and family investments and the resulting benefits that accrue to school leavers.

SOCIAL IDENTITY VERSUS COMMODITY ECONOMICS

A fourth conception of the economic character of schooling—social identity formation—is described in column D of Tables 10.1 and 10.2. At first glance, social identity formation presents itself as the antithesis of an economic theory rather than an alternative to the production, service-delivery, and investment theories discussed previously. Identity formation is certainly not amenable to the sort of cost-benefit analysis used to define rationality in the other models. In part, this is because social identities are not easily sorted and graded. Social alienation can be the beginning of political or artistic success for some individuals, even though it presages personal disaster for others. At the societal level, alienation and anomie serve as wellsprings of creative change and development, even while creating personal pain and suffering.

More important than the ambiguous value of the social identity formation process, however, is the fact that moral values and cultural norms are at stake. Social identities are morally evaluated and sanctioned, making it very difficult to subject them to an economic assessment. When goodness and honor are at stake, no price seems too high, and any pragmatic compromise with truth and righteousness seems to utterly destroy the worth of the outcome. Moreover, core conceptions of the good social identity to be generated by the schools are perpetually being contested by competing cultural groups seeking to have the schools embrace and reproduce divergent values. The culturally contested and ambiguous character of social identity leads directly to the need for sharply divergent school experiences and outcomes—even to the desirability of privatizing the relationship between teachers and students to keep bigotry and jingoism from overrunning pluralistic cultural goals.

Though the culture-specific, contested, and ambiguous character of social identities at first appearance put this view beyond the pale of economic discussion, there is at least one important respect in which this appearance is misleading. The essential economic question confronting this view is: How important is it to make public provision for the function of social identity formation, and how closely is this function linked to schooling as we now know it? Until the modern period, education was largely a private matter, generally outside the purview of government support and regulation. Family and religious life, key institutions of cultural identity formation, were more closely aligned with governmental action than education. In modern American society, however, we have embraced the view that family life and religious exercises are simultaneously (a) crucial to a healthy culture, and (b) beyond government management. This view has led to government support and protection, but relatively little regulation. As cultural institutions, contemporary schools occupy a compromised position. The cultural contributions of the schools may be private (or at least complex and multifaceted), but the importance of this institution as a primary source of common cultural values in a pluralistic society is sufficiently clear to make the delicate task of governmental support and management seem both necessary and appropriate. Thus, from the cultural identity formation perspective, the economic value of schooling lies in the contributions made by education to the overall quality of life for both individual students and society as a whole. Although the mission of enhancing our quality of life is easily supported in the abstract, the concrete results of specific school programs are often the objects of intense political debate. Conflicts over freedom of student expression and the place of religion in the schools have, for example, reached the U.S. Supreme Court on numerous occasions. Success in the formation of social identities for the nation's children is measured in terms of specific cultural norms and values, enabling any given school program to be viewed as wildly successful by some observers and deeply flawed by others.

What are the parameters of a rational or politically effective resource allocation system within the culturally contested framework associated with social identity formation? Key terms for responding to this question are shown in column D of Table 10.2. As indicated in the first row of the figure, justice and fairness in the treatment of divergent subcultural groups are the primary touchstone for a rational approach to social identity development. In the last quarter of a century this has been the most fundamental meaning of the term "equal educational opportunity." Educational equity has meant assuring that all cultural groups— racial, ethnic and language minorities; women; and children with various handicapping conditions—have been the object of rational allocation of resources aimed at improving educational services. Alienation of individuals or whole social groups is the result if rational resource allocations fail to direct school efforts toward just and fair attention to identity formation for all children.

When political power rather than rational planning dominates resource allocations aimed at enhancing social identity formation, elitism is the operative principle of decision making. Political elites operate to assure that resources are allocated toward the support of their own cultural norms and values and away from the social values of others. Elitism has been the driving force behind the formation of restrictive residential neighborhoods with their own schools. It has also motivated the formation of many private schools. Elite culture support is not damaging to children if political power is distributed in a fairly equitable manner. Where political power is out of balance, however, elitism gives way to domination and exploitation of minority cultures by the political faction that gains control over school resources.

As shown in the last two rows of column D in Table 10.2, the human capital resource of greatest val ie to an educational system operating on the basis of social identity formation is public confidence in the efficacy and goals of the schools. Public confidence not only endorses the work of the school in shaping the cultural values and norms of the students, it also protects the schools from overly close scrutiny that would invariably identify controversial elements in the social identities being developed. Finally, to keep this public confidence alive, identity formation-oriented schools must constantly expend resources on public confidence—engaging parents and community members in various forms of boosterism, communicating about the virtues of the school programs, and carefully attending to challenges to the values and norms being taught. In sum, cultural identity-oriented policymakers and managers can be expected to view devoting at least some resources to nurturing public interest and support, even if the result is less student achievement on scholastic measures, as rational and important.

SUMMARY

To summarize the foregoing discussion: The research reported in the earlier chapters of this volume approaches the issue of school resource analysis from the perspective of rational planning in a product-manufacturing industry. Not surprisingly, therefore, the question of whether resources are being allocated rationally is approached by asking whether the pattern of resource allocation is reasonably linked to measured student achievement. The evidence presented convincingly demonstrates that, viewed from this perspective, school resource allocation decisions are dominated by political forces and bureaucratic routines rather than rational planning processes. This conclusion must be tempered, however, by the recognition that production of measurable achievement is only one way of defining the economic mission of the schools. Very different pictures of both rational and political power approaches to resource allocation emerge when we view schools as social service, personal investment, or cultural identity formation institutions. It is still important to distinguish between rational and political approaches to resource allocation within each of these other three conceptions of schooling, but the criteria for rationality, as well as the sources and aims of political power utilization, differ dramatically as we move from one perspective to another.

Before we conclude unequivocally that school resources are subject to political control and bureaucratic inefficiency because they are not rationally linked to measured student attainment, it would be well to determine whether they are being used in ways that rationally link allocation decisions to student engagement and participation, improved life chances in the search for jobs and college admissions, or to social identity formation among students. If any of these latter three goals are being rationally pursued, the issue is not so much the politicizing of the resource allocation process as a disagreement about the economic character of schooling.

By the same token, even though the politics of accountability for student achievement may be failing, school resources may still be serving important political ends if they are being effectively utilized to co-opt clients, assure the success of personal investments in education, or promote the enculturation of children into the common culture. Thus, unless resource utilization has been examined in relation to these political goals, it is premature to conclude that the dominant political forces at work in the schools are those expressing the self-interest of the professional staff.

TOWARD AN INTEGRATED THEORY OF RESOURCE ALLOCATION

The existence of at least four competing conceptions of the economic value of schooling suggests that conflict surrounding resource allocation decisions will be governed by two distinct forces. First, as in any human endeavor, disagreement over economic values will lead to disagreement about the most-desirable goals of education. Productivity analysts will find test scores desirable measures, but cultural identity advocates will find them irrelevant or even repugnant measures of attainment.

Even where a common set of economic goals is embraced, however, conflict over resource allocation will continue. Schooling is a complex activity, hence the effectiveness and efficiency of alternative means of pursuing specified goals will remain uncertain and context sensitive. Children respond very differently to the same instructional programs, complicating selection of the most-appropriate pedagogical techniques. New techniques are constantly being developed, and new research evidence requires regular reappraisal of previously accepted instructional strategies. The existence of continued disagreement about both educational goals and the means of realizing those goals makes it essential that educational leaders and policymakers provide mechanisms of conflict management that will permit development of stable school operations in the midst of continuing disagreement and conflict.

As conflict over the means and ends of education ebbs and flows within a school or community, we can expect the resource allocation process to develop the four distinctive forms described in Figure 10.1 (next page). In the upper-left cell of Figure 10.1 is the rational planning model, which can operate in situations where there is general agreement about both the economic values to be realized and the pedagogical means to achieve them. Note, however, that the basis for rational decision making varies sharply as public and professional agreement about the economic goals of high-quality schooling shift from production of student achievement to servicing family needs, investing in human capital, or creating cultural identities for children. Production function analysts may study the most effective way to raise test scores, but service advocates are more likely to look for ways to reduce drop-

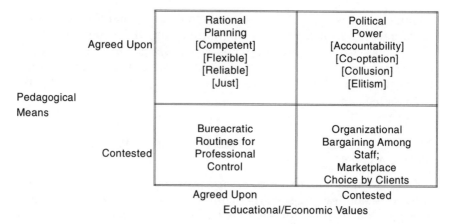

Figure 10.1. A Resource Allocation Model.

outs or raise the level of enthusiasm among students.[2] Investment-oriented observers will emphasize assessing the degree of risk and rate of return for those who finish school, and cultural analysts will probably emphasize responding to the legitimate interests of all client groups or the importance of modeling democratic values within school operations.

Because conflicting goals change the definition of what constitutes a rational decision, it is not surprising that rational planning processes are painfully absent just when public and professional debates are focusing on whether schools are adequately realizing the goals for which they have been created.

As indicated by the terms in the upper-right cell of Figure 10.1, political power is used to control resource allocation when it is not possible to reach agreement about the economic goals to be pursued. Confronted with intractable disagreements about ends, interested groups can be expected to seek control over both participation in the allocation process and access to resources. As described in previous sections, the mechanisms of these power-based control strategies include accountability, co-optation, collusion, and elite domination.

Rational decision making changes in a very different way when disagreements are focused on the appropriate means of attaining agreed upon economic ends. The key mechanism for controlling this type of conflict is to specify who gets to control the selection of pedagogy. The simplest such control is certification of professional roles. By certifying professionals, the state narrows the circle of those who need to be consulted about programs and teaching techniques. The certification strategy occasionally breaks down—over such issues as the phonics approach to reading, adoption of controversial textbooks, or teaching subjects like sex-education and creationism—but on the whole it has worked well to keep pedagogical controversies within the profession.

Because there continues to be ample professional disagreement about the effectiveness of various schooling programs and practices, successful professionalization of these conflicts can create serious organizational stresses within the schools. Bureaucratization is the mechanism for keeping these professional stresses in check. Whatever their economic merits might be, the principal political value of the modern bureaucracy is its capacity to standardize work routines—coordinating the work of individuals whose differences in orientation and belief would otherwise prevent cooperation. Bureaucracies don't guarantee adoption of the most effective or most efficient work strategies, but they do provide a basis for joint action where confusion and disagreement would otherwise prevail.

To succeed in fulfilling their basic coordination functions, however, bureaucracies require that members share a common set of goals and objectives. Management by objectives is possible only where the objectives are not themselves contested. Bureaucratic goal setting is reserved to executive management (or elected public officials) and works best when the goals are intrinsically appealing to most organization members.

As suggested by the terms in the lower-right cell of Figure 10.1, if educational goals are not broadly supported, bureaucracies lose their capacity to define standard procedures. As a result, confidence in the organization breaks down, and all its participants begin to seek independent control over their own behavior. A similar desire for private, independent control over system operations arises if confidence in the efficacy of prevailing pedagogical methods disappears in a setting where political processes are being used to allocate resources during a period of goal conflict or uncertainty. Within a work organization, the desire to take independent control over work activities leads to a separation between workers and managers. Outside the organization, it encourages client groups to oppose institutional control of the work and to seek expanded marketplace choices. Goals and methods are redefined as matters of personal preference rather than as either technically or politically universal. As a result, staff bargaining dominates internal resource allocation decisions, and freedom of choice appears as the only way for clients to secure the kind and quality of education they are seeking.

CONCLUSION

The central point in this chapter is simply this: It should not be viewed as surprising to discover that evidence of rational resource allocation within schools and districts is weak or absent in most re-search studies. First, there are several different definitions of rational, and evidence that one form of rationality is absent does not mean that other definitions might not apply. Second, the capacity for schools, or any other complex organizations, to use rational decision strategies depends upon their developing a reasonably broad-based consensus on both the economic values to be optimized and the pedagogical means for pursuing them.

Although it is important to document the neglect of production function rationality in the schools, it is equally important to inquire into the frequency with which public service provision, personal invest-ment, or cultural identity formation conceptions of rationality are being pursued. Additionally, it is important to examine whether the current conditions of public education might not be more conducive to politi-cal, bureaucratic, or market choice approaches to resource allocation. And, if conditions warrant the use of these nonrational mechanisms, it will become increasingly important to ascertain what consequences for students and their families follow, without assuming that the results are necessarily less desirable just because they are arrived at using nonra-tional mechanisms.

NOTES

1. The controversial "Sandia Report" (1991) produced by the Sandia National Laboratory (Sandia, New Mexico) argues that school failure claims are overstated and possibly misdirected.

2. Even the issue of test score production is being made more complex as cognitive psychologists urge redesigning assessment instruments to measure higher-order thinking skills.

REFERENCES

Meyer, J. W., & Rowan, B. (1978). The structure of educational organizations. In M. W. Meyer and associates (Eds.), *Environments and Organizations*, pp. 79–109. San Francisco, Calif.: Jossey-Bass.

Sandia National Laboratories. (1991). *Report on the status of education.* An unpub-lished technical report submitted to the U.S. Department of Energy.

Index

About the Editors and Contributors

WILLIAM T. HARTMAN is a professor of education in the Educational Administration Program at the Pennsylvania State University and is Director of Research for the Center for Total Quality Schools. He is the author or coauthor of two previous books and many articles and technical reports on school finance and budgeting and microcomputer models for educational policy analysis.

WILLIAM LOWE BOYD is Distinguished Professor of Education at the Pennsylvania State University. He has published over 100 articles and has co-edited ten books. He has served as a Fulbright Scholar in Australia and in Britain, and as a visiting scholar at Gothenburg University, the University of British Columbia, and the University of Wales at Cardiff. He also has served as president of the Politics of Education Association, vice-president in charge of Division L of the American Educational Research Association, and on numerous editorial boards.

ELAINE M. CHICHURA is the Coordinator of the Family and Consumer Sciences Education Program for Marywood University. She is currently a member of the Pennsylvania Department of Education's Family and Consumer Sciences/Home Economics Education Task Force Steering Committee to set academic standards for family and consumer sciences education in Pennsylvania.

PETER COLEMAN has been a teacher and department head, a school trustee, and a school superintendent. He is currently a professor on the Faculty of Education at Simon Fraser University. Since 1971, he has published three books and a wide variety of articles on educational finance, organizational theory, and school improvement in Canadian, American, British, and Australian journals and books.

BRUCE S. COOPER is professor of administration, policy, and urban education at the Fordham University Graduate School of Education in New York City. He is an active member of the Politics of Education Association (PEA) and has a special interest in government policies, programs, and finance in the US and UK, where he was visiting professor at the Institute of Education University of London. He is co-editor, with E. Vance Randall, of the 19th Yearbook of the PEA, *Accuracy or Advocacy? The Politics of Education Research,* which will also be a special issue of the journal, *Education Policy.*

STEPHEN EASTON is professor of economics at Simon Fraser University. He has written extensively in the fields of international economics and economic history, as well as on the economics of Canadian education. He recently edited a series of monographs on public policy perspectives in Canadian education for the Institute for Research on Public Policy, Montreal.

LINDA LaROCQUE is an associate professor on the Faculty of Education at Simon Fraser University. She has conducted research and published in the areas of school district ethos, shared leadership, staff collaboration, and professional learning. She is currently a participant in a national project on student engagement in learning.

DOUGLAS E. MITCHELL is professor of education and Director of the California Educational Research Cooperative at the University of California, Riverside. He is past president of both the Politics of Education Association and the Sociology of Education Association, and recipient of the Stephen K. Bailey Award for research contributions to the Politics of Education. As founding director of the California Educational Research Cooperative he has led in the creation of a major research center supported by substantial contributions from more than twenty local school districts, county offices of education, and UC, Riverside.

DAVID H. MONK is professor of educational administration and chair of the Department of Education at Cornell University. He has taught in a visiting capacity at the University of Rochester and the University of Burgundy in Dijon, France. Monk is the author of *Educational Finance:*

An Economic Approach (1990) as well as numerous articles in scholarly journals. He serves on the editorial boards of *The Economics of Education Review*, *The Journal of Educational Finance*, *Educational Policy*, and the *Journal of Research in Rural Education*. He is a past president of the American Education Finance Association.

E. VANCE RANDALL is an associate professor and Chair of the Department of Educational Leadership and Foundations at Brigham Young University. His experience includes seventeen years as a teacher and administrator in religious education. He is the author of *Private Schools and Public Power: A Case for Pluralism*, and served as the principal consultant for an equity study sponsored by the Utah State Office of Education.

DEBORAH ROSENFIELD is Senior Research Director in the K-12 Education Team at Coopers & Lybrand L.L.P., Chicago.

RICHARD A. ROSSMILLER is Emeritus Professor of Educational Administration at the University of Wisconsin-Madison. Rossmiller has served as a consultant to local, national, and international institutions; as Director of the Wisconsin Center for Education Research; as Director of the National Center for Effective Schools; and as Chairperson of the Department of Educational Administration at the University of Wisconsin-Madison. He is the author or coauthor of over 100 books, articles, and monographs, and has testified as an expert witness in court cases dealing with school finance and employment discrimination issues.

M. BARBARA SARTORI has been a high school administrator in three different school districts in Pennsylvania. She has attended the Principal's Center at Harvard University and an education symposium in China.

SHEREE T. SPEAKMAN is principal, partner, and head of the K-12 Education Team at Coopers & Lybrand L.L.P., Chicago.